THE HOMOSEXUAL PERSON

New Thinking in Pastoral Care

JOHN F. HARVEY, O.S.F.S.

The Homosexual Person

New Thinking in Pastoral Care

IGNATIUS PRESS   SAN FRANCISCO

Cover by Roxanne Mei Lum

To the memory of Cardinal Cooke
and the members of Courage,
who continue to witness by
their lives to the truth
of Catholic teaching

CONTENTS

PREFACE

I thank John Cardinal O'Connor, Archbishop of New York, who encouraged me to take a six-month sabbatical from my work in New York to write this book. I am also grateful to Brother Stephen Olert, F.S.C., who assumed my responsibilities in New York and Arlington, Virginia; to the Very Reverend Richard Reece, O.S.F.S., Provincial of the Wilmington Province of the Oblates of St. Francis de Sales, for granting me permission to go to Malvern Institute for the Comprehensive Treatment of Alcoholism and Drug Addiction in Malvern, Pennsylvania, to write this manuscript.

I thank Mr. Joseph Driscoll, and the entire staff of the Malvern Institute, who went out of their way to provide the solitude for research; Father John Sibel, Director of Communications, Archdiocese of Philadelphia, and his Secretary, Mrs. Marie Kelly, who introduced me to the perils and wonders of Word Processing; Doctor Richard Fitzgibbons, a Philadelphia Psychiatrist, who provided very helpful advice at the beginning of this project; the late Doctor John Kinnane, Professor of Clinical Psychology at the Catholic University of America, with whom I have shared many retreats to priests and brothers with homosexual difficulties and who guided me through the chapter on pedophilia; Father Jeffrey Keefe, Clinical Psychologist, for contributing a chapter on emotional factors; Doctor Elizabeth Moberly and Doctor Gerald van den Aardweg, with whom I shared much correspondence as I wrote the manuscript; Father Benedict Groeschel, O.F.M., Cap., my reader and mentor, for his encouragement and invaluable suggestions; Sister Mary Cronin, Daughter of Mercy, and Mrs. John A. Harkins, who composed the Index; and Miss Kathy Joyce, who wrote numerous letters to publishers asking permission to use their materials.

John F. Harvey, O.S.F.S.

INTRODUCTION

Everyone needs love—and, tragically, many may find little or no true love in this life. This is because there are many counterfeits of love. Some are simply insincere, like manipulation or narcissistic projection, which is self-love looking like love for someone else. Other counterfeits are more sincere and honest enough, but they are not true love. They may be sympathy or indulgence or even affection built on mutual concern and attraction, but they fall short of being true love. For as St. Paul reminds us, love never fails (1 Cor 13:13). Love seeks not its own but rather bears all things, endures all things, hopes all things. Modern psychology has at times recognized in true love something that was only implicit in St. Paul's great description; love can be tough.

True love has to be tough at times because it seeks something for the beloved that is beyond appearances and far more radical than the needs and hungers of the passing moment. For the Christian, love must consistently and ultimately be directed toward the salvation and sanctification of the beloved. True friendship seeks the best for one's friend. The best for the Christian is the road to holiness, however painful that road may be, however great the sacrifices it may demand.

If there is any group of people who are aware of the painful need for love, it is those who, for want of a better name, are called homosexuals. In working with this part of the human family for more than a decade, I have come to appreciate that they more than most others experience a profound hunger for love, for love that does not fail. Deprived of marriage and family life, the closeness that brings love to most human beings, they often embark on a painful, frustrating, and futile search for real love. Frequently this search has been described in literature in most agonizing ways, as it was by Marcel Proust and Thomas Mann. For this reason I have found homosexually oriented people to be on average more aware of the hunger for God than most people, even when their religious desires take the form of bitter cynicism or rage. When homosexually oriented people finally find their way to God through a genuine conversion, they are often among the most devout and faithful friends of Christ. I have long suspected that there are several of them hidden away in the calendar of saints: a few as penitents, and many others who endured a lonely struggle for chastity surrounded by people who never recognized their secret battles or their secret victories.

It is the duty of the Catholic Church in her historically appointed responsibility as the guide and teacher of the path laid down by her Founder to indicate the road of authentic moral conduct in season and out of season. This responsibility often calls for tough love. Anyone who has had a parent who really cared knows that tough love is not always easily expressed. The New Testament—especially the Gospels and Pauline Epistles—suggests that tough love is seldom appreciated, often criticized, and frequently rejected. Words like *rough*, *hard*, *straight* and *burdensome* characterize the evangelical descriptions of the way to God, while the word *nice* does not occur in the Gospels at all. Tradition has summarized all of this in a most appropriate term—*the cross*.

Tough Love does not run away from the cross. However, the expression of that love is not free from the vagaries of human sentiment that affect the lives of us all, including those who represent the teaching voice of the Church. No student of Church history would ever think of denying that those who speak for it are children of their own generation. They are molded not only by the Gospels but by the social context in which they live. The active membership of the Church is largely made up of devout, personally conservative and conforming people who dutifully care for their families, worry about their children, and try to do some good work while keeping the wolf away from their door.

Most of the other active believers are clergy, religious, and single lay people who differ little from the main body of married faithful. It is the sons and daughters of these devout Christian families who usually speak for the Church. When they address a question such as homosexuality, they are at a disadvantage even when they try to be compassionate, because they usually do not speak from within the situation. Their words, though true, may strike the person who has struggled with sexual attraction toward the same sex as abstract, unsympathetic, and even lacking in charity and understanding. Yet these are the people who as a rule are given the responsibility of speaking for the Church.

Another group has emerged in our challenging times: those who attempt to speak for the Church from within the world of homosexual experience. This new group is extremely varied. Its members range from people who openly say that homosexual genital behavior is morally acceptable—or even a blessing—to those who for years have lived a homosexual lifestyle and who now repent of this and stand strongly by the teaching of the Church.

This latter group offers chaste celibacy and even the healing of homosexual orientation as an alternative. I addressed a sizable part of the message of my own book *The Courage to Be Chaste* (Paulist Press, 1985) to this latter group because I have been deeply impressed by the vibrant spiritual lives and inner peace of many Christians converted from the homosexual lifestyle. Furthermore, I have known many people, married and single, religious and lay, who have experienced a vibrant spiritual life while avoiding the indulgence of homosexual or bisexual inclinations.

Those who argue that homosexual behavior can be an acceptable part of Christian life have had a lot of notoriety in recent years. The best representatives of this group have tried to present their position with all sincerity as part of the gentle love of Christ. They have tried to bind up wounds caused by prejudice, homophobia, and ignorance of psycho-dynamics. In a cultural situation where the mass media consistently campaign for complete sexual freedom and license, and where overt homosexual behavior has been made to appear more and more socially acceptable, they have tried to move the moral teaching of various religious groups toward complete acceptance of a respectable and dignified homo-sexual lifestyle.

After years of experience as a spiritual director and psychologist, I must admit that I find their efforts, however sincere, really a form of soft love that is neither spiritually nor psychologically productive in the long run. Over and over again I have seen soft love lead to bitter personal frustration at the failure to find a lasting loving relationship in God.

Sometimes the homosexually indulgent have sadly settled for a melan-choly acquaintanceship that is socially dignified enough but lacking in the depth and generosity that marriage can and often does afford in the later years of life. Obviously these attempts can never lead to family life, the ultimate goal of marriage and the highest expression of sexuality.

On the other hand, I have seen the tough love taught by the Church lead many to a vibrant spiritual life and to the true dignity of an adult who is not enslaved by sexual need. It should be said that large numbers of Christians in many denominations have found healing and spiritual growth in the acceptance of the tough love of the Gospel. This volume will provide much information about these individuals and groups. At the same time, a number of psychiatrists and psychologists have written about the successful resolution of the homosexual conflict; some of their thoughts are summarized by the author in the following chapters. Groups built on the powerful experience of Alcoholics Anonymous (A.A.) are helping men and women with sexual compulsions to lead chaste and integrated lives after years of sexual conflict and despair. Out of all of this, the value of the tough love contained in the official teaching of the Catholic Church is beginning to become clearer to large numbers of young people who are seeking to follow the Gospel in our grossly decadent counter-culture.

In the midst of this struggle there have emerged a few people of genuinely heroic stature in the various Christian communities. Some of these are identified in this book; others are largely unknown except to the people they have helped. One of the great heroes of tough love is Father John Harvey. He began working with homosexually oriented persons over thirty years ago when few even used the word *homosexual* in public. He risked and experienced a good deal of criticism and disdain for doing what was considered a fringe apostolate at best. More than any other person I know, he has largely succeeded in helping homosexually oriented Christians who want to live a chaste life to do so. Although he does not speak as one coming from within the homosexual experience, he presents what may be even more important: the experience of a non-homosexual person who knows, loves, and serves Christians who have homosexual inclinations. In this way his book, which is a summary of a life's work, can be of great help to clergy, religious, and laity who are seeking to help in a compassionate and loving way.

Father Harvey is a most gentle and patient man. He has learned over the years to accept criticism and even abuse with great equanimity because he understands that those who have not yet accepted the challenge of Christian chastity may be deeply hurt and angry. More than anyone else I know, he prays for and desires the conversion and sanctification of the very people who reject his message out of hand. A loyal Catholic and orthodox theologian, he has borne the criticism of others who do not understand what he is trying to do to help homosexually oriented brothers and sisters in the Faith. Among other things the recent letter to bishops of the Congregation for the Doctrine of the Faith (October 1, 1986) contained a vindication of his attempts over the years, often misunderstood and criticized, to assist struggling persons in groups that were loyal to the teaching of a Church that seemed often to fail to recognize their needs.

If you believe that love sometimes has to be tough for everyone, and if you take seriously Christ's admonition to walk on the straight way and to enter by the narrow gate, then this book will be helpful. If you are concerned to be compassionate and loving to the ever-growing number of fine people who are suffering from sexual identity confusion, then this volume will provide you with invaluable information. If you are a Christian who has suffered from a conflicted sexual identity and frighteningly uncontrollable impulses, then this book can be a program of life that may lead you to a faithful and joyous spiritual life.

Finally, if you desire and are courageous enough to follow the way of love, even tough love, then this book will be a special grace for you.

Benedict J. Groeschel, O.F.M., Cap., Ed.D.
Director of the Office of Spiritual Development
Archdiocese of New York

CHAPTER ONE

THE VATICAN DOCUMENT
AS A STARTING POINT

One can hardly write about a more emotional topic than homosexuality. Gay Pride parades, homosexuals demanding that their unions be regarded in the same way as marriage, homosexuals insisting that AIDS is as rampant among heterosexuals as among homosexuals, homosexuals upset by the Supreme Court decision (June 30, 1986) that homosexual persons do not have a constitutional right to anal or oral sex, and, on the other hand, many who condemn all homosexual persons as perverts—all these make it very difficult to consider the issues in the light of reason. No matter what one writes, it will displease many. When, for example, the Congregation for the Doctrine of the Faith wrote a letter to the bishops of the Catholic Church, the American media and homosexual spokesmen greeted it with general hostility. Yet I make this study in the hope that I can contribute some insights into the development of effective pastoral programs for homosexual persons. I shall begin with an overview of the Vatican letter of October 1, 1986, postponing detailed commentary on certain sections until subsequent chapters.

First of all, this letter is not a mere repetition of the statement in the Vatican's 1975 *Declaration on Certain Questions concerning Sexual Ethics*, section 8. It was written because the Congregation legitimately believed that the confusion generated by numerous dissenting theologians on the morality of homosexual acts has had ramifications in the pastoral care of homosexual Catholics throughout the world. In presenting the Catholic moral teaching, moreover, the document expands the argument of 1975. It adverts to the widespread argument of dissenting theologians that the traditional teaching of the Church on sexuality and the family should yield to opinions based upon empirical data: for example, that the Church should allow remarriage after divorce because the practice of sexual abstinence is practically impossible for most of the faithful. The document responds that the Church welcomes the findings of empirical science and uses them in developing a theological perspective, but her more global vision rooted in revelation "does greater justice to the rich reality of the human person in his spiritual and physical dimensions. . . ."[1] Before presenting new facets of the phenomena of homosexuality the document

---

[1] "Letter to the Bishops of the Catholic Church on the Pastoral Care of Homosexual Persons", Oct. 1, 1986 (hereafter abbreviated PCHP), 1–2.

reviews the Congregation's teaching in 1975, in *The Declaration on Certain Questions in Sexual Ethics*, 8.

In the 1975 document the Congregation emphasized understanding the homosexual condition and noted that culpability for homosexual acts should be judged with prudence. It also recognized the distinction, previously drawn by theologians, between the homosexual condition, or tendency, and individual homosexual actions. Such actions were described as lacking in their indispensable and essential finality, or as being "intrinsically disordered". Under no circumstances could they be approved.[2]

After the publication of the 1975 statement, however, some authors called the homosexual orientation neutral, or even good. The 1986 statement corrects this evaluation, pointing out that "although the particular inclination of the homosexual person is not a sin, it is a more or less strong tendency ordered toward an intrinsic moral evil; and thus the inclination itself must be seen as an objective disorder" (PCHP, 3). Unfortunately, the homosexual activists, supported by the media, consider the description of the homosexual condition as "disordered" to be an affront to the dignity of all homosexual persons. They claim that it will increase the level of hostility toward homosexual persons in our society, that it contradicts the American Psychiatric Association's removal of the homosexual condition from the category of neurosis, and so on.

But the clarification had to be made. To say, as do some Catholic moralists, such as John J. McNeill, S.J., that the homosexual orientation is good and should be allowed genital expression is at least consistent with the premise, which happens to be false. Some homosexual persons wanted to say that the inclination was psychologically good but could not legitimately be actualized because the Church *called* the action immoral. Such reasoning gives the impression of an authoritarian Church that makes decisions arbitrarily, without considering the nature of things. Nothing could be farther from the truth. As I shall point out later, one may develop strong arguments against homosexual activity from the very nature of human sexuality, apart from revelation and the magisterial teaching.

The document next adverts to a new exegesis of Holy Scripture that sees all scriptural references to the immorality of homosexual activity as "culturally conditioned" or as non-applicable to stable same-sex genital relationships. A few authors even try to find in certain scriptural accounts a tacit approval of homosexual relationships. John's putting his head on the breast of Christ and Jonathan's swearing undying love to David are examples cited. The response of the Congregation to these sophistries is truly enlightening, introducing a much more comprehensive scriptural

---

[2] *Declaration on Certain Questions in Sexual Ethics*, 8.

argument against homosexual activity than is found in the 1975 document. Since I shall develop the moral argument from Scripture in Chapter Six, in this overview I shall merely mention several insights of the new document.

It first agrees that the interpretation of biblical literature must take into consideration the different epochs in which the books were written, together with the varied patterns of thought and expression. Indeed, it points out, the world of the New Testament was very different from that of the Old Testament. Yet despite this remarkable diversity of times and places, "there is nonetheless a clear consistency within the Scriptures themselves on the moral issue of homosexual behavior."[3] The Church bases her teaching, then, not on isolated passages, but on the general thrust of both Testaments. Today's Church stands in unbroken continuity with the Jewish and Christian communities within which the Scriptures were written. Furthermore, the Holy Scriptures, the Tradition within the Church from the time of the Apostles, and the Magisterium of the Church "are so connected and associated that one of them cannot stand without the others. Working together, each in its own way under the action of the one Holy Spirit, they all contribute effectively to the salvation of souls."[4]

This preface to the scriptural argument must be understood. While the Church will continually use the latest research of exegetes, she is conscious also of the sacred Tradition that has been within the Church from the very beginning and conscious that her interpretation of any part of her teaching relies upon Tradition as well as upon the Scriptures. Under the guidance of the Holy Spirit, the Church provides an authentic interpretation of matters of faith and morals, and certainly homosexual activity is a matter of morals. As the details of the scriptural argument will be considered in Chapter Six, at this point it is enough to say that the argument is not an argument from Scripture alone, but from Scripture and Tradition together, as they have been understood by the living Magisterium (PCHP, 5).

The document, moreover, adds a new argument against homosexual behavior. It is drawn from the *dogmatic* teaching of the Church concerning the sacramental nature of the marital union. Marriage is of the divine plan, and sexual-genital intercourse is morally good only in this state. From this teaching it follows logically that one who engages in homosexual behavior "acts immorally" (PCHP, 7). Noteworthy also in this document is the development of arguments of a personalist character showing that homosexual activity thwarts the Gospel call to a life of self-giving. This does not

---

[3] *Ibid.*, 5.
[4] Vat. Council II, *Dei Verbum*, quoted in PCHP, 5.

mean that homosexual persons are not often "generous and giving of themselves". It means rather that homosexual activity in itself is essentially self-indulgent and proceeds from a disordered sexual inclination; it cannot but prevent one's own fulfillment and happiness. In condemning homo-sexual activity the Church is really upholding personal freedom and dignity (PCHP, 7).

The document next adverts to the phenomenon of massive pressure from certain groups within the Church to persuade the Magisterium that the homosexual condition is not disordered and that under certain circum-stances homosexual behavior is licit. These groups often agree with similar organizations outside the Church that do not share with Catholics the vision of the human person as made in the image of Christ. This places upon the ministers of the Church a serious responsibility to teach clearly what the Church holds on the immorality of homosexual activity. Unless the leaders of the Church repudiate these false views, the faithful will continue to be confused, and this will be to the advantage of the false prophets (PCHP, 8). These pressure groups within the Church like to give the impression that they represent all Catholic homosexual persons, but, as I shall show in Chapter Six, this is far from the truth. The document goes on to say that these groups generally use a tactic of protesting any kind of criticism of homosexual lifestyle or behavior and that they regard all criticism as unjust discrimination.

One example of this tactic of protest is the gay civil-rights movement, to which I shall advert in Chapter Six in evaluating the civil rights of homosexual persons. It suffices here to point out that many Catholic clerics and religious have been hoodwinked by the Gay Catholic Liberation propaganda. Whoever refused to sign their statements was regarded as "against the rights" of homosexual persons. This is what the document means when it says that in some countries there has been an effort to "manipulate the Church". The implied premise of such pressure groups is *gay is good*. Therefore, it is said, homosexual persons have a right to homosexual acts so long as they are performed in a responsible way (cf. PCHP, 9). Father Enrique Rueda has already documented this infiltration of the Catholic Church in America in *The Homosexual Network*.[5]

Then comes a statement that has infuriated homosexual organizations: "Even when the practice of homosexuality may seriously threaten the lives and well-being of a large number of people, its advocates remain undeterred and refuse to consider the magnitude of the risks involved" (PCHP, 9). During the first week after this document was published, numerous references in the secular press and media by Catholic homo-

[5] (West Greenwich, Conn.: Devin Adair Co., 1982), pp. 269–283.

sexual spokesmen (self-appointed, to be sure) accused the Church of inciting violence against the "homosexual community". In my judgment, the document is referring to the numerous attempts of homosexual groups to oppose any restriction on their sexual activity; for example, their attempt to forestall the closing of gay bathhouses by civil authorities, who fear the spread of AIDS through promiscuous anal and oral intercourse. The risk of spreading AIDS in this fashion is a matter of common knowledge that many homosexuals continue to ignore.[6] Larry Kramer, who has written the drama *The Normal Heart*, confronts both prejudice against homosexual persons and the "sexual mores" of the homosexual community. Those indulging in bathhouse promiscuity are the victims and the creators of the bad image that homosexual persons have. He charges the promiscuous with spreading a deadly disease.[7]

As I shall show in Chapter Eight, many doctors, including the Surgeon General of the United States, Dr. C. Everett Koop,[8] agree with Larry Kramer. Unfortunately, in the media these facts are generally ignored, and the Church is regarded as tyrannical. While the Church is not concerned about the pressure from society to change her teaching, she is solicitous that the faithful not be deceived by pro-homosexual propaganda. She realizes also that there are many homosexual persons not represented by the gay movement who need her support to live a chaste life. Again, she is aware that any attempt to place homosexual relationships on the same level as marriage and family jeopardizes the family and ultimately the common good.

In section 10, the document states clearly that the Church is opposed to any violence or hatred shown to homosexual persons, because this is a direct violation of the intrinsic dignity of each person. Nevertheless, opposition to such homophobia must not lead to the conclusion that the homosexual condition is not disordered. Whenever a society condones the active homosexual lifestyle, introducing legislation to protect such behavior, it will come as no surprise to either the Church or society at large that "other distorted notions and practices gain ground, and irrational and violent reactions increase."

While the document gives no specific examples of *how* distorted practices lead to violent reactions on the part of others in society, one can recall the murder of a pro-gay political leader in San Francisco, violent responses to the annual Gay Pride march in New York City, or the irrational way some

[6] Katie Leishman, "Heterosexuals and AIDS: The Second Stage of the Epidemic", *The Atlantic Monthly*, February 1987, pp. 39–58.

[7] "Kramer vs. Cruising", *The Economist*, April 5, 1986, p. 104.

[8] *Surgeon General's Report on Acquired Immune Deficiency Syndrome*, U.S. Department of Health and Human Services, October 1986, pp. 4, 15.

health-care workers responded to those infected by the AIDS virus. The Church does not *approve* such reactions, but merely points out that when a society justifies and protects a homosexual lifestyle it will engender a negative and violent reaction by other elements in society who believe that the homosexual lifestyle is a threat to them and to society at large. It is a psychological reaction in places where homosexual groups have been placed on the same level as Christian marriage. Unfortunately, this distinction has been lost in media confusion.

Doubtless, many virtuous homosexual persons have allowed themselves to be hurt by the two document statements that (1) homosexual groups refuse to acknowledge the harm they can do to the rest of society in pursuing their alleged right to sexual activity and that (2) it is no surprise that such promiscuous activity may provoke a violent reaction by other elements of society. While both statements are empirically verifiable, they became inflammatory when they were quoted out of context by the media and homosexual organizations. In my efforts to explain this document to Catholic celibate homosexual persons I ran into strong opposition by persons faithful to the Church. They felt that such statements would be used against *all* homosexual persons and that the authors of the document either should have omitted them or should have expressed them in a more delicate way. I believe that the first statement about homosexual promiscuous activity had to be said, and indeed has already been said, as the reader will see in the section on AIDS in Chapter Eight. The second statement could have been omitted with no loss to the pastoral purpose of the document.

In section 11 the document addresses the fallacy that if one did not choose a homosexual orientation, he has no choice but to behave in a homosexual fashion and that such a person is not responsible for his homosexual acts. At the root of this fallacy of non-culpability is the unstated assumption that every person must have physical-genital sex to be healthy and happy. The document goes on to stress a basic principle of pastoral theology: avoid generalizations in judging individual cases. Circumstances may now exist or may have existed in the past "which would reduce or remove the culpability of the individual in a given instance."

In Chapter Two I shall describe the problem of compulsive activity to which the document here alludes. Where such compulsion has been proven to exist, one must judge culpability with prudence and mercy. On the other hand, it happens, says the document, that "other circumstances may increase it [culpability]". There are times when a person who ordinarily acts compulsively acts freely and other times when one who ordinarily acts freely acts compulsively. For this reason the document stresses this principle: "What is at all costs to be avoided is the unfounded and demeaning assumption that the sexual behavior of the homosexual person is always and totally compulsive and therefore inculpable." The homosexual person must be seen as possessing the dignity of freedom. While he may not be able to extricate himself from homosexual activity without the grace of God, nevertheless his conversion is always a mysterious collaboration between the grace of God and the free will of the homosexual person.

Section 12 offers to the homosexual person an ascetical perspective within which he can understand the deeper meaning of his life. He is urged to join his life to the Cross of Christ after the example of St. Paul, who says in Galatians (5:24), "You cannot belong to Christ unless you crucify all self-indulgent passions and desires." This self-denial in imitation of Christ is in service to the will of God, who empowers those trusting in Him to practice virtue instead of vice. Those, however, who refuse to sacrifice their own will in obedience to the will of God are effectively preventing their own salvation.

The document proceeds to explain this strong statement. Just as the Cross is central to the expression of God's redemptive love for us, "so the conformity of the self-denial of homosexual men and women with the sacrifice of the Lord will constitute for them a source of self-giving which will save them from a way of life which constantly threatens to destroy them." Part of that self-denial consists in leading a chaste life. One pastoral and practical way to understand the nature of God's personal call to the homosexual person is to make frequent use of the sacrament of Confession. This will lead to a deeper conversion of heart.

From sections 13 to 17 the document highlights the role of the bishops in communicating the truth of the Church's teachings to his priests and people. Section 13 states: "Bishops have the particularly grave responsibility to see to it that their assistants in the ministry, above all the priests, are rightly informed and personally disposed to bring the teaching of the Church in its integrity to everyone." The document recognizes that many ministers in the Church are already helping homosexual persons to lead a chaste life.

But ministers need some kind of program to guide homosexual persons, and section 14 takes up this issue. Here the Congregation asks the bishops to be particularly cautious of any programs that may seek to pressure the Church to change her teaching, "even while claiming not to do so. A careful examination of their public statements and the activities they promote reveals a *studied ambiguity* [emphasis added] by which they attempt to mislead the pastors and the faithful. For example, they may present the teaching of the Magisterium, but only as if it were an optional choice for the formation of one's conscience. Its specific authority is not recognized." The document goes on to challenge these organizations calling themselves "Catholic" when not only do they not support the Church but attack it. It is typical of these organizations that they make a vague appeal to the teaching of Christ while ignoring the teaching of the Church. For this reason bishops should not support these organizations in any way. I shall describe several organizations of this type in Chapter Seven.

Section 15 elaborates upon section 14, pointing out that no authentic pastoral program will include organizations that do not *clearly* teach that homosexual activity is immoral. The principles concerning the near occasions of serious sin should be taught. To remain silent about the teaching of the Church on the plea of providing pastoral care is "neither pastoral nor caring. *Only what is true can ultimately be pastoral*" (emphasis added). Thus, failure to present the teaching of the Church to homosexual men and women is to deprive them of the care they need and deserve, and their first need is for truth. The document goes on to list the various spiritual aids that the Church can provide for the homosexual person—"the sacrament of Reconciliation, prayer, witness, counsel, and individual care". In this way the entire Christian community can realize its duty to assist its brothers and sisters "without deluding them or isolating them".

In section 16 the Congregation adverts to what is known as the holistic approach, which is based on the realization that a homosexual person, "as every human being, deeply needs to be nourished at many different levels simultaneously." This is a wonderful statement, implicitly acknowledging that we must minister to the physical, psychological, and spiritual levels of the human person. Such needs will also include the need for *spiritual group support systems* that the document does not mention explicitly but implicitly refers to, as in section 15, where one of the spiritual aids is "witness". That is exactly what a Catholic support system does—*witness* to the *truth* of the Church's teaching. But I shall describe group spiritual support systems in Chapter Seven.

It is clear in the second part of section 16 that the Congregation wishes to explode the myth of *homosexual identity* that is usually expressed in calling oneself "gay". In the last twenty years *gay* has come to mean not only that a person has a homosexual orientation, but also that he accepts an active homosexual lifestyle. In other words, being gay is one's fundamental attribute. The Congregation reminds us that we are made to the image and likeness of God and that there is no way that our mysterious complexity can be reduced to a sexual orientation. Thus, the Church asks all persons to get beyond the *superficial* identities of being "heterosexual" or "homosexual" and contemplate one's *fundamental* identity as a creature of God, and, by grace, His child and heir to eternal life.

One sentence in section 16 cautions the homosexual person not to exaggerate the suffering that his condition brings to him: "Everyone living on the face of the earth has personal problems and difficulties, but challenges to growth, strengths, talents, and gifts as well." I see this as a reference to the tendency found in many homosexual persons to indulge in self-pity, to feel that "no one else has to suffer the way I suffer". Dr. Gerald van den Aardweg perceives this self-pity as a manifestation of deeply rooted feelings of being inferior as a man. In Chapter Three I review his thought and practice.

In paragraph 17 the Congregation exhorts the bishops to communicate the teaching of the Church on this important question to all the faithful. One hopes that in sermons to adults as well as in spiritual conferences during retreats the truth of the Church's teaching as reaffirmed in this document will be made known. After the bishops have considered the points already made, they may wish to make "intervention" in their own dioceses. While the specifics of intervention are not mentioned, section 17 is an obvious reference to homosexual organizations that do not support Church teaching. In this regard "further coordinated action at the level of their National Bishops' Conference may be envisioned." In my judgment, this would be very effective in communicating the message of the Church.

The Congregation, however, goes beyond condemnation, urging the bishops "to support, with the means at their disposal, the development of appropriate forms of pastoral care for homosexual persons. These would include the assistance of the psychological, sociological, and medical sciences in full accord with the teaching of the Church." Here again the Congregation encourages those who have a ministry to homosexual persons to use the insights of the empirical sciences to understand and guide those to whom they minister. It certainly includes spiritual group support systems. Theologians are likewise urged to explain the meaning of human sexuality and marriage and the implications for homosexual activity. Ministers chosen to serve homosexual persons should be selected with special care by the bishop. They should possess a high degree of spiritual and personal maturity and be known for their fidelity to the Church. I would add that they should be aware that an individual joining the group may be seeking a liaison with just one person, with its destructive emotional and moral consequences. Leaders should take due measures to prevent such an occurrence.

Furthermore, bishops should promote "appropriate catechetical pro-grams based on the truth about human sexuality in its relationship to the family as taught by the Church". In this context one should deal with the question of homosexuality.[9] This catechesis should also extend to the families of homosexual persons to help them deal with this problem. Earlier in this letter the Congregation had warned the bishops that homosexual organizations claiming to be Catholic were undermining Church teaching; now in section 17 it is recommended that "all support should be withdrawn from any organizations which seek to undermine the Church, which are ambiguous about it, or which neglect it entirely." The document argues that even the *semblance* of support can be *gravely* misinterpreted. It requests bishops not to schedule religious services for such groups in Church buildings or in the facilities of Catholic schools and colleges. Permission to such groups to use Church property contradicts the purpose for which these institutions exist. It is often scandalous, says the document. Finally, the document briefly refers to gay rights legislation, advising bishops that in their evaluation of such ordinances they keep in mind primarily the promotion of family life. In the following chapters I shall develop in greater detail some of the points made in the document.

In concluding this overview I offer this suggestion to those who want to use this document in their teaching and preaching. The document does not sufficiently elaborate upon the need for spiritual support groups loyal to Church teaching, such as Courage. Aided by the media, gay propagandists have spread the message that the Church is against homosexual persons. To disprove this claim, Church leaders need to establish spiritual support groups for Catholic homosexual persons who desire to live chaste lives. Priests and religious should come to such meetings as often as possible to give concrete evidence that they care for the psychological and spiritual welfare of homosexual persons.

There are also difficulties in terms. Many homosexual persons do not like the term *homosexual* because they feel it connotes some kind of abnormality; they prefer the term *gay*. But, as we have seen, *gay* has come to mean that one accepts an active gay lifestyle. For this reason the culture looks with suspicion on anyone who claims to be a gay celibate, because celibacy is not part of the gay lifestyle. *Gay*, *gay rights*, and *gay liberation* have become politicized terms.

[9] The Archbishop of San Francisco, Most Reverend John R. Quinn, responds to the constant negative criticisms of homosexual organizations by explaining the nature of the document as an act of the teaching Church addressed to the bishops, and thus phrased in precise and technical language. He also shows that its central affirmation that homosexual acts are immoral is based on Holy Scripture, as the Church and the best of contemporary exegesis understand it. He stresses the pastoral nature of the document in its respect for the personhood of the homosexual and in its careful assessment of culpability. The Church really cares. ("Toward an understanding of the letter 'On the Pastoral Care of Homosexual Persons' ", *America*, Feb. 7, 1987, pp. 92–95, 116.)

If one accepts the gay lifestyle, one must also reject sexual abstinence. This explains why gay propagandists vehemently oppose any proposal that homosexual persons live a life of sexual abstinence. Of course, our culture rejects the idea that persons can live a celibate life that is at the same time a life of joy and intimacy with both God and others. The contemporary bias is that both homosexual and heterosexual persons have a right to choose any kind of sexual pleasure, provided that no one is hurt by the choice.

CHAPTER TWO

PSYCHOLOGICAL CONSIDERATIONS

I. DEFINITIONS OF HOMOSEXUALITY

In speaking of the condition of homosexuality one could mean many things. Sex researchers such as Wardell Pomeroy and others refer to the heterosexual-homosexual continuum, that is to say, the fact that, besides those who are exclusively heterosexual or homosexual, there are some who are predominantly heterosexual and only incidentally homosexual; others who are predominantly heterosexual but more than incidentally homosexual; others who are equally heterosexual and homosexual, and so on, to the other end of the spectrum. A married man, for example, may engage in heterosexual intercourse but be predominantly homosexual in his fantasy life. Thus homosexuality is not always an all-or-none condition.[1] Keeping the complexity of homosexuality in mind, I proceed to consider some definitions.

Traditionally, homosexuality has been described as a persistent and predominant attraction of a sexual-genital nature to persons of one's own sex. I use the term *predominant* to indicate that there may be a lesser degree of erotic interest in the other sex, as described above. I use the term *persistent* to indicate that these erotic feelings toward someone of the same sex have persisted beyond the adolescent phase.[2] Dr. Gerald van den Aardweg expresses this view when he writes, "We shall reserve the word homosexual (homophile) here for *erotic wishes* directed to members of the same sex accompanied by a reduction of erotic interests in the opposite sex. Then we have to distinguish between *transitory homosexuality*, which may be a phase of development, especially during adolescence, and *chronic homosexuality*, the latter being the type of homosexuality that is generally meant when one uses the term. According to this definition, the criterion lies in one's feelings, not in one's manifest behavior."[3]

Recently, however, this traditional understanding of homosexuality has been challenged by Dr. Elizabeth Moberly in *Psychogenesis: The Early*

[1] Wardell Pomeroy, "Homosexuality", in *The Same Sex*, ed. Ralph Weltge (Philadelphia: Pilgrim Press, 1969), pp. 3–13. See also Alfred Kinsey, *Sexual Behavior in the Human Male* (1948). The Kinsey Group demonstrated the continuum with much evidence.

[2] John R. Cavanagh, *Counseling the Homosexual* (Huntington, Ind.: Our Sunday Visitor Press, 1977), pp. 38–40. Cavanagh discusses a series of definitions.

[3] *On the Origins and Treatment of Homosexuality* (New York: Praeger, 1986), p. 3.

Development of Gender Identity and in *Homosexuality: A New Christian Ethic*. Moberly holds that a homosexual orientation "does not depend on a genetic dispositional hormonal imbalance or abnormal learning processes, but on difficulties in the parent-child relationship, especially in the early years of life."[4] Admitting the complexity of the homosexual phenomenon, Moberly singles out as one underlying principle that the homosexual man or woman "has suffered from some deficit in the relationship with the parent *of the same sex* and that there is a corresponding drive to make good this deficit through the medium of same-sex or homosexual relationships".[5]

The term *deficit* does not in itself imply any willful neglect or maltreatment of the child by the same-sex parent, yet some kind of trauma has disrupted the normal attachment, leaving the child unfulfilled in its need for same-sex attachment.

Involved also are the dynamics of repression. Repressing the normal need for attachment strengthens the opposite drive for restoration of the attachment. This reparative urge is involved in the homosexual impulse; that is, this impulse is essentially motivated by the need to make good earlier defects in the parent-child relationship. Says Moberly: "The persisting need for love from the same sex stems from, and is to be correlated with, the earlier unmet need for love from the parent of the same sex, or rather the inability to receive such love, whether or not it was offered."[6] This defensive detachment, coupled with the urge for renewed attachment, implies that the homosexual condition is one of same-sex ambivalence. This holds for both males and females. In Moberly's view this same-sex ambivalence is primarily a *gender*-identity problem rather than a *sexual*-genital one.

According to Moberly, the very term *homosexuality* begs the question because it describes the homosexual condition primarily in terms of sexual desire and activity; thus, she substitutes a nonsexual definition, such as same-sex ambivalence, since this condition exists prior to, and independent of, any sexual activity; and, most importantly, the needs involved can and should be met independently of any sexual activity.

Moberly's definition and theory of homosexual orientation will be analyzed later. At this point it should be stressed that there is a vast difference between her definition, based upon considerations of gender, and the classical view of persistent and predominant attraction to persons of one's own sex. The classical view does not do justice to the psycho-

---

[4] Elizabeth R. Moberly, *Homosexuality: A New Christian Ethic* (Cambridge, England: James Clarke, 1983), p. 2.

[5] *Ibid.*, p. 4.

[6] *Ibid.*, p. 6.

logical data. In particular, the classical view is one-sided in its neglect of the data on same-sex animosity. "Same-sex love" is a partial and misleading definition; "same-sex ambivalence" is the central issue. Moberly's view focuses on the meaning of such orientation and behavior in terms of gender identity during the early years of life.

In my pastoral work with homosexual persons I have noted that younger men and women value Moberly's insights because they help them to come to a better understanding of themselves. They find particularly appealing her emphasis on the point that attraction to one's own sex is not pathological, but rather that early hostile detachment from a parental figure of the same sex is, and that one can repair, as it were, the deprivations of the past through the endeavor to cultivate same-sex celibate friendships. Van den Aardweg challenges this definition. On the other hand, older homosexual persons tend to resist any theory of homosexuality that makes the slightest suggestion that one may change one's sexual orientation; they accept their orientation as a given, although usually with reluctance.

In any consideration of definitions of homosexuality one must seek an explanation of the phenomenon of bisexuality. Many persons engage in both heterosexual and homosexual acts. How do we classify them? This is a controversial question on the theoretical level. On the practical level, many persons engage in both kinds of acts in adult life. I personally agree with those authors who hold that apparently bisexual persons are either homosexual or heterosexual.[7] From pastoral experience in dealing with bisexual men and women I have discerned that the emotional attachment to persons of one's own sex and the absence of the same degree of emotional attachment to persons of the other sex identify the person as homosexual in orientation. I shall enlarge on this in the pastoral perspectives. It should be noted that the ability to engage in sexual intercourse with persons of the other sex is not the determining criterion of sexual gender identity. Far more significant in the determination of that identity is the history of one's fantasy life and the emotional quality of one's relationships to persons of one's own sex and to the persons of the other sex. Later when I consider individual histories I hope to show how these latter characteristics are more significant than the capacity for sexual intercourse with a person of the other sex.

In discussing definitions of homosexuality it is necessary to distinguish transsexuality. Transsexuals are persons who anatomically are one sex but perceive themselves to be of the opposite one. "Such persons do not doubt their anatomical identity, but they are convinced it is the wrong one and

[7] Cavanagh, *op. cit.*, pp. 69–72.

therefore desire their anatomy to correspond with their perceived gender identity. The condition can become acutely painful, leading to severe disruption of their lives and even suicidal tendencies."[8]

Unlike authors such as Robert Stoller in *Sex and Gender*, Moberly sees homosexuality and transsexualism as differing only in degree and not in kind. Starting with the premise that the homosexual condition is one of same-sex ambivalence, she develops her own homosexual spectrum in the sense that the deficit involved will vary in degree from person to person. Where the deficit is less marked one is likely to find the bisexual.

> To the extent that same-sex love is still needed the person is homosexual and the psychodynamic structure here is the same as in all homosexuality, varying only in degree. True bisexuality implies a greater degree of fulfill-ment of same-sex attachment needs, prior to defensive detachment, than in most homosexuals.[9]

Moberly cautions that a married homosexual is not necessarily a bi-sexual, "and indeed is not a bisexual if his or her chief emotional needs are for the same sex".[10]

At the other end of the spectrum is the person in whom the same-sex relational deficit is extremely marked. In this person the normal process of physiological growth has been accompanied by very little of the normal corresponding psychological growth. The blocking of the identificatory process is so severe that it leads to disidentification: "not just an absence of identification, but a reaction against identification".[11]

The persons in whom this radical disidentification has taken place do not feel themselves to be members of their own anatomical sex. This sense of gender dislocation is entirely realistic if physical growth has not been accompanied by requisite psychological growth. In brief, transsexualism is a more radical break with the parent of the same sex and is rooted in early childhood trauma. This same-sex deficit is so great that it is more accurate to speak of actual gender dislocation. Such is Moberly's under-standing of the transsexual.[12]

---

[8] Donald McCarthy and Edward Bayer, *Handbook on Critical Sexual Issues* (Garden City, New York: Doubleday, Image Books, 1984), pp. 164–168.

[9] *Ibid.*, p. 12.

[10] *Ibid.*

[11] *Ibid.*

[12] *Ibid.*, pp. 13–14.

2. THE DISTINCTION BETWEEN HOMOSEXUAL ACTIVITY
AND ORIENTATION

Homosexual orientation includes not only one's conscious physical attraction for members of one's own sex, but also the fantasy life that has preceded it for years. It is sometimes called the homosexual condition that is not consciously willed by the person. It would be more accurate to say that the person discovered it than that he chose it. Sometimes this inclination or attraction is not recognized by the person, because unconsciously he does not want to admit that he has homosexual inclinations. Usually when he does become aware of these feelings he is filled with sentiments of self-hatred and guilt, because he has accepted the harsh verdict of society against even the inclination itself.

Whether the orientation is recognized or not, it is not sinful in itself. It is, however, an *objective* disorder because it inclines one to perform an evil act.[13] Theologians have always made a distinction between spontaneous inclinations and the deliberate nurturing of the inclinations, which would be sinful. Hence one makes the moral distinction between orientation and activity. Only when one freely gives in to such inclinations does one commit a sin of homosexuality, which can take the form of deliberate fantasizing or masturbation, or an act with another person of the same sex. As we shall see in the next chapter, Moberly holds that the inclination toward persons of one's own sex is something good and positive, while hostile detachment from a same-sex parental figure is the real evil, albeit not a moral evil. She also holds that such a person ought to strive to become heterosexual in orientation.

Not all authors, however, agree that the tendency to homosexual acts is not in itself sinful. Some Protestant writers tend to see this inclination as an effect of original sin; thus, Colin Cook writes that Jesus' death was God's judgment and punishment of one's sin, one's homosexuality. In effect, God says, "I do not charge your sinful nature, your homosexuality, against you any more. It has been condemned and punished in Christ".[14] I shall return to the thought of Cook in Chapter Three and again in the pastoral section in Chapter Seven.

[13] PCHP, 3.

[14] *Homosexuality: An Open Door?* (Boise, Idaho: Pacific Press Publishing Association, 1985), p. 28.

3. DISTINCTION BETWEEN COMPULSIVE AND NON–COMPULSIVE ACTIVITY

Since over the years professionals continue to learn more and more (but seemingly never enough) about compulsive (addictive) behavior, it is necessary to clarify the distinction between compulsive and non-compulsive homosexual activity. I understand compulsion and addiction as referring to patterns of behavior either within the thought and feeling patterns of the individual or in his relations with others and with the culture that show clearly that the individual concerned is out of control, and this despite the fact that he tries often to live an ordered life, but with little or no success. Step One of A.A. refers to compulsive activity: "I am an alcoholic and I am powerless over this condition." One can adapt Step One to the compulsive homosexual: "I am a homosexual, and I am powerless over this condition." But in doing so one is not stating that all homosexual persons are compulsive. Indeed there are no reliable statistics concerning what percentage of homosexual persons are compulsive.

It will be profitable, however, to explore some of the nuances of compulsive activity in general in order to understand the nature of homosexual activity among homosexual persons. With a deeper understanding of their own compulsions, homosexual persons can perceive the value of a pastoral program whose objective is to help the individual regain control over his actions.

The Sexual Addiction by Patrick Carnes[15] is perhaps the first book to identify and define sexual addiction. It deals not only with the sexual addict but also with his family and the whole network of people affected by the addict's compulsiveness. Carnes describes the origins of sexual addiction, the addictive cycle with its progressive intensity, and the terrible loneliness of the double life the addict must lead. He also discusses programs of recovery that we shall consider later in the pastoral perspectives.

Turning to a consideration of the compulsive homosexual person, one notes the squalid circumstances coupled with risk that characterize his sexual behavior. The fact that a person in public life risks his career for the sake of a quick sexual "fix" indicates the gravity of the problem. We need to consider the many degrees of compulsion among homosexual persons.

The extremely compulsive homosexual person tends to contemplate solicitation of every male he meets; others are compulsive only with certain kinds of persons; still others are compulsive only under a certain set of circumstances. For example, a person discovers that whenever he

---

[15] Stephen Olert, F.S.C., and Ruthann Williams, O.P., "In a Plain Wrapper—Help for the Sexual Addict", *The Priest*, Nov. 1986, pp. 29–36, clearly describes the sexual addict and provides practical guidelines for both the counselor and the addict.

enters a certain restroom he is overcome by the sight of an exposed or scarcely concealed phallus of another person who may be there for seduction. Part of the dynamics of compulsion in this example is the person's motive for visiting the restroom in the first place. Frustration, guilt, anger, loneliness, and despair are contributing factors in compulsion.

We have no way of categorizing the kinds and degrees of compulsive homosexual behavior. Each person reveals a different degree of compulsion in a different pattern of personality traits. One needs to look at the strength of the compulsion and the nature of the object of sexual desire. One also needs to consider the mood of the person, a point we shall consider in the pastoral perspectives. In this respect there are valid comparisons between alcoholism and compulsive homosexuality. The fact that a person stops drinking after he joins A.A. is not proof that he was not a compulsive drinker in the first place; likewise, the fact that a compulsive homosexual person avoids homosexual activity for several weeks after making a retreat with other homosexuals does not prove that he was not compulsive from the beginning. At the same time it is almost impossible to say that a given action was the result of a compulsive urge.

A person who acts freely one day may act compulsively the next, and his neighbor would be none the wiser.[16] As Rudolph Allers points out, "We cannot know anything about the nature of alleged irresistible impulses unless we know all we can find out about the total personality."[17] Oftentimes the compulsive person seems perfectly free in what he does despite the fact that he is under the influence of one dominant purpose which shuts out all other thoughts from his mind, thereby eliminating at the time any chance of any counteracting motives from having their efficacy. The mind is filled with one big idea or image: a bathhouse, a movie theatre, or a pornographic bookshop. That is all he thinks about until he succeeds in arriving there. His actions seem deliberate and free, yet they are the result of a narrowing of consciousness to but one idea.[18]

In another form of compulsion one finds that as a result of intense concentration of the person's faculties on the object of desire (usually a quick impersonal act) great tensions build up, with a craving for release from this tension so overwhelming that the person feels he either has to give in or suffer an intolerable situation. He has to have a quick "fix" at a truckstop restroom or he must masturbate. In such instances there is more freedom than in the previous situations where the principal factor is the

[16] John Ford and Gerald Kelly, *Contemporary Moral Theology*, vol. 1, *Questions in Fundamental Moral Theology* (Westminster, Md.: Newman Press, 1958), p. 230.
[17] "Irresistible Impulses: A Question of Moral Psychology", *American Ecclesiastical Review* 100 (1939):219.
[18] *Ibid.*, pp. 214–215.

narrowing of consciousness. The person is more aware that he can resist, but only with great tension. He is also conscious that the more he gives in to the temptation, the less control he will have.

Finally, there is an insight in Allers' article that I have seen verified not only among many homosexuals but also among heterosexuals prone to grave sins of impurity either with themselves or with others. The passage merits quoting in full.

> There is one very curious and very important feature worthy of mention in these irresistible impulses. They become irresistible, so to say, before they have fully developed. People have a presentiment of the impulse arising; they know that within a short time they will become entangled in a situation from which there is no escape, much as they desire one. They know that they are still capable, at this very moment, of turning away and that by doing so they will avoid the danger—but they do not. There is a peculiar fascination, a lurid attraction in this kind of danger, and there is evidently some anticipation of the satisfaction that the *partes inferiores animae* will derive from indulging in the irresistible action. The action itself may, therefore, not carry any responsibility and nevertheless not be excusable, because, in fact, the person has assented to its development.[19]

Commenting on this passage, Ford and Kelly hold that the development of the impulse is "often the disguised expression of a desire for sexual satisfaction".[20] This is an insight that Christian counselors should make with the homosexual counselee who may not realize the latent insincerity of his protestation that he really did not want this to happen. I shall return to the homosexual person's need for complete honesty in the pastoral section.

It should be noted that compulsive traits are not understood as the mere strength of the impulse as it is commonly supposed among those who regard all homosexual persons as super-sexed, because in general the sexual tendencies of the homosexual person are no stronger than those of the heterosexual person. Finally, there is another and less exact sense in which the term *compulsion* is used. It is the conviction, born of bitter failures to control their sexual impulses, that the urge is irresistible, and of the ready acceptance of the same false idea as the result of indoctrination. I have met many homosexual persons who have been seduced by such teaching.

More will be said about compulsion among homosexual persons in the pastoral perspectives. At this point I summarize the thought of Allers, as well as my own pastoral experience of over thirty years, by saying that

---

[19] *Ibid.*, pp. 216–217.
[20] Ford and Kelly, *op. cit.*, p. 233.

one can know little about a compulsive person until one knows his personal history. Patrick Carnes has developed the insights of Allers by showing the mind-set found in many compulsives—that is to say, their unreal view of themselves, their loved ones, and the world in which they live. In the pastoral section I shall draw out the implications of compulsion within a pastoral program.

I turn now to the consideration of some recent theories concerning the origin of the homosexual condition with the hope that certain aspects of these theories will help both the counselor of homosexual persons and homosexual persons themselves.

CHAPTER THREE

SOME RECENT THEORIES CONCERNING THE ORIGINS OF HOMOSEXUALITY

Since it does not serve my purpose to review and evaluate the variety of etiological theories concerning homosexual orientation, I shall refer the readers to professional sources on the subject.[1] From even a cursory reading of the contemporary literature it is clear that many professionals no longer regard homosexuality as a disease or mental illness but as a perfectly normal variant of sexual desire. The controversial decision of the American Psychiatric Association (1973) does not go so far as to say that homosexual orientation is a perfectly normal alternative to marriage and a heterosexual lifestyle, yet that is the way it has been understood by the public. In the *Diagnostic and Statistical Manual of Mental Disorders*, third edition, the category of homosexuality is replaced by Ego–dystonic Homosexuality, described in this fashion: "The essential features are a desire to acquire or increase heterosexual arousal, so that heterosexual relationships can be initiated or maintained, and a sustained pattern of overt homosexual arousal that the individual explicitly states has been unwanted and a persistent source of distress."[2]

In 1974, during the height of the controversy, a significant minority of the members of the A.P.A. did not accept *D.S.M.*'s revision of the category of homosexuality. Representative of the minority, Dr. Irving Bieber objected to the revised classification on the score that it is a developmental abnormality, although not a disease or mental illness. It might be called heterosexual dysfunction or inadequacy.[3]

---

[1] Arno Karlen, *Sexuality and Homosexuality* (New York: W. W. Norton and Co., 1971). His series of critical bibliographies, pp. 619–646, are excellent. Other useful and more contemporary references include: M. P. Feldman and M. J. MacCulloch, *Homosexual Behaviour and Assessment* (Oxford, England: Pergamon, 1971; John R. Cavanagh, *Counseling the Homosexual* (Huntington, Ind.: Our Sunday Visitor Press, 1977); Judd Marmor, *Homosexual Behavior* (New York: Basic Books, 1980); *Sex and Gender*, ed. Mark Schwartz, Albert Moraczewski, and James Monteleone (St. Louis, Mo.: Pope John Center, 1983).

[2] *Diagnostic and Statistical Manual*, 3rd ed. (Washington, D.C.: American Psychiatric Association, 1980). p. 281. The manual goes on to describe *ego-syntonic homosexuality* as no longer "classified as a mental disorder" (p. 282). In this form the individual is not upset by his orientation. In Chapter Four Father Jeffrey Keefe questions whether homosexuality is a normal alternate psychosexual development or a disorder.

[3] John F. Harvey, O.S.F.S., "Changes in Nomenclature and Their Probable Effect", in Cavanagh, *op. cit.*, pp. 30–36 at 32.

Since I concur in Bieber's view that homosexuality is a developmental abnormality, I see the necessity of finding some explanation for such a development. I turn now to a more complete analysis of both Moberly's and Gerald van den Aardweg's thought. In presenting this summary I hope to draw from each insights valuable for pastoral practice. Each has a distinct perspective, with many elements that can be useful in understanding the meaning of homosexuality and in providing pastoral guidance.

1. MOBERLY'S THOUGHT

Moberly presents a radical reassessment of the data of depth psychology. Traditionally, these data have been held to support an understanding of same-sex love as pathological and deviant. By contrast Moberly insists that these very data actually indicate that same-sex love is a normal and legitimate developmental need. The capacity for same-sex love is neither problematical nor pathological. However, this valid and universal love-need has not been fulfilled on the usual developmental time-table. Paradoxically, the homosexual's capacity for same-sex relating is damaged. For this reason, therapy is still desirable for the homosexual, but it must be a therapy that focuses on *same*-sex relational needs and difficulties.[4]

According to Moberly's data, the homosexual person—whether male or female—has been unable to meet the normal developmental need for attachment to the parent of the same sex. There has been some difficulty in relationship in the earlier years of life: permanent or temporary separation, the emotional unavailability of the parent, neglect or other difficulty in relationship. The child experienced hurt, even if the parent was *not* deliberately hurtful, and this hurt resulted in the repression of the child's attachment to the parent of the same sex. Here Moberly develops John Bowlby's well-known work on child attachment and separation. As a major innovation, she applies these principles to the development of gender identity and sexual orientation.[5]

As a result of early difficulties in relating to the parent of the same sex, the attachment-need is repressed and remains unfulfilled. Hence the child's normal needs for love, dependency, and identification remain unfulfilled, since their fulfillment depends on an uninterrupted attachment. However, the attachment-need may well emerge from repression and seek further fulfillment. When this occurs, a renewed same-sex relationship

---

[4] This summary of Moberly's thought is taken from her two books on homosexuality: *Homosexuality: A New Christian Ethic* (Cambridge, England: James Clarke, 1983, and Greenwood, S.C.: Attic Press), a popular version; and *Psychogenesis: The Early Development of Gender Identity* (London: Routledge and Kegan Paul, Ltd., 1983), a scholarly work.

[5] *Psychogenesis*, pp. 9–12, 21, 60, refers to Bowlby's writings.

is established. This means that a so-called homosexual relationship is not deviant but is based on the drive to fulfill a legitimate developmental need. What Moberly stresses is the validity of the needs involved: "What the male homosexual seeks is what he should have received from his relationship to his father. What the female homosexual seeks is what she should have received from her relationship to her mother. What is sought is the fulfillment of attachment needs which are a *normal* part of the developmental process, but which have *abnormally* been left unmet in the process of growth."[6]

On Moberly's developmental perspective, the homosexual's need for a same-sex attachment is the need to make up for missing growth. It is the reparative attempt to fulfill unmet developmental needs. In other words, same-sex love is not an obstacle to development, but is itself the drive to resume and further the developmental process. Moberly stresses that same-sex love is the *solution* to a developmental problem. Contrary to the traditional viewpoint, it is *not* itself that problem. Same-sex love is not an abnormal sexual drive, but a normal developmental drive. To be sure, it may be less easily recognized as such whenever it is expressed in sexual activity, but the point is that it is possible for same-sex needs to be fulfilled apart from sexual expression.[7]

The early damage to the relationship with the same-sex parent results in an abiding difficulty in the child's own relational capacity, persisting into adult life. This leads us into a highly significant point. If homosexuality is defined as the capacity for same-sex love, why is there so much evidence of hostility toward members of the same sex? Moberly explores the evidence for this hostility in her major psychological study, *Psychogenesis*. She notes that this same-sex antagonism may often be unconscious but emerges into consciousness with resulting difficulties in same-sex relationships, whether sexual or social. Found both within the psychoanalytic literature and elsewhere, such evidence leads to the conclusion that the homosexual condition is one of same-sex ambivalence, not just same-sex love. Paradoxically, homosexuality involves a conflict between positive and negative attitudes toward members of the same sex. As already noted, this conflict is not always conscious, but it does imply a persisting deficit in the homosexual's capacity for relating to the same sex.[8]

[6] Moberly, "Counselling the Homosexual", in *The Expository Times*, June 1985. See also *Psychogenesis*, p. x: "Need for love, dependency and identification which are normally met through the medium of an attachment to a parental love source have remained unmet. The capacity for same-sex love is an attempt to restore this disrupted attachment and hence to make up for missing growth."

[7] *Homosexuality: A New Christian Ethic*, pp. 18–22.

[8] *Psychogenesis*, pp. 14–16.

This same-sex difficulty deserves therapeutic attention. The persisting unmet need for same-sex love presupposes this underlying problem, but it must be emphasized that same-sex love *is not in itself problematical*. It is a normal developmental need, and as such it deserves fulfillment. The therapeutic task must therefore be to resolve same-sex hurts and difficulties and to improve the capacity for same-sex relating so that these legitimate developmental needs for same-sex love may be fulfilled.[9]

By contrast with the traditional approach, Moberly advocates gender-specific therapy for homosexuals. Firstly, it is essential that the therapist be of the same sex, a man for a male homosexual, a woman for a lesbian. The purpose of gender-specific therapy is to coordinate the solution with the nature of the problem. Where the unmet need is one of fathering and masculine identity, only a male therapist can help, since only a man can be a father. Where the unmet need is one of mothering and feminine identity, only a female therapist can help, since only a woman can be a mother. With the same-sex therapist, there is a twofold therapeutic goal: to meet the same-sex relational needs and, equally important, to resolve the underlying antagonism toward members of the same sex. Within the therapeutic relationship, the same-sex ambivalence is to be resolved, and the need for a same-sex attachment may be fulfilled. Because of the moral law, such an attachment ought not to be expressed sexually.[10]

Since same-sex developmental needs can only be fulfilled—by definition —in a relationship with a member of the same sex, Moberly's gender-specific principles offer a marked contrast to traditional therapy. She insists that increased opposite-sex contact is entirely inappropriate for the homosexual: "Attempted heterosexual relationships or social contact with the opposite sex are not the solution to homosexuality, since increased opposite-sex contact can do nothing to fulfill same-sex deficits. Relationships with the opposite sex are, literally, by definition, irrelevant to a problem of this nature."[11] For this reason it is important—indeed, in Moberly's method, essential—*not* to counsel the homosexual in the direction of dating or marriage. To encourage increased opposite-sex contact for homosexuals is quite simply irrelevant to the therapy of homosexuals, because the homosexual condition involves *same*-sex developmental deficits. There are no shortcuts to heterosexuality. The attainment of genuine heterosexuality is possible for those who wish it, but, paradoxically, it depends on the fulfillment of the *same*-sex developmental process.[12]

[9] *Ibid.*, pp. 66–77.
[10] *Homosexuality: A New Christian Ethic*, pp. 18–22.
[11] *Ibid.*, p. 18.
[12] *Ibid.*, p. 21.

Moberly is not concerned to promote heterosexual behavior in homosexuals. Many homosexuals can and do function heterosexually, with or without therapy, but heterosexual behavior is a superficial criterion. Moberly does not regard such behavior as an adequate measure of basic sexual orientation or of psychological needs. From her perspective, the homosexual's deepest need is quite rightly and genuinely for relationships with members of the same sex. Before heterosexuality is reached, it is vital to do justice to the developmental stages that must precede it. The need for same-sex love is an essential part of this process, and as such it is a normal and legitimate need. Moberly reiterates that this legitimate developmental need cannot be superseded unless and until it has been fulfilled.[13]

The need for same-sex relationships is entirely realistic and needs to be accepted and assisted by the therapist. Same-sex love is a legitimate developmental drive. Please note how Moberly shifts the focus away from the sexual to the developmental. One cannot bypass same-sex developmental needs; justice must be done to them. Moberly's view is quite different from viewing same-sex relationships as intrinsically wrong. According to Moberly, same-sex relationships are inherently healing relationships: "If fulfillment is seen as merely sexual or if healing is seen as merely the suppression of sexual activity, both of these approaches miss the heart of the matter. There are legitimate needs involved in the homosexual condition. These ought not to be met sexually, but they ought to be met."[14] In other words, Moberly indicates that it is the blocking of the same-sex developmental process and the desirability of resuming it that is the main point at issue. Same-sex love is the *solution* to unmet developmental needs. It is not the problem.

Here it will become evident how Moberly's position differs from that of other counselors and contemporary therapists who assert that there is no problem at all in homosexuality, and hence no need of therapy.[15] This position, however, simply ignores the evidence of depth psychology and fails to respond to its claims. By contrast, Moberly bases her position on the evidence of depth psychology but draws radically new conclusions from it. Same-sex needs are *not* problematic in themselves. The fact that they have been left unfulfilled since the earlier years of life is problematic.[16]

[13] *Ibid.*, pp. 22–24.

[14] *Ibid.*, p. 39. It should be noted that the Church does not hold that same-sex relationships are intrinsically wrong, but only same-sex *genital* relationships.

[15] C. A. Tripp, *The Homosexual Matrix* (New York: McGraw-Hill, 1975), is representative of this point of view. Ruth T. Barnhouse, *Homosexuality: Symbolic Confusion* (New York: Seabury Press, 1977), offers a critique of Tripp's position, pp. 38–40, 54–59.

[16] See *Psychogenesis*, pp. 14–38, for a deeper analysis of the structures of same-sex ambivalence.

Moberly's position also contrasts sharply with that of traditional therapists who insist there is a problem in homosexuality: the need for same-sex love. She insists that traditional therapy has been utterly misdirected, not because homosexuals need no therapy at all, but because the solution has been mistaken for the problem. Depth psychology offers clear evidence of legitimate developmental needs in the homosexual condition. This is detailed in *Psychogenesis* and in *The Psychology of Self and Other*, in which she develops her principles further.[17] Moberly indicates that no one is an ex-homosexual, as distinct from an ex-practicing homosexual, unless and until same-sex developmental deficits have been resolved and fulfilled:

> To stop being a homosexual means to stop being a person with same-sex developmental deficits. A non-practicing homosexual is still a homosexual. Sexual activity may not be appropriate to the working out of the problem, but sexual abstinence in itself does not begin to meet the problem of the underlying deficits.[18]

Moberly believes it is hardly surprising that many homosexuals have rejected or resented what has been offered to them in the name of therapy. The relatively limited success of traditional attempts to cure or change homosexuals stems from a fundamental misunderstanding of the nature of the homosexual condition. The goals and methods of traditional therapy have been seriously mistaken, and Moberly believes that this accounts for the widespread pessimism concerning therapy to cure homosexuals. It is pointless to try to cure something that is not a problem. Moberly stresses that this is a major and radical shift of therapeutic focus and that it affects both the goal and the methods of therapy.[19]

Significantly, Moberly notes that "healing and fulfillment may no longer be regarded as polar opposites in the homosexual debate, for the healing of same-sex developmental deficits takes place precisely through the fulfillment of the need for same-sex love."[20] In offering therapy to the homosexual there is no longer an obligation to choose between the alternative goals of change *or* fulfillment, because ultimately the two goals coincide. The checking of homosexual activity should not be equated with the elimination of homosexual needs. Paradoxically, to block their fulfillment blocks the possibility of progress toward heterosexuality: "It

[17] (New York: Methuen, 1985).

[18] *Homosexuality: A New Christian Ethic*, p. 40.

[19] *Ibid.*, pp. 29–32. See my review of Moberly's *Psychology of Self and Other* in *The Linacre Quarterly*, Feb. 1986, pp. 87–90.

[20] "Homosexuality: Restating the Conservative Case", in *Salmagundi*, Fall 1982–Winter 1983.

must be understood very clearly that to thwart the fulfillment of such needs implies that the person is forced to remain homosexual."[21]

Many homosexuals may not consciously seek heterosexuality or may even stress that they do not wish to become heterosexual. In Moberly's view a major reason for this is rooted in a misunderstanding of what it means to become heterosexual—a misunderstanding that has, unfortunately, been promoted by traditional therapists. Moberly holds that heterosexuality does not imply the checking of same-sex love-needs. Justice must be done to developmental needs; they cannot be bypassed. She sees the apparent fixity of the homosexual orientation as due to the need to give attention to the same-sex developmental process. Genuinely heterosexual response is based on the fulfillment of same-sex love-needs and on the resolution of the same-sex ambivalence that hinders the adequate fulfillment of same-sex love-needs. Moberly notes: "This is what is implied by the phrase 'becoming heterosexual': the fulfillment of same-sex attachment-needs, and hence the fulfillment and not the checking of the homosexual's own deepest emotional longings."[22]

Analysis of specific points in Moberly's theory

While heterosexuality is the goal of human development, it will take place only through the fulfillment of homo-emotional needs and not their abrogation. For this reason therapy should aim at undoing the defensive detachment from the same-sex love source and in bringing the reparative drive to its fulfillment. Thus, Moberly devotes a significant section of her book to the lesbian, whom she sees as suffering from the same kind of ambivalence as the male homosexual, and she recommends a similar therapy, which we will outline.[23]

We need to look also at the persisting love-need of the homosexual person. As long as the defensive barrier is a dynamic force within the personality (and this holds for the adult as well as for the child), he or she will block the capacity for the fulfillment of the love-need. One will not be capable of receiving love from the mistrusted love-source. Thus the presence of the unmet need for love reveals an underlying conflict. The love-need of itself implies an ambivalence toward the needed love-source. The love-need cannot be isolated from the defensive process that has shaped it and caused it to persist unmet. The need for love, and hate for the

---

[21] *Homosexuality: A New Christian Ethic*, p. 40.

[22] *Ibid.*, p. 25.

[23] See my review of *Psychogenesis* in *The Linacre Quarterly*, May 1984, pp. 185–188.

hurtful love-source, are inextricably tied together. Hence the reality of ambivalence, with its two faces. Applying these concepts to the phenomenon of homosexuality, one notes that it has frequently been defined as love of the same sex. From Moberly's analysis it would be more accurate to define it as ambivalence toward the same sex. There is a love-need involved, but it is based on defensive detachment from the needed love-source. "In one and the same condition we find both defensive detachment from a love-source and an abiding need for attachment to that love-source, which the defensive barrier has blocked."[24]

An important detail of Moberly's theory is that one of the components of the structure of ambivalence is hostility, overt or latent, toward parental figures and toward other members of the same sex. This hostility may be a component of actual sexual relationships. Moberly refers to Bieber's major study of male homosexuals in which it is noted that where the man's father has been hostile to his son, as distinct from merely neglectful or ambivalent, the homosexual partner was invariably identified with the father who had been hated and feared.[25] Hostility may also be expressed in the form of antagonism toward colleagues of the same sex, or in a marked tendency toward bemoaning injustice or fault-finding, or in authority problems. In all these situations, notes Moberly, the unresolved animosity, which was originally a response to hurtful behavior by the parent of the same-sex has been generalized and can be reactivated in any interpersonal relationship with members of the same sex.[26]

These negative signs of ambivalence are not really adult behavior, although they may be manifested in adult life. They represent the reemergence of the child's repressed defensive response. While the person may have realistic grounds for complaint in the present, one is essentially motivated by the hurts of the past. One allows the present to be unreasonably conditioned by the past. It is really a transference—the reactivation of genuine interpersonal difficulties, carried over from the relationships of the past to those of the present.

Moberly stresses the search of the male homosexual person to fulfill hitherto unmet needs by a restored attachment. It is really an attempt to complete the process of identification, and it is obvious when homosexual persons seek virile partners to get a shot of masculinity through identification with the partner.[27]

The homosexual love-need is essentially a search for parenting, but this

[24] *Psychogenesis*, p. 23.

[25] *Homosexuality: A New Christian Ethic*, p. 7. The reference is to I. Bieber et al., *Homosexuality: A Psychoanalytic Study* (New York: Basic Books, 1962).

[26] *Homosexuality: A New Christian Ethic*, p. 7.

[27] *Ibid.*, p. 9.

does not mean that the same-sex partner must be an overt parent figure. It should be remembered also that we are here concerned with the homosexual condition and not with its translation into sexual activity. While the psychological needs of the homosexual person are often expressed sexually, these needs exist independently of sexual expression, according to Moberly. They can be fulfilled by a good non-sexual relationship with a member of the same sex.

Not all the structures of same-sex ambivalence are visible in all cases or at all times. Many of them remain latent on the unconscious level. Either side of the ambivalence may be predominant. The homosexual love-need may often be the only conscious manifestation of this total structure. What often happens is that the person forms a renewed attachment while defensiveness toward the same sex remains repressed. Unfortunately, the reparative attempt may be thwarted by this defensiveness from the unconscious level. The relationship may be subject to instability and disruption. This happens frequently in homosexual relationships.

As I continue to analyze Moberly's thought, it will be helpful to turn to the female homosexual person, because I believe that Moberly has given one of the best, perhaps the best, explanations of the origin of female homosexuality, also known as lesbianism. The psychodynamic structure of female homosexuality is analogous to that in the male in that it also involves same-sex ambivalence. The defensive detachment from the same-sex love-source will be marked by hostility, whether latent or overt, toward the mother and toward other members of the same sex. This defensive detachment implies a blocking of the normal process of identification, which leads to an absence of femininity, an absence which in turn is rooted in a defensive anti-femininity. In some instances this will reveal itself in a quasi-masculine identity.[28]

Yet in spite of the defensive detachment there is in women as in men a drive toward reparation of the broken libidinal attachment. Thus the female homosexual seeks female love, which is an essentially maternal love. Many studies have commented on the mother-daughter character of the lesbian relationship. This need for the mother, however, is often misunderstood as a mother fixation, i.e., as an abnormal attachment. It is more correct to interpret it as an abiding need for attachment, consequent on actual detachment. In the female, as in the male, homosexuality marks a defect in the capacity for relating to the same sex.

Moberly refers to the pathological mourning response which follows an early separation of the little girl from the mother or the little boy from the father, and she believes that its long-term effects on identity and

[28] *Psychogenesis*, p. 52.

homo-emotional needs have not been studied sufficiently. She postulates that female homosexuality always stems from some actual difficulty in the mother-child relationship, whether or not it is possible to identify this difficulty retrospectively. Be it noted that Moberly is the first to make the link between such early trauma and homosexuality.

Moberly and others note that the father-daughter relationship for the disidentified female is not as intense as the mother-son relationship for the disidentified male.[29] She goes on to comment on the *immaturity* of the disidentified person. If a normal channel of attachment has remained blocked since early infancy, the person is in certain important respects still a child psychologically, although he may be mature in many ways. Citing Storr, who speaks of how the lesbian may demand the kind of love and attention that a child of three or less may justifiably demand from its mother, Moberly comments that this was one of the most important clues at the very beginning of her investigation into homosexuality. "If someone behaves like a child of two or three, might this not imply that they genuinely have the actual needs of a child of that age and that something occurred at that age to prevent further maturation? The evidence gathered in this study would seem to confirm this hypothesis."[30]

The perpetuation of ambivalence is due to the disruption in early childhood of the girl's normal and necessary attachment to her mother. It is hardly surprising that the lesbian relationship takes on the character of a mother-child relationship in which an effort is made to restore the broken attachment. Moberly cites instances of this immaturity within the context of a restored attachment. She adds that jealousy and possessiveness are related characteristics in many lesbian relationships—and, may I add, in many male homosexual relationships. I have witnessed the kind of immaturity to which Storr refers in a thirty-two-year-old man who also manifested jealousy and possessiveness in his relationship with another member of the support group. Not surprisingly, moreover, Moberly mentions the sense of inferiority in the lesbian. If the child's capacity for attachment has been repressed, it lacks the sense of personal worth that comes from accepting its parents' love.

Often the relationship is disrupted from within, with the negative side of the ambivalence causing the disruption. The perennial problem of the homosexual ambivalence is that the reparative attempt may at any time be thwarted by the reemergence of the defensive barrier. The tendency toward renewal of loss through renewal of detachment is inherent in the

[29] *Ibid.*, p. 59.
[30] *Ibid.*, p. 60. See also Moberly's *Psychology of Self and Other* (New York: Methuen, 1985).

very structure of homosexuality. This is the reason why active homosexual relationships are unable to fulfill developmental deficits.[31]

Moberly concludes her observations concerning female homosexuality by reaffirming that the fundamental requirement for same-sex identification is an uninterrupted attachment to a figure of the same sex. The interruption of a relationship with a mother, whether she is heterosexual or homosexual, is pathological, while on the other hand an uninterrupted relationship will itself guarantee basic gender identity.

In summary, Moberly says that homosexuality is marked by incompletion, i.e., the absence of some degree of normal growth, so that the homosexual cannot—unless superficially—act as if the growth had been completed. At this point, then, it is unrealistic to expect the homosexual person to act in a heterosexual way:

> But homosexuality involves both a state of incompletion and also a striving for completion. The homosexual response is itself the reparative attempt toward completion. It must also be recognized that completion cannot be attained without the fulfillment of homosexual needs. Homosexuality may not be the goal of human growth, but it is certainly the normal, and indeed only, means toward the goal.[32]

Moberly's thought provides much insight for pastoral guidance, inasmuch as her understanding of the homosexual person helps one to see what is good in a relationship with a person of the same sex and to strive to form non-genital friendships with persons of the same sex as the first step to forming heterosexual relationships later when one's homosexual needs have been met. Same-sex friendships are good, but not enough by themselves; otherwise, you get only non-practicing homosexuals, and not genuine ex-homosexuals. Again, one notes that Moberly is placing the emphasis, not on physical same-sex attraction, but on the process of gender-specific therapy. Fulfilling one's homosexual needs on the gender level is only the first, but necessary, step toward the development of heterosexual orientation. As I complete this analysis of Moberly's theory, I still have the same difficulty I had when I first read her works in 1984: the need for more empirical verification.

The research of Moberly, however, must be compared with that of other authors, all of whom help us to see some aspect of this complex problem. For this reason I have added several more-recent findings before I present a summary of van den Aardweg's thought. I ask the reader to reserve judgment until he has studied all these related viewpoints. I believe

[31] *Ibid.*, p. 63.
[32] *Ibid.*, p. 66.

we can draw something valuable for pastoral practice from all these studies.

Richard Green cites several retrospective studies linking boyhood cross-gender behavior with late adolescent and adult homosexual orientation. Saghir and Robins found that 65% of 89 homosexual men, but only 3% of 35 heterosexual men, recalled a "girl-like" syndrome, which was characterized by an aversion to playing with boys, an aversion to boys' games and activities, and an interest in playing with dolls. A larger study by Bell and others of 575 homosexual and 284 heterosexual men found "that the most significant correlate of adult homosexuality recalled from boyhood was 'gender non-conformity', which was characterized by a preference for girls' rather than boys' activities and cross-dressing."[33] An even larger study by Harry, involving 1,400 homosexual men and 200 heterosexual men, found that significantly more homosexual than heterosexual men recalled being called "sissy", being social loners, wanting to be girls, playing with girls, and cross-dressing.[34] Because of the fallacies of retrospective recall, Green made an experimental study of the same phenomenon and came to the conclusion that "the association between extensive cross-gender behavior in boyhood and homosexual behavior in adulthood, suggested by previous retrospective reports, can be validated by a prospective study of clinically or family-referred boys with behaviors consistent with the gender-identity disorder of childhood."[35]

Another cross-cultural study runs counter to the theory that male homosexuality is the result of conditioning by pleasurable erotic events, especially first experiences at puberty, with the pleasure reinforced by repeating these pleasures as time passes. To the contrary, Robert Stoller and Gilbert Herdt point out that such a theory leaves out "an appreciation for the power of early non-erotic events in shaping the character structure that, once formed, in itself, and weightier than chance encounters, leads people to erotic preferences."[36] The authors go on to show from a case history of a Sambian homosexual man that the gender-identity factor was far more crucial in his psychosexual development than his indulgence in ritualistic fellatio with prepubertal boys and youths.

[33] Richard Green, "Gender Identity in Childhood and Later Sexual Orientation: Follow-up of 78 Males", *Amer. J. Psychiatry* 142:3 (March 1985):339–341 at 339.

[34] *Ibid.*, p. 339. Green also points out that a cross-cultural study by Whitam in U.S.A., Brazil, and Guatemala came to the same conclusion.

[35] *Ibid.*, p. 340.

[36] Robert J. Stoller and Gilbert Herdt, "Theories of Origins of Male Homosexuality", *Arch. Gen. Psychiatry* 42 (April 1985):399–404 at 304.

2. AARDWEG'S THOUGHT

Now I turn to the analysis of another contemporary writer on homosexuality, Gerald van den Aardweg. He has authored *Homosexuality and Hope* (Ann Arbor, Mich.: Servant Books, 1985) and *On the Origins and Treatment of Homosexuality* (New York: Praeger Publishers, 1986).

Aardweg's books have been chosen for study because, like Moberly, he offers hope that persons can free themselves from a homosexual orientation. We will consider this aspect of Aardweg's work in the pastoral perspectives; now I describe his theory concerning the origins of homosexual orientation. In general, Aardweg holds that homosexuality is an expression of inferiority feelings that usually emerge in prepuberty or puberty. Filled with self-pity and feeling inferior to the same-sex persons whom he comes to admire and idolize from his own inferiority feelings, he desires to have contact with such persons. His craving to have contact is not so much an attempt to get rid of inferiority feelings as a passionate attempt to possess what he thinks he lacks. These feelings persist into adult years.[37]

From his research and long clinical experience Aardweg concludes that homosexual inclinations are learned, not innate. In considering hormonal factors as possibly contributing to homosexual orientation, Aardweg cautions the reader concerning the limitations of studies which claim that differences in hormonal levels between heterosexual and homosexual persons indicate that such levels are contributing causes of homosexual orientation. It could just as easily mean that psychological factors and habits of the given homosexual person influence their hormonal levels. In short, sometimes one cannot distinguish between cause and effect.[38]

Aardweg specifically criticizes the theory that there is a critical prenatal period in the development of the brain in which androgen can influence the masculinization of the brain's sexual response center *only*, with the exclusion of its influence on sexual responses to related brain centers. This theory has not been demonstrated as applying to humans. Aardweg sums up the objections to an endocrine theory of homosexuality:

> Not only are the theoretical objections to an endocrine theory of homosexuality impressive, the reported hormonal differences between groups of homosexuals and controls on which such a theory must be based are in all

[37] *Homosexuality and Hope*, pp. 17–21. Aardweg refers to the depressing fatalism in labeling oneself homosexual. "The young person does not think, 'It is true that I have occasional or regular homosexual feelings, but basically I must have been born the same as anyone else.' No, he feels that he is a different and inferior creature, who carries a doom: he views himself as tragic" (p. 21).

[38] *On the Origins and Treatment of Homosexuality*, pp. 9–11.

likelihood either artifacts of the compositions of the groups under investigation or they reflect effects of behavior (sexual and other) rather than causes. The conclusion of Perloff some twenty years ago (1965), that no convincing demonstrations of endocrine causation of homosexuality have been forthcoming, still holds.[39]

Homosexuality, moreover, cannot be explained by a genetic theory. In commenting about the various studies that claim that homosexuality is a matter of inheritance, Aardweg considers Kallmann's homosexual twin research, which points to a genetic factor.[40] Kallmann had reported that 11.5% of the twin brothers of homosexuals who were members of dizygotic pairs rated themselves as "predominantly" or "exclusively" homosexual on the Kinsey scale, whereas a group of homosexuals who were members of monozygotic twin pairs had a homosexual twin brother in 100% of the cases. But Aardweg observes that the criteria for calling a monozygotic twin brother a homosexual were less strict than those used for the dizygotics. Too many unknown variables are involved.

First, it is well known that selection plays an important role in these studies of twin concordance. The investigator starts with those homosexuals of whom it is known that they are members of a twin pair; thus, he is likely to collect a biased sample. Further, we have to reckon with the effect in monozygotes to show themselves identical—it is rather peculiar that Kallmann observed many of them to be similar even in small behaviors, in gestures and demeanor, which under the assumption of a hereditary factor would imply that their behavior was genetically programmed into details, an inference which cannot be upheld unless we forget all that we know about the influence of upbringing, self-image, and habit formation in childhood and adolescence; . . . the higher concordance between monozygotes might well be explained by a psychological theory which stresses the mutual identification of monozygotic twins. Everyone knows of examples of supposedly monozygotic twins who live as each other's duplicate, and thus it would be highly interesting to explore cases of homosexual monozygotes as to their whole psycho-biography, their self-view in function of their vision of their twin counterpart, and their psychic reactions to childhood experiences.[41]

Aardweg concludes that endocrinological and genetic research has failed to substantiate the theory of constitutional endowment. Not even a

[39] *Ibid.*, p. 13. Aardweg points out in note 11 on p. 13: "I do not agree with the opposite extreme that the choice of the sexual orientation is solely dependent on the sex role which the child has 'learned'; if reared as a boy, he would become sexually interested in girls and vice versa, irrespective of his genetic endowment. This extreme position is taken, among others, by Masters and Johnson (1979). If this were true there was no inherited preference for heterosexuality."

[40] F. J. Kallmann, "Comparative Twin Studies on the Genetic Aspects of Male Homosexuality", *Journal of Nervous and Mental Disease* 115 (1952):283–298.

[41] *On the Origins and Treatment of Homosexuality*, pp. 14–15.

physical or physiological predisposing factor has been demonstrated.[42] In this regard Judd Marmor comments on studies that attempt to show that homosexuality is the result of endocrinological or genetic factors. His view is really a theory of *convergence* of factors in any given person:

> This interpretation of the new research, however, represents a failure to appreciate the complex way in which nature and nurture interact in human beings. . . . A probable answer to the nature-nurture question, then, is that in all instances of human homosexuality, both constitutional and experiential factors are involved. These may include social and economic factors as well as hormonal and familial ones.[43]

In opposition to the homosexuality-is-inherited theories, Aardweg argues that homosexuality is a form of self-pitying neurosis. To understand self-pity, however, one must study the nature of an inferiority complex. From his clinical experience Aardweg observed a psychic structure that had been described for the first time by J. L. Arndt under the name of *autopsychodrama* or *autonomic psychic structure* with a *dramatic* content. Arndt had discovered this dynamic structure in the mind of persons suffering from inferiority complexes, but in the course of time he noted that it operated as well in the mind of many homosexuals.

Aardweg has observed the same phenomena in homosexuals of different cultural backgrounds and in well-documented biographies of Wilde, Proust, and Gide. Autopsychodrama means infantile self-pity turned autonomous. A child or adolescent who has experienced self-pity over a long time usually cannot get rid of it; it becomes firmly fixated in his mind, leading a life of its own, independent of later experiences. This infantile self-pity recurs time and again, both with and without an external motive. It is like a closed circuit in the brain, "emitting impulses [of self-pity] on its own initiative and remaining unaltered during a life-time. This infantile self-pity, which does not change in intensity or form, is always active as an emotional force that influences a person's sentiments, thoughts, and self-consciousness, and in this way his actions and reactions."[44]

The person with this infantile self-pity may now be an adult, but he continues to think, feel, and act as a self-pitying child; hence Aardweg uses the expression "the self-pitying child in the adult".[45] This results in a double personality, the adult ego with his will, thoughts, and feelings, and this self-pitying child. It may also be called a compulsion to complain.

---

[42] *Ibid.*, p. 17.

[43] "Homosexuality: Nature vs. Nurture", *Harvard Medical School Mental Health Letter*, October 1985, pp. 5–6.

[44] *On the Origins and Treatment of Homosexuality*, pp. 19–20.

[45] *Ibid.*, p. 20.

Although found in many neuroses, it throws new light on the genesis, structure, and functioning of homosexuality in its various forms; for this reason it would be more accurate to speak of the "homosexual neurosis" than of "homosexuality", thus linking this particular neurosis to the many other forms of neurosis, and emphasizing that the similarities between homosexuality and other neuroses are far more essential than the differences."[46]

Before describing the specific elements of self-pity in the homosexual person, Aardweg explains the processes that lead to the autonomization of self-pity in neurosis and the general laws by which it is controlled. Following Arndt, Aardweg sees the beginning in early childhood trauma. If a child perceives himself as rejected, discriminated against in one way or another, less respected, or not loved, he will usually react with self-pity. "No one loves me"—this self-view automatically elicits the warm, comforting tears of self-pity and an attitude of complaining about oneself. Self-pity, as pity, is elicited *instinctively* whenever one sees oneself in one's present circumstances as pitiable. Usually this self-pity occurs when a person makes comparisons between self and others and concludes that he is inferior to others. Most painful is the perception that one is less appreciated than others or that one is inferior in worth. This particularly applies to children: "The decisive factor for the development of intense self-pity in childhood is often the *comparison* with other children which turned out negative for the child concerned."[47]

A child who is frequently told he is good for nothing will come to believe he is worthless and not worthy of the love of others, while other children are. This leads to self-pity, which is really love directed toward the self, and in pitying oneself one finds consolation. Thus self-pity can be seen as a mechanism of self-defense meant to restore mental equilibrium. That is probably why this instinctive emotion is so powerful, and it is something a child may easily fall into, particularly when we remember that children are naturally ego-centered and see themselves as the *dramatic* center of the world: "No one suffers as *I* do."

This dramatic self-view does not fade away in the course of time, but remains fresh and active, even if the objective circumstances of a person's life are later excellent. Good circumstances do not change one's view of being a "poor me", while bad circumstances become a reason for complaining. Learning theory does not explain this phenomenon, because self-pity functions without eliciting stimuli. Thus, a sixty-year-old feels exactly the same self-pity he felt as a child, and his way of complaining has remained exactly the same over the years. In summary, neurotic self-pity

---

[46] *Ibid.*
[47] *Ibid.*, p. 21.

"is in all likelihood not normally learned or conditioned—precisely, therefore, it is atypical, pathological, and inadequate. It *is* a habit in the sense of a persistent way of emotional functioning, but one that has been formed and is preserved in exceptional ways."[48]

Before describing how self-pity or autopsychodrama is at the root of homosexual orientation, Aardweg reviews important characteristics of the compulsion to self-pity that he has discovered in research and clinical practice. This compulsion to complain is continuous; there is a constant stream of complaints moving forward in one's mind. There is little profit in exploring the content of a complaint, hoping to find all kinds of hidden meanings after the fashion of classical psychoanalysis. The only function of the contents of the complaint is to justify the need for complaining. The "inner" child has to have something to complain about. Of course, the person's chief complaint (that of being homosexual) will fill his mind.[49]

If, however, the counselor endeavors to get the complainer to recognize that he is filled with self-pity, the complainer will be indignant. This is too painful, an attack on his infantile pride. He fears any effort to put his complaints in perspective, because he would no longer be a tragic hero. Since he is so preoccupied with himself, moreover, he lacks sensitivity to the needs of others. He is discontented with himself and with the circumstances of his life. Others are doing so much better than he. He ardently wishes to be rich and famous, to have social prestige, and so on. He constantly compares himself in a negative way to others and feels jealous of them. Significantly, he will not let go of any annoying incident or moment of humiliation or blunder of the past. He must reinvoke them in order to suffer anew. This tragic and fatalistic view of one's past is a distortion of the facts. In therapy the person comes to realize that there were many happy moments in his life. Unfortunately, however, the compulsion to self-pity is so strong that it resists therapy.[50]

The compulsion to self-pity causes the person to believe that no one has ever suffered like him and that his suffering is going to get worse. "My situation is different" means that my situation is more serious than that of others. Aardweg calls this a Christ-complex, telling of a homosexual who was moved to tears by the image of Christ as the victim of the hatred of the Jews. But what he thought were deep religious feelings were feelings of infantile self-pity; he liked the tragic role of identifying with Christ as the unique sufferer.

Often the complaining person feels like a child and would like to act like

---

[48] *Ibid.*, p. 25.

[49] *Ibid.*, pp. 28–31.

[50] *Ibid.*, p. 39. Aardweg quotes Freud, who had the feeling "that there is a force at work that defends itself with all possible means against cure and that obstinately clings to illness and sufferings" (p. 32).

one. Aardweg cites the example of some homosexual men who wish to be treated as "boys" instead of as adults: "They show uneasiness in the role of the adult when they insist on being addressed as 'Bobby', 'Tommy', etc. at the same time as their need to be treated with sympathy like little boys."[51]

Another characteristic of the complainer is his lack of dynamism. He is always fatigued; or, more accurately, he complains that he is tired. While he may do his work in his profession, he becomes tired when he is asked to do something he does not want to do. Lack of persistence and feelings of being exhausted can be observed in the majority of male homosexuals, who, as a fact of Aardweg's experience, nourish the specific complaint of being weak and unable to cope with the difficulties of life. For this reason they may not achieve in accord with their capacity.[52]

Again, sometimes there is a foundation in reality for a complaint. Then the "inner child" will cling to his rights, arguing that he has good reasons for complaining. Thus the homosexual who feels sorry for himself because society rejects him, because he is subject to ridicule behind his back, may be right, but at the same time he may be childishly complaining to himself that everyone ignores him. What he needs to learn in therapy and in spiritual support groups is how to cope with real suffering and how to make the difficult situation as bearable as possible.

In the next sections of his book Aardweg discusses the concept of "the inner child in the adult" or the "child in totum". Aardweg holds that only the self-pity of the former child remains active and that this self-pity emerged during a circumscribed period of childhood or adolescence. The "inner child" preserves the former child's habits of thinking and feeling insofar as they are part of his drama or are associated with it. This is the "child in totum", the complaining child. To understand the childhood inner drama of the complainer, we must understand the inner child's view of significant persons at that time; likewise, we need to study the childhood views of homosexuals in order to understand their specific ways of viewing other people and of relating to them. A homosexual male, for example, who had a habit of behaving overcharmingly toward older women really harbored the "little boy" who was treated by older women (particularly his mother) as the "sonny boy". He really wanted attention, and every child in his place would have done the same.[53]

Thus the "child in totum" means the continued existence of all varieties of childish thinking. Over and over again Aardweg has noted in his clients

[51] *Ibid.*, p. 41.

[52] *Ibid.* In conducting group spiritual support sessions in New York City I have noted this lack of dynamism or enthusiasm in some homosexual persons, but previously I did not understand it.

[53] *Ibid.*, pp. 43–47.

the tendency to project their own thoughts, inclusive of their self-view, into the minds of others. Such projection is rooted in infantile self-centeredness. Children relate everything they perceive to themselves, because their ego is the center of the universe. They see everything in terms of feelings; and these emotions of fear, anger, or joy tend to be exaggerated. In an adult such emotionality is really a weakness. Childish emotionality leads to irresponsibility and a variety of egoistic behaviors, predominantly because it is ego-centered. It prevents the development of more mature feelings. Having remained children for a considerable part of their emotionality, some homosexual persons manifest many of these emotional infantilisms, especially in their relations with their partners. [54]

At this point in his treatment of the compulsive complainer Aardweg reminds his readers that, with all the emphasis on the signs of infantile behavior in such a person, as well as in other neurotics, one must not lose sight of the datum that the total person is more than his neurotic part. Although we find many marks of the "inner child's" behavior in everyone with an inferiority complex, this does not mean that the total person is completely identified with it. Although the inner child is a powerful force that undermines the adult's will, it cannot kill it. That is why a homosexual person with this "inner child" may nonetheless manage to live in a reasonably satisfactory way. Through the use of his will he will be able to overcome the very strong impulses from his complex and to maintain a certain behavioral equilibrium. Such self-discipline is by no means easy. In many instances the person reaches a compromise, with the "inner" child prevailing at one time and the adult at another. [55]

Among the common reactive behaviors of the compulsive complainer are *compensation* and *imitation*. The child who feels deplorably inferior wants to show off, to make an impression. It is not enough to be esteemed; one must be "the greatest". It may even appear as if he has a superiority complex. He pretends to be what he is not. Such role-playing is well known in social life and among homosexual persons. One notices one homosexual person with a narcissistic attention to physical appearance and dress, another showing off his intellectual acumen, or another playing the role of the superior sensitive and artistic person. Such overcompensators tend to enjoy dominating others.

Imitation is closely related to overcompensation. The child who is impressed by someone's behavior will imitate him: dressing like him, speaking like him, and adopting his opinions. Such patterns of imitation

[54] *Ibid.*, pp. 48–50.

[55] *Ibid.*, p. 51. In dealing with any kind of compulsion it would seem that more than strength of will is required. Spiritual support groups for homosexual persons, modeled on A.A., such as Courage or Homosexuals Anonymous, can help the homosexual person to maintain control over such tendencies.

are common among homosexuals. The inner child follows an anachronistic style of clothing, hairdressing, etc., believing he will be admired for that. Generally, homosexual men adopt non-aggressive compensatory roles. They do not fight, but try in a more indirect way to impose their image of being important, assuming roles such as that of the "artistic genius", the "clown", or the "nice person". In Aardweg's view these roles are chosen because such persons lack self-confidence in being masculine or feminine. Moreover, related to overcompensation is the quest for love and sympathy.[56]

Some "inner children" stick to other people like leeches, compelling other people to accept them. This insatiable striving after love derives from the feeling that one is not loved and no amount of affection can satisfy it. This is one of the reasons why homosexual relationships are usually accompanied by conflicts. The "inner children" in these persons want love for themselves, regardless of the reactions of their partners: "The tendency to *be* loved can always be detected in homosexual love; also if it hides behind a fathering or protecting attitude toward a partner. The tragic infantile ego has the leading part in any homosexual love affair. This happens not on purpose, but follows a compulsive pattern."[57]

Another common reaction to the self-image of being rejected is self-pampering. Thus habits of overeating, compulsive eating of sweets, drinking, masturbating, etc., can be understood as forms of childish self-comfort. Another form of pampering is the collection of fine objects of art, the joy of "having things".

Infantile self-pity is often, indeed almost always, accompanied by rage or *protest*. In the adult person it has various manifestations, particularly in expressions of hatred and rancor. Because of strong moral principles in the adult ego these manifestations are tempered, but one sees signs of infantile hatred in acid criticisms, cynicism, and hostile behaviors that disturb interpersonal relationships. The "inner child" wants revenge in some way. This desire may lead to calumniating articles against those who oppose such persons. Therapists are familiar with homosexual patients who are still very angry at their parents, particularly the father, and express this anger in a generalized way against any father figure. Sometimes this anger, more disguised, shows up in dreams. Such disguised forms of aggression and resentment are found in most homosexuals.[58]

In lesbians overt aggression is sometimes more obvious, particularly in those who want to express their masculinity. With regard to both male and female homosexuals Aardweg suggests the following rule to account

[56] *Ibid.*, pp. 52–56.
[57] *Ibid.*, p. 56.
[58] *Ibid.*, pp. 57–59.

for the quantity of infantile hatred: "The more he felt *unjustly* humiliated, treated with injustice in childhood, the more aggression will live on in him."[59]

Aardweg next shows how feelings of self-pity are connected to homosexual orientation. He describes the *autopsychodrama* of the male homosexual. As we have seen, the whole infantile personality remains alive in the mind of the adult, fueled by self-pity. The male homosexual harbors a "self-pitying" child whose chief drama is that he is not virile like other boys or men. This is his specific form of inferiority feeling:

> In one variant or another this specific inferiority feeling was evident in every male homosexual I have analyzed and this corroborates the observations of Adler (Ansbacher and Ansbacher, 1958). The unmanliness complex of male homosexuals is increasingly recognized by specialists in the field. It is implicit in the case histories described by Socarides (1978); also Bieber focuses in his later publications more than in his earlier ones on the nuclear importance of the male homosexual's "sense of impaired masculinity" (Bieber and Bieber, 1979). In many cases we can rightly call it a *psychophysical* feeling of unmanliness . . . as the homosexual feels inferior to others of his sex both as to the mental and physical aspects of virility. He feels inadequate in those things he associated in his youth with "being a real man". . . . As a child or adolescent he felt a painful inferiority and self-pity concerning his manly role.[60]

Various environmental factors and childhood experiences have contributed to this drama of inferior manliness, but these factors are not the strict causes of homosexual longings, but only *precipitating factors* that create in the boy a certain predisposition to develop his specific self-view. In some cases the relationship with the mother has been the prevailing precipitating factor; in others, the attitude of the father, and in others a combination of the relationships with both of them. Yet there are other factors as well: rearing by elder siblings or by grandparents or special treatment due to the boy's chronic illness. In summary, Aardweg's clinical findings indicate a variety of precipitating factors, most important of which is that the boy passed through a period of loneliness and inferiority because he found himself "different from other boys", *not belonging* to their community.[61]

Even if he were objectively a group member, he nevertheless felt himself a stranger and inferior to the rest. Aardweg goes on to detail memories of his homosexual clients to substantiate his argument. The

[59] *Ibid.*, p. 58.

[60] *Ibid.*, p. 64. Aardweg argues for his position from his own clinical experience, as well as from the clinical experience of others.

[61] *Ibid.*, p. 65.

greatest number of such memoirs center on the boy's feeling isolated from his peers, and inferior to them.

> Feeling not one of the other boys and not manly like them is very painful for a boy. . . . This smarting feeling of exclusion triggers the defense reaction of self-pity, and this may have been felt for a longer period so that our so-called sensibilized structure is formed. The child is unable to tear himself free from his self-pity and remains attached to it with bonds of addiction.[62]

But how does this recurring, autonomized complaint produce *homosexual* interests? Aardweg responds that the complex of the homosexual is not a sexual matter in its essence, but a continued specific self-drama of inferiority. Therefore, therapy for homosexuality is not sex therapy, but anti-inferiority complex therapy or, better, anti-complaining therapy. If a homosexual person can free himself from infantile self-pity about his inferiority feelings, he would no longer feel physically attracted to his own sex.[63]

The question of therapy, however, will be considered in the pastoral section of this book, together with other views on the subject. Aardweg next considers the three steps involved in the development of erotic feelings:

1. The boy or adolescent feels inferior as a man and therefore indulges in self-pity.

2. He looks up to those who, in his eyes, possess the manly qualities (strength, sturdiness) he thinks are lacking in himself. Usually he is interested in specific types in regard to age and physical appearance. He admires these other persons, but he admires them in the manner of a child: he *idolizes*. Actually the admiring boy is concentrating on himself, thinking "I'm not like him." Thus, idolization of the other is a way of complaining about himself. It is to be noted that this admiring attention paid to other boys and young men frequently precedes homosexual feelings in the strict sense by some years. "The self-pitying boy who feels inferior already looks too often at other boys or men, *comparing himself with them*, thinking and dreaming about them before the awaking of sexual imagery proper."[64]

3. He falls in love with his admired objects, longing to touch and caress them and *to be caressed*, to be near them, to seek their attention for himself, and to possess their warmth. During preadolescence and adolescence this need for warmth leads to sentimental and erotic longings for a member of his own sex. This is understandable in light of the child's feelings of being excluded from intimacy with members of his own sex. His interest in this

---

[62] *Ibid.*, pp. 65–66.
[63] *Ibid.*, p. 67.
[64] *Ibid.*

other person of his own sex assumes erotic dimensions. Daydreams and masturbation fantasies center around the idolized one, and the homosexual wish comes into being. This infatuation acquires a special force whenever the self-pitying child is overwhelmed by inferiority complaints concerning his sexual identity. The child or adolescent sees bodily contact with the adored ones as fulfillment of his passionate desire for love and acceptance. The fact that he imagines that such contacts will bring him happiness is part of his infantile thinking. Moreover, since adult homosexual relationships share in this kind of thinking, they are fundamentally infantile affairs. [65]

From Aardweg's analysis it is clear that the homosexual wish is something desperate and pathetic; it is really a complaint: if only the loved one would cherish me! Such a wish has its pleasant side, being close to the desired person, but its satisfaction is never permanent and never enough, because the source of this wish, feelings of self-pity, never dries up. Although being with the beloved may bring temporary jubilation, the wish cannot be satisfied. It is in essence unfulfilled longing that tends to create a chain of restless inner dramas in the life of the homosexual. Thus, after he has found his loving friend the homosexual person will continue to complain about not being appreciated by him—or by men in general. Soon he will complain about the unfaithfulness of his partner, or he will lose interest in him and fall in love with another man. Thus quarrels and jealousy are normal in homosexual "marriages".

Aardweg goes on to compare the homosexual wish to an obsession like the perfectionistic compulsion of the obsessive-compulsive neurotic. Observing behaviors at a gay bar is evidence of this; one sees men eying every person who comes into the bar, not satisfied with attention from only one friend, since they feel inferior with regard to manhood in general. Such preoccupation with pursuit of the perfect male cannot be compared with heterosexuality. While heterosexual men may look at women on the street, their feelings are usually far less obsessive than those of homosexual men. Yet this homosexual hunger for men can be compared with some forms of neurotic heterosexuality; it is like the impulses of the Don Juan, who compulsively chases women in order to feel accepted and admired by them. A woman who observed a homosexual acquaintance at a party staring at some young men described his look aptly: "It seemed as if he were in a *trance*." [66] As one homosexual said, "It's like a hypnosis."

Many homosexual persons believe they can find one person with whom they can form a faithful relationship and be completely satisfied.

[65] *Ibid.*, pp. 67–68.
[66] *Ibid.*, p. 70.

Aardweg does not believe that this is in practice possible. His research indicates that the typical pattern is that "the homosexual with a steady friend also looks for others, even if his friendship would objectively give reasons to expect that his emotional needs would be satisfied."[67]

Consistently with his general premise concerning the origin of homosexuality, Aardweg regards homosexual "love" as infantile romanticism. He is aware that many homosexual persons regard their homo-eroticism as an expression of the deepest and purest love, but in his view this love amounts to self-centered sentimentality, an asking for love for "poor me", who unconsciously is conceived as an innocent child in need of warmth and understanding: "This 'self-pitying' child clings to his friend in a purely egocentric way—'You must love me'; but very soon he may act very coolly toward his partner after a row or seeming betrayal."[68] For this reason the modern pastoral advice to homosexuals to be faithful to one lover only must be called *naive*: "This is exactly what many homosexuals cannot achieve and what others would never accept as an ideal because they are just interested in short-term contacts; emotionally they could not tolerate a homosexual 'marriage' any more than a heterosexual could."[69]

3. RELATIONSHIPS BETWEEN THE THOUGHT OF MOBERLY AND AARDWEG, AND THE RELATIONSHIP OF COOK'S TEACHING TO PSYCHOLOGICAL THEORY

Both Moberly and van den Aardweg develop their theories within traditional frameworks. Moberly draws upon the psychoanalytic tradition, while adding her own interpretation of parental relationships. Aardweg comes from the school of Alfred Adler, which stresses interpersonal and social relationships and the concept of inferiority complex. Both consider at length the poor image the homosexual has of himself. Both believe in the power of unconscious dynamisms, in the destructive effects of traumatic childhood or infant experiences. Moberly sees the origin of homosexuality in developmental deficits during the process of gender-identity, beginning with hostile detachment from the parent of the same sex. Aardweg relates homosexuality to the more general phenomenon of inferiority feelings, although he is careful to point out that inferiority feelings lead to homosexual orientation only under certain specified

[67] *Ibid.*, p. 75.
[68] *Ibid.*
[69] *Ibid.*

circumstances that we have noted. Both see the adult homosexual person as still harboring the thought patterns and feelings of the child. Both hold that the homosexual person can move toward heterosexuality. They differ *significantly* in their explanations of the origins of homosexual orientation and in their forms of reorientation therapy.

Moberly stresses proper gender identification with a parental figure of the same sex as necessary to fulfill true homosexual needs; where this does not take place the child is a psychological orphan, and later in adolescence he or she will seek to fulfill identificatory needs with same-sex persons under the illusion that physical contact will help one to be masculine or feminine. Seeking intimacy with persons of one's own sex is good and normal; what is abnormal and pathological is the previous and unconscious hostile detachment from the parent or parental figure of the same sex. At that point the child cuts himself off from the process of identification with the parent of the same sex, thereby depriving self of growth into masculinity or femininity. Thus the confused longings of the adolescent boy or girl to contact physically members of one's own sex are reparative urges. It is necessary, then, to explain to such persons that physical–genital satisfaction is not the answer to their true needs. Learning to form non–genital and chaste friendships with persons of the same sex is the first step toward fulfilling homosexual needs, according to Moberly.

On the other hand, Aardweg makes feeling inferior *as masculine* the focus of his theory. From his clinical experience he views the constant complaining of the homosexual person as a manifestation of these feelings. As a remedy to this condition Aardweg proposes an anti-complaining therapy that he has developed over the years with some success.[70] Aardweg, moreover, puts more emphasis on peer relationships of persons between the ages of eight and sixteen than Moberly does, seeing them as a very important factor in the genesis of homosexuality, whereas Moberly sees feeling inferior to one's peers of the same sex as a *result* of the deprivation brought on by hostile detachment from the same-sex parent. Finally, Aardweg does not accept the gender-specific therapy of Moberly, with its stress on same-sex friendships as the first step toward heterosexuality; he believes that same-sex identification comes about through the *felt* approval of one's gender identity by both parents.[71]

In presenting the thought of both Moberly and van den Aardweg, and some of the differences between them, I hope to stimulate further analysis of their theories; originally, I conceived of devoting a section of this book to an interchange between them, but perhaps that will follow after

[70] *On the Origins and Treatment of Homosexuality*, pp. 252–258.
[71] *Correspondence*, Oct. 1, 1986.

publication of this work. Valuable as many of their insights are for pastoral practice, I also realize that their therapeutic approaches are inadequate in themselves to effect the full spiritual rehabilitation of the homosexual person. This is not so much a criticism of their theories as an assertion of the inadequacy of psychiatry and clinical psychology to provide a complete pastoral program for the spiritual healing of the homosexual person.

Without neglecting the findings of psychology, I should like to turn to the spiritual program of Colin Cook. A brief note about him is necessary to understand his position, the full details of which will be given in the pastoral section. Resigning from a Seventh Day Adventist pastorate in 1974, Cook reflected upon his life and behavior and began to see that much of his homosexual feelings and behavior was based on a misinterpretation of God, self, and the world that had produced within him a sense of incompleteness and isolation.

Later he wrote: "I know of nothing that gives such a deep sense of incompleteness, of being divided, as the feeling of being homosexual while wanting to love God."[72] He sees his homosexual condition as being part of his sinful nature: "Basically, deep down, you are a heterosexual being, as your first parents were. No matter how deep your homosexual feelings are, deeper still, buried under all the confusion and feelings and habits lies your heterosexuality."[73]

With the exception of his view that homosexuality is part of our sinful nature, Cook is in agreement with Catholic teaching that homosexual activity is always immoral. As I have shown in Chapter One, the Congregation for the Doctrine of the Faith describes the inclination to homosexual activity as an *objective disorder*. It may be argued (and I concur in the argument) that the homosexual condition is not the way the human person ought to be; it does not lead to the ordered expression of genital sexuality in marriage, but to actions that are always objectively immoral. In this respect it can be conceived of as placing a difficult burden upon the homosexual person: the practice of chastity. But since the person did not will to be homosexual and since some homosexuals who try to change their orientation do not succeed in doing so, one must be careful not to say that the homosexual person is in sin simply because of the condition in itself, which is an objective disorder but *not* a sin.

More importantly, Cook sees the struggle of the homosexual person to reach heterosexuality as a spiritual confrontation similar to that of the

---

[72] *Homosexuality: An Open Door?* (Boise, Idaho: Pacific Press, 1985), p. 25. A more complete account of Cook's teaching can be found in the ten-tape set (20 parts), "Homosexuality and the Power to Change" (American Cassette Ministries, P.O. Box 922, Harrisburg, Pa., 17108).

[73] *Homosexuality: An Open Door?*, p. 37.

alcoholic striving for sobriety. But he sees it in the profoundly spiritual context of divine creation and redemption through Christ. His H.A. Fourteen Steps,[74] detailed in the pastoral section, are really a form of spiritual strategy to help the person avoid Satan and sin and find a life of union with Christ. Already we have seen Aardweg describing the compulsive element in the homosexual condition and pointing out that the road back to heterosexuality is hard work, demanding not only the acceptance of psychological insight but the practice of virtue as well.

Cook's Fourteen Steps clearly assume that the road back to virtue and, in some cases, to heterosexuality depends on constant cooperation with the grace of God, and in this regard he is in harmony with Catholic teaching on grace. Indeed A.A. has taught us that there is no psychological answer to addiction and that only a truly spiritual program such as the Twelve Steps can enable one to regain control over one's life. To the extent that the homosexual condition involves addictive elements, one may adapt the Twelve Steps to the healing of the homosexual person. This is the aim of the Fourteen Steps of H.A. Moberly and Aardweg help us to understand many of the psychological factors involved in the homosexual condition.[75] Cook proposes a spiritual program to help the person to live virtuously in spite of the temptations that flow from the condition. So also does Courage.

[74] Cook is the co-founder of Homosexuals Anonymous (H.A.), a Christian fellowship of men and women who have chosen to help each other live free from homosexuality. This nonsectarian organization has approximately fifty chapters in the United States and Canada.

[75] Subsequent to the writing of this manuscript I received news of the resignation of Colin Cook as the director of the Quest Learning Center in Reading because of admitted sexual misconduct over the last six years. He has publicly expressed sorrow for his conduct and has sought spiritual and psychological guidance. Tragic as this is, it does not cast into doubt the validity of the Fourteen Steps of H.A., which an estimated 600 people throughout North America follow. The criticism, however, that greater accountability should be built into these steps should be considered.

CHAPTER FOUR

A SHARPER FOCUS ON HOMOSEXUALITY

by Jeffrey Keefe, O.F.M. Conv., Ph.D.

Homosexuality was once the love that dare not speak its name, as Lord Alfred Douglas poignantly expressed it. Today homosexuality is spoken of quite openly in books, journals of science and opinion, and the media, as well as from podium and pulpit.

Much discussion about homosexuality is marred by error or lack of precision and nuance. These shortcomings are hard to avoid because sexual orientation is a complex condition that does not lend itself to general statements.

Therefore I will focus on certain issues that, in my opinion, are not sufficiently attended to either by those sympathetic to the personal plight of homosexuals or by those who react with fear and prejudice that stems from ignorance. When prejudice stems from personal dynamics, information alone will not have much impact.

My aims are: (1) to present a schema of sexuality for fuller appreciation of the complexity of sexual development, (2) to show that the term *homosexuality* is an oversimplification, (3) to explain an essential criterion of psychological health and disorder and its application to homosexuality, and (4) to comment briefly on change from homosexuality and change in attitude toward homosexuals.

I. PHYSICAL AND MENTAL SEXUALITY

Human sexuality has both physical and psychological characteristics. Through empirical research and accumulated clinical experience many functions and factors, physiological and psychological, innate and acquired,

Father Jeffrey Keefe is a Conventual Franciscan friar ordained in 1952. He received a doctorate in clinical psychology from Fordham University and interned at Bellevue Psychiatric Hospital in New York City. Father Keefe has worked in clinical settings at Staten Island Mental Health, a children's service; St. Vincent Medical Center, Staten Island; and Onondaga Pastoral Counseling Center, Syracuse. He has taught at the University of Notre Dame summer sessions and is adjunct professor of pastoral psychology at the Franciscan theologate, St. Anthony on Hudson, in Rensselaer, New York. Currently he is in private practice in Syracuse, New York, and serves as consultant on candidacy for two dioceses and several religious communities. He has contributed to various periodicals and has a monthly column in *Catechist* magazine.

have been differentiated within the aggregate of interacting forces that constitute an individual's developing sexuality.

Physical sexual history begins at conception and continues in a definite sequential pattern until birth. There are three principal stages in uterine sexual development: genetic sex, gonadal sex, and sexual differentiation in the brain.

Genetic sex is determined at conception by the pair of sex chromosomes. The ovum or egg of the mother always provides an X-chromosome. Depending on whether the single sex chromosome in the fertilizing sperm of the father is X or Y, the offspring will be genetically female (XX) or male (XY). Thus an individual is female or male in every body cell. However, genetic sex alone does not guarantee proper physical sexual development.

In humans the next phase of sexual development begins about the seventh week of fetal life. As yet, the rudimentary sexual tissues remain undifferentiated. These tissues, in animals and humans, will develop into female organs unless there is some physiological intervention. The biological axiom is "Nature prefers females". In genetic males the Y chromosome provides this intervention by producing a protein that covers or coats the tissues otherwise destined to become female sexual organs, and initiates the formation of male sexual anatomy.

A third phase occurs in the second trimester of human fetal life, following sex-organ development. In the male the now-formed testes produce the male hormone testosterone that masculinizes clusters of cells in the hypothalamus, thalamus, and limbic systems of the "old brain", the brain structures humans share with lower vertebrates. Estrogen and progesterone, hormones produced chiefly by the ovaries, feminize counterpart sites in the female's brain. This neurohormonal programming of brain-cell clusters influences many later functions and behaviors, among them the reproductive cycle and nurturant tendencies in the female and aggressiveness in the male.

In summary, three aspects of physical sexuality develop before birth: genetic or cytological sex, gonadal or anatomical sex, and sexual differentiation in the brain. Obviously, physical sexual development continues after birth, especially in adolescence.

Psychosexuality, that is, sexualized consciousness, is a postnatal development. Psychosexuality is sexuality as it manifests itself in the mind. It is a pervasive and fundamental personality feature that includes three interwoven components: one's basic conviction of being male or female; behaviors and attitudes that are culturally associated with masculinity and femininity; an individual's preference for male or female sexual partners.[1]

---

[1] Richard Green, *Sexual Identity Conflict* (New York: Basic Books, 1974), p. xv.

These components, variously labeled in the literature, are core gender identity, gender role identity, and psychosexual orientation.

Core gender identity is the belief "I am male", "I am female." It begins to crystallize in the second year of life as the infant undergoes "psychological birth", the separation from its symbiotic relationship with the mother, and acquires a dawning sense of individuality.

Gender role identity is the subtly different belief "I am masculine", "I am feminine." The individual gradually attains the felt conviction that he or she matches or falls short of the gender role expectations of one's particular environment. Gender role identity may vary on a fairly wide spectrum without infringing on core gender identity or orientation. Conversely it may occasion a sense of inadequacy antagonistic to the other two constituents of psychosexuality.

The third eventual psychosexual component is orientation, preferential erotic attraction to members of the opposite sex, the same sex, or to both sexes in varied degree. This is the defining element of heterosexuality or homosexuality.

Sexuality, therefore, cannot be viewed as a simple or single phenomenon. Freud noted that the physical and mental characteristics of sexuality, including orientation, may vary independently of one another *up to a certain point* [italics added] . . . and are met with in different individuals in manifold permutations."[2] However, these characteristics also influence one another.

Complications may occur in any of the interacting physical and mental elements of sexual development. Scientific literature contains numerous reports of animal experimentation in which the normal sequence of uterine development was manipulated by various techniques such as castration of fetal males or injection of male sex hormones to pregnant females at the critical period prior to anatomical differentiation of fetal sex tissues or just prior to the subsequent phase of masculinization or feminization of the fetal brain.

Experimental interference with normal hormone function prior to anatomical differentiation results in variously intersexed offspring, that is, animals genetically one sex, but with the external genitals of the other sex. When hormone manipulation follows anatomical differentiation, offspring of one sex demonstrate the temperament and behavior typical of the other sex. These behavioral results are less clear-cut in animals such as monkeys, which have higher development of the cortex of the brain.

For obvious ethical reasons such experiments cannot be carried out with humans, but nature has provided some "experiments" of its own.

---

[2] Sigmund Freud, *Collected Papers*, vol. 2, trans. Joan Rivière (New York: Basic Books, 1962), p. 230.

There are chromosomal anomalies, XXY and XYY among others, and syndromes of endocrine functioning gone awry in prenatal development.

Experimental findings with animals and some of the data from prenatal endocrine dysfunction in humans have led to loose generalizations. One is the firm claim that psychosexual orientation in humans is due to prenatal chemical influences and neurohormonal patterning.

Yet the researchers themselves are much more cautious in drawing conclusions from their findings. There is fair agreement among these biological and medical researchers that postnatal social experience in humans is prepotent over possible biological predispositions in developing psychosexual identity.

Animal studies report only *observed* behavior, which is at best analogous to behavior in humans. Psychosexual orientation in humans is a mental characteristic. To assume the same "mentality" in animals is an unwarranted inference. It should be noted that *exclusive* homosexuality is a phenomenon that does not appear to have any counterpart in the animal world.[3]

The unconditional transfer of behavioral findings from animal studies to humans ignores the radical discontinuity between the animal brain and the human brain. Humans adapt by learning. Humans function with minimal dependency on instinctive programming. Arno Karlen remarks that "humans almost seem to be an experiment by nature to see whether sexuality can be left minimally to programming and mostly to learning."[4]

John Money has followed for many years a substantial number of "human experiments", that is, persons who were born with ambiguous genitalia or who suffered some prenatal endocrine disorder that affected their sexuality. He summarizes scientific research and clinical experience in the field of gender disorder with this comment: "Whatever may be the possible unlearned assistance from constitutional sources, the child's psychosexual identity is not written, unlearned, in the genetic code, the hormonal system or the nervous system at birth."[5] He does suggest possible biological vulnerability to homosexual orientation, not in any preordained sense but as dependent on postnatal environmental circumstances.

Garfield Tourney, reviewing prenatal and postnatal hormonal research, states that a correlation of sexual hormones with sexual behavior is true

[3] John Bancroft, "A Psychiatric Perspective", pp. 102–124, in *Sex and Gender*, ed. Mark Schwartz, Albert Moraczewski, and John Monteleone (St. Louis: Pope John Center, 1983), p. 109.

[4] Arno Karlen, *Sexuality and Homosexuality* (New York: Norton, 1971), p. 389.

[5] John Money, "Sexual Dimorphism and Homosexual Gender Identity", pp. 42–79, in *Perspectives in Human Sexuality*, ed. Nathaniel W. Wagner (New York: Behavioral Publications, 1974), p. 68.

"to some extent" in lower species but that for primates "the hormonal theory of sexual regulation, particularly in terms of orientation toward the sexual object, lacks evidence."[6] Allowing for "the hypothesis of some hidden predisposition to homosexuality, somehow lurking in the brain", he adds, "this would occur providing the social environment, particularly the early relationships within the family, provide the dynamic circumstances which result in overt homosexuality."[7]

Psychosexuality has its own developmental course. Psychosexuality is a learned characteristic, though not acquired simply by direct teaching, as one might learn arithmetic. One's sense of being male or female, masculine or feminine, is absorbed rather than formally learned, primarily from parents, with later influences from siblings, relatives, peers, and various adults. Psychosexuality is learned largely through affective interpersonal experience filtered through the child's fantasies and conceptualizations. We learn psychosexuality much as we learn all our basic orientations: trust or mistrust, autonomy or dependency, self-esteem or inferiority. These convictions about oneself are precipitated out of experience and woven into the warp and woof of personality. The nucleus of these convictions is structured before we can understand or reflect on, cognitively label or verbally express them. We know them intuitively; we sense them, feel them.

At birth the infant is assigned its sex on the basis of its external genitals. The formation of psychosexuality, however, begins with "psychological birth", around the eighteenth month. Psychological birth is the infant's passage from the original symbiotic, blissful fusion with the mother to a sense of being a separate self. Even at one-and-a-half the child is not convinced of the merits of separateness *vis à vis* oneness, a conflict ordinarily resolved by age three with definite individuality.[8]

With the dawning of consciousness as a separate person, and the initial capacity to fantasize, interpret (or misinterpret) experience, the child forms an individual and gender identity. The child formulates psychosexual as well as personal identity out of the unending series of messages from parents and others by word, behavior, and attitude. Core gender identity is irreversibly established during the third year. But untoward events in the child's life up to this point may leave him or her with a sense of threat to the integrity of gender identity, as will be discussed later.

Gender identification, which is much deeper than imitation, requires that the same-sex parent be seen as nurturant. Identification can be

---

[6] Garfield Tourney, "Hormones and Homosexuality", pp. 41–58 in *Homosexual Behavior*, ed. Judd Marmor (New York: Basic Books, 1980), p. 41.

[7] *Ibid.*, p. 57.

[8] Louise Kaplan, *Oneness and Separateness* (New York: Simon and Schuster, 1978).

impaired when the parental model is experienced as hostile or detached and unresponsive. Closely allied is the need for the child to see the same-sex parent as competent and respected by other important persons in the child's life. The most significant other person is that parent's spouse. A wholesome parental marriage is one of the better guarantees of proper psychosexual identification.

Gender role identity is the ongoing internalization of the role typical of a given sex in a particular culture or, closer to home, in a particular family.

Labeling behaviors as more typical of one sex may be done narrowly or with great latitude. There is no doubt that stereotypic labels, past and present, have fostered caricatures of both masculinity and femininity.

However, a society that completely blurs the differences in sex roles distorts the complementary features of the sexes by which they ultimately become two in one flesh and united in communal life and love. A unisex approach clouds sex differences and makes it difficult for either sex to establish a clear gender role identity.

The denial of differences makes it especially hard for boys to confirm their sexual identity through their sexual role. Boys first identify with their mothers, the original source of security, and therefore they have a greater need of role reinforcement for a sense of manhood. Robert Stoller, a clinician with twenty-five years of specialization in gender–identity disorders, proposes that in boys the period of marked intimacy between mother and child necessary for healthy development leaves behind "a trace, a touch of uncertainty that their masculinity is intact."[9] While overstated to make the point, boys have to shift identity; girls do not. Cultures intuitively have realized this need, which is one reason why most societies are less tolerant of cross-over of sexual roles by boys than by girls.

The child learns what is judged appropriately masculine or feminine from the example of parents (and others) and from their positive or negative reinforcement of manifest interests, attitudes, and activities. The fact that a girl is energetic and competitive or a boy aesthetically inclined may help or hinder gender role identity, depending on the affirmation or disapproval shown by parents. To a child praise and approbation confirm appropriateness; harsh criticism is likely to spawn self-doubt about one's acceptability as a person and one's adequacy as feminine or masculine. I recall a client whose boyhood interest in music met with crude teasing from his athletic brothers; he felt his father was distant and indifferent to him in general. His mother suggested kindly that he would do well to be out with the other boys, but in the context of the isolation he felt from father and brothers he perceived her stance as one more disaffirmation. He

---

[9] Robert Stoller, *Presentations of Gender* (New Haven: Yale University Press, 1985), p. 8.

felt he did not measure up as a boy, and this was a contributing factor in developing a homosexual orientation.

2. HOMOSEXUALITIES

A vast corpus of clinical literature and child-development research points to impairment of core gender identity or gender role identity in the etiology of homosexuality.

Pro-homosexual apologists point out, rightly, that many clinical research findings do not apply to all homosexuals, but they wrongly argue that lack of universal application invalidates these findings. A child may undergo experiences that traumatize psychosexual development at different periods of growth, some more critical than others. These conflicts deflect, in varying degree, the strong cultural and environmental forces promoting heterosexual development. On this account various dynamics may contribute to homosexual orientation, some more in one person than another. Every person has a unique, rich, and dramatic psychic history.

Bell and Weinberg titled their massive study *Homosexualities* because they found diversity in lifestyle and personality type among the nearly one thousand homosexual men and women interviewed for the study.[10] I suggest three broad categories of homosexuality as a useful framework for those who minister to homosexual persons pastorally or in supportive counseling: compulsive, symptomatic, and episodic homosexuality.

Charles Socarides maintains that the first category, the *compulsive homosexual orientation*, has its origins in the second and third year of life as a result of disturbed mother-child relations at the time of individuation. This disturbance in the resolution of psychic separation from the mother may have consequences for one's core gender identity, the formation of which coincides with initial ego development.[11]

Should the mother's relationship be experienced as markedly ambivalent during psychological birth, the child's developing ego becomes ridden with anxiety. The child may experience a double message—maternal rejection and close-binding intimacy—and be caught in a bind. The trend to separate, to be an individual, is hampered by a fear of abandonment, while the trend to remain united arouses fear of engulfment. This conflict, with its dread of dissolution, ultimately is repressed, only to be triggered in later life situations wherein one feels slighted, criticized, humiliated, or weakened. Because individual identity is so interwoven with gender

[10] Alan Bell and Martin Weinberg, *Homosexualities* (New York: Simon and Schuster, 1978).

[11] Charles Socarides, *Homosexuality* (New York: Aronson, 1979).

identity, perceived assaults on self as a person are experienced in deep psychic levels as assaults on one's sexual integrity as well. The individual pursues homosexual contact in a driven manner as a reparative device: the male homosexual gets a shot of manhood; the lesbian, an infusion of womanhood. The compulsive homosexual protects ego and gender identity by a sexual fusion with another person of the same sex.

The main dynamic is not sexual gratification. Rather, it is the anxiety arising from a deep-seated threat of isolation, helplessness, and even distintegration.

This fear may break into consciousness. The person will say of the homosexual act, "I'll fall apart if I don't have it", and protest, "It's not an indulgence; it's something I *have* to do." Homosexual acts discharge this primary anxiety for the time being, but if homosexual acts are against one's values, the person is then suffused with guilt, anguish, self-hatred, and remorse.

Even when the compelling anxiety remains unconscious because of effective repression, it is still evident in the driven character of the pursuit. A man may be single or married—perhaps the father of a family—and find himself driving miles to homosexual haunts, taking what he knows are ridiculous, insane risks, and later saying that something stronger than he just seemed to pull him toward it. The confessor who presumes the motivation to be ordinary sexual desire or the sympathetic mentor who advocates a monogamous homosexual relationship as a better lifestyle does not begin to fathom the addictive nature of the problem; nor does the critic who sees the Church's refusal to sanction such relationship as contributing to promiscuity.

This dynamic explanation of compulsive homosexuality may seem fanciful. We all feel at times that we cannot cope with a situation, that we "can't make it". In a person afflicted with an unresolved individuation conflict, and consequently tenuous ego structure, even minor distress activates extraordinary inner tension, a sense of overwhelming helplessness and fear of annihilation. Individuality and psychosexual identity are so enmeshed that homosexual activity is resorted to in an attempt to stave off the threat of psychic disorganization.

Moreover, it is precisely because the homosexual symptom is so effective in the short term in neutralizing anxiety that it allows the compulsive homosexual to function well socially and occupationally. Many compulsive persons are highly productive and are generally adjusted in areas of life apart from the compulsive symptom itself.

Following individualization, a child's experiences may strengthen or undermine its sense of maleness or femaleness, its core gender identity. One of the more negative factors is the perception that one's sex is a disappointment to a parent or parents. It is less than affirming for a child to hear, "I (we) wanted a girl (boy), but I (we) took you because God sent you." Elizabeth Moberly has clarified defensive detachment from an already-underway same-sex identification as a principal dynamic in homosexuality. (See Father Harvey's review of Moberly's position in Chapter Three.)

The second category is *symptomatic homosexuality*, that is, homosexuality as a symptom of a more general personality problem. This does not imply that there is no impairment of psychosexual identity, only that the stronger impetus toward homosexual activity is to resolve some ancillary conflict that became sexualized. Symptomatic homosexuality has a driven quality also, but it falls short of the intensity of compulsive homosexuality. Ruth Barnhouse summarizes the unresolved issues that may lead to homosexual adaptation: problems of unsatisfied dependency needs, unresolved power or dominance needs, and fear of heterosexuality.[12]

Some youngsters, feeling unaffirmed and deprived of affection, come to look for acceptance on any terms. They may drift to homosexuality hoping for affirmation and may thereby solidify homosexual leanings.

For others, homosexuality may be a quest for dominance, a sense of power. A man in his late twenties sought treatment because he feared growing old in a subculture where youth is idolized even more than in society at large. He pitied the forty-year-olds who hung around gay bars, trying to look twenty, searching desperately for a pickup. As his story unfolded, his anger emerged against a father who had rejected him. His parents had been divorced when he was three. As a teenager he sought out his father in another city and camped on his doorstep all night with the hope of starting a father-son relationship. When his father finally showed up, he gave the boy bus fare for the return trip and told him to get lost.

Upon reaching eighteen, the young man's first act was to change his surname legally, thereby announcing to the world his disidentification with the father he had desired so keenly. He was equally contemptuous of his mother, who had indulged him with whatever he wanted as a child and who in his teens had insisted that he should not get a job because it would require mingling with supposedly inferior-class youth. The message he had absorbed was that he was weak, useless, unmanly, and unable to make it on his own. During early therapy he said with disdain, "I could never have a woman lead me by the hand", but later he came to see his collusion in enjoying the comforts of indolence.

---

[12] Ruth Tiffany Barnhouse, *Homosexuality: A Symbolic Confusion* (New York: Seabury Press, 1979), p. 51.

Eventually he admitted that his homosexuality was a passive-aggressive ploy, a declaration to his parents, "Look what you did to me." He acknowledged his motivating hatred: homosexuality was a way to strike back at parents he resented implacably and at a self he demeaned as weak. In a tearful burst of insight he declared, "I've always treated sex as a degradation of the other person. I wanted to tear down the other person, to prove he's just as bad as I am. When I'm with some man I'm interested in, I want to share life with, I know it's not right; it's not meant to be this way." In my clinical experience, it is not uncommon that a male homosexual cannot continue having sex with a partner as affection deepens.

Fear of heterosexuality may arise from many sources. Too often a parent's sexual maladjustment spawns a child's feeling that sex is dirty, that heterosexual relations are gross and coarse. Hearing themes such as "your father only thinks of one thing" can contribute to heterosexual aversion in a child of either sex. Sexual abuse of a child is patently traumatic. A girl abused in childhood by a male family member may turn, from an abiding heterosexual revulsion, to homosexuality. Others turn to lesbianism with the unspoken conviction, "I could never destroy a man as my mother destroyed my father."

Finally, I propose a third category of homosexuality, variously called *situational, variational,* or *episodic homosexuality*. It includes those who engage in homosexual activity occasionally or those who engage in it regularly but whose basic orientation is heterosexual.

Episodic homosexuality may occur in situations where heterosexual behavior is not possible—for example, in prison. Adolescents may engage in homosexual activity out of experimental curiosity, not psychosexual conflict. Some persons engage in homosexual acts for money, in search of a new kick, or from nothing more than indifferent sexual moral values. Homosexual behavior may simply express a counter-culture protest against conventional standards and inhibitions, a declaration of liberation by having erotic adventures.

3. THE QUESTION OF DISORDER

Is homosexuality a normal alternate psychosexual development, or is it a disorder? In late 1973 the board of trustees of the American Psychiatric Association voted to drop homosexuality per se as a mental disorder. This decision, which erased a hundred-year-old psychological definition, was confirmed by a referendum among the membership, who voted approximately six to four.

Psychiatrist Ruth Barnhouse observed that many members felt caught between either upholding an appraisal based on scientific evidence or contributing to discrimination—a dilemma, she says, born of muddy thinking.[13] Interestingly, in a medical journal survey four years later, 69% of responding psychiatrists agreed that "homosexuality is usually a pathological adaptation, as opposed to a normal variation."[14]

The A.P.A. explained its decision by stating:

> The crucial issue in determining whether or not homosexuality per se is to be regarded as a mental disorder is not the etiology of the condition, but its consequences and the definition of mental disorder. A significant proportion of homosexuals are apparently satisfied with their sexual orientation, show no significant signs of manifest psychopathology (unless homosexuality, by itself, is considered psychopathology), and are able to function socially and occupationally with no impairment. If one uses the criteria of *distress* or *disability*, homosexuality per se is not a mental disorder. If one uses the criterion of *inherent disadvantage*, it is not at all clear that homosexuality is a disadvantage in all cultures or subcultures.[15]

I shall comment mainly on what seems to be the central argument: that etiology is not a criterion of psychopathology.

The critical *psychological* criterion of normality or abnormality, distinct from cultural norms or ethics, is not the act itself, its cultural setting, or the subjective comfort of the agent; rather, it is the psychological mechanisms involved.

Lawrence Kubie, delineating the essential criterion of health or dysfunction, points out that every act is influenced by a constellation of motives. Insofar as an act, thought, feeling, or impulse proceeds predominantly from conscious and preconscious motives, that is, forces within oneself *accessible* to consciousness, it is healthy. To the degree that an act is determined primarily by anxiety and conflict of which an individual is unaware and cannot, unaided, become aware, the act is unhealthy. It is unhealthy to the degree that it is cut off from possible conscious control, ranging from minor determinism to inflexible repetition.[16] This criterion is proper to psychology itself. Extended from single acts to patterns and general trends of behavior, it is the essential consideration for assessing mental health or disorder.

Does this criterion mean we are all somewhat disordered and neurotic? We may find this possibility repugnant, yet it is a rare person who has not asked himself, "Why do I keep doing that?" when he feels nearly helpless

[13] *Ibid.*, p. 46.

[14] *Time*, Feb. 20, 1978, p. 102.

[15] *Diagnostic and Statistical Manual of Mental Disorders*, 3rd ed. (Washington, D.C.: American Psychiatric Association, 1980), p. 380. Quoted with permission.

[16] Lawrence Kubie, "The Fundamental Nature of the Distinction between Normality and Neurosis", *Psychoanalytic Quarterly* 23 (1954):167–204.

to shift to more constructive behavior. The challenge of life (and the specific task of depth therapy) is to know oneself, to become more deeply aware of one's inner workings, to discover the reasons reason does not know, the motivations that we keep from ourselves through defensive maneuvers.

It is also true that anyone afflicted with a psychological disorder has reserves of health. Psychological health and illness are not mutually exclusive terms. The balance between the alliance of conscious and preconscious forces on one side, and unconscious processes on the other, is intricate and complex in every person. For this reason only God finally can judge a person. In terms of this *psychological* criterion, any activity good in itself may be healthy or neurotic, and even acts evil in themselves, like stealing, may be "healthy" in this restricted sense of not being compulsive. The morality of such behavior rests on other criteria and is the province of other disciplines.

The A.P.A. statement ruling out etiology as a criterion of disorder (or health) simply ignores the accumulated literature on psychodynamics that has demonstrated the connection between unresolved unconscious conflict and disordered functioning. This literature, wrought from clinical experience, sees compulsive and symptomatic homosexuality as a sexualized resolution of conflict in which the particular experiences of an individual became interwoven with psychosexual development. Episodic homosexuality usually is not psychologically disordered, because its motives are accessible to consciousness.

4. THE POSSIBILITY OF CHANGE FROM HOMOSEXUALITY

Can homosexuals change their orientation? The fact, reported in the literature, proves the possibility. I have seen some homosexuals in treatment —and have met more former homosexuals (including those who were exclusively so)—who now respond physically and emotionally as heterosexuals in successful marriages. Movement toward the heterosexual end of the Kinsey scale ordinarily requires strong motivation on the client's part, a skilled therapist, and unfortunately more often than not, financial resources. In my judgment, Homosexuals Anonymous, a recent movement begun by Colin Cook, provides the most effective program, because it combines needed group support, which in turn fosters self-acceptance and self-insight, with the spiritual dimension essential for any radical personal change. Individual therapy may be needed to supplement group therapy.

5. A NEEDED CHANGE
TOWARD HOMOSEXUALS

One's position regarding homosexuality as a normal or abnormal development is a separate issue from one's treatment of homosexual persons. No matter what a person's problems are, he is deserving of compassion and respect.

We too easily dismiss the pain that any person with psychosexual problems suffers. This was brought home to me as a fledgling psychologist by a homosexual young man who helped me more than I helped him.

He was a candidate for a religious community for which I was a consultant. In the course of the psychological evaluation it became clear that he was homosexual and unhappy about it. At his request, I arranged for him to enter a therapy group for homosexuals conducted by one of my former teachers, a psychiatrist in New York City. At the end of our meeting he told me gratefully that I was the first person in his Catholic experience who had discovered his orientation and treated him with respect.

He then related some rough experiences in the confessional and described how he cringed inwardly when the nuns on the faculty of the school where he taught would tell jokes about homosexuals. He was left with little hope of compassion or attempted understanding from Church functionaries. I appreciated his compliment, but I am more grateful for his helping me toward some affective appreciation of the devastating hurt, isolation, shame, and self-hatred felt by many homosexuals. Some homosexuals cover these feelings with militant anger or flaunting behavior, but the pain is still underneath.

Recent times have brought progress in our attitude toward alcoholics. Alcoholism is now more widely viewed as a disease. It is a physical disease, and prior to admitting one's problem, it is the psychological "disease of denial". We need a corresponding shift in attitude toward homosexual persons. I do not think, however, that denying the disorder is the way to accomplish this turnabout. Nor need one compromise personal moral conviction. Our primary task is to deal with whatever personal prejudice or visceral fear of homosexuality constricts the gospel law of love of neighbor.

CHAPTER FIVE

MAJOR DISSENTING THEOLOGICAL VIEWS

I. MAJOR DISSENTING THEOLOGICAL VIEWS

It is not our purpose to make a complete survey of moral perspectives on homosexuality and homosexual activity. In recent years several studies have been published on this issue. Batchelor's overview in *Homosexuality and Ethics* presents a wide spectrum of views, ranging from the thesis that homosexual acts are natural and good to the view that homosexual acts are always morally evil.[1] While these views are presented fairly, there is not one author who shows the credibility of official Roman Catholic teaching. Edward Malloy's *Homosexuality and the Christian Way of Life* provides a perspective in which the Church's teaching is presented ably. At the same time Malloy does justice to positions of Catholics, Protestants, and non-believers who are not in agreement with official Catholic teaching. I believe, however, that the teaching of the Church demands a more complete presentation so that her pastoral practice can be seen to be viable, workable. It is my intent to present the arguments in favor of the Church's teaching after I have reviewed major objections to it.[2]

Beyond the full consideration of the morality of homosexual activity are other questions such as the subjective responsibility of the homosexual person for his orientation, the necessity of a pastoral program to help the homosexual person to live chastely, and the real possibility that some persons may become heterosexual in orientation through appropriate therapy. The critical exploration of these pastoral programs, however, will be in vain unless one is convinced from the start that homosexual activity is always objectively immoral. I proceed now to various schools of thought that are in various ways opposed to Church teaching.

In Chapter One I have given an overview of the most recent official document of the Church on homosexual activity, showing how it goes beyond paragraph 8 of the Vatican's *Declaration on Certain Questions Concerning Sexual Ethics*. After making the distinction between homosexual acts and the condition of homosexuality, the new document states

---

[1] *Homosexuality and Ethics*, ed. Edward Batchelor, Jr. (New York: Pilgrim Press, 1980), Edward Malloy, *Homosexuality and the Christian Way of Life* (Washington, D.C.: University Press of America, 1981).

[2] John F. Harvey, O.S.F.S., "An In-Depth Review of *Homosexuality and the Christian Way of Life* in *The Linacre Quarterly* 50, no. 2 (May 1983):122–143.

that even the condition is an *objective* disorder, because it predisposes the person to intrinsically evil acts. The new document also gives a more comprehensive argument from Holy Scripture, which I shall incorporate into my argument in Chapter Six. Before considering specific dissenting views it will be useful to state some general propositions common to many dissenting theologians.

1. The Church in practical moral questions is not able to make an infallible statement. All such statements are non-infallible and therefore subject to revision and change. Accordingly, the opinions of learned theologians, particularly large numbers of them, when in conflict with official Church teaching, constitute a solidly probable opinion in favor of freedom. Consequently, confessors and spiritual directors of the faithful may use such opinions in the guidance of the faithful, whether this refers to the use of contraceptives to space births or to the encouragement of steady lover relationships between two homosexuals.[3]

2. Specific texts of Scripture, traditionally used to demonstrate the immorality of homosexual activity, such as Leviticus 18:22 and 20:13; 1 Corinthians 6:9–10; 1 Timothy 1:9–10; and Romans 1:26–27, have no probative value for the homosexual person today, because they do not apply to contemporary situations of homosexuals. The sacred writers were concerned with the condemnation of cultic prostitution rites and promiscuity, not with faithful love relationships.[4]

3. The concept of natural moral law binding universally and holding that certain actions such as direct abortion are always immoral is repudiated; for such abstractions society has substituted cultural norms based upon the customs and needs of the people. The goodness or evil of an action, then, is largely determined by the intention of the person and the circumstances of the action.[5]

4. The data of the empirical sciences dealing with human behavior—such as psychology, sociology, anthropology, and the like—should be the

---

[3] Germain Grisez, *The Way of the Lord Jesus Christ*, vol. 1, *Christian Moral Principles* (Chicago: Franciscan Herald Press, 1983), pp. 831–856, gives a cogent rebuttal of this presupposition. See also Benedict Ashley, "The Use of Moral Theory by the Church" in *Human Sexuality and Personhood* (St. Louis: Pope John Center), pp. 223–242, for a scholarly exposition of magisterial teaching with due respect to theological approaches.

[4] John J. McNeill, *The Church and the Homosexual* (Kansas City, Kans.: Sheed, Andrews and McMeel, 1976), would follow this line of reasoning, which would also be accepted by Anthony Kosnik et al. in *Human Sexuality* (New York: Paulist Press, 1977), pp. 188–196, as well as many Protestant scholars.

[5] John Boswell, *Christianity, Social Tolerance and Homosexuality* (Chicago: University of Chicago Press, 1980), pp. 303–332, attempts to demolish the natural moral law arguments against homosexual activity. I comment on his thesis in *Linacre Quarterly*, Aug. 1981, pp. 265–275.

determinative factor in forming moral norms for concrete situations such as homosexual lifestyles. In the event of conflict between the findings of such data and traditionally held moral norms, the conclusions of the empirical scientists should prevail.[6] (Note that this presupposition fails to take into account that the conclusions of empirical sciences, as such, are limited and particular, and that norms for free human behavior must be rooted in a sound philosophy of the human and in the teachings of Revelation.)

5. Determination of moral norms should be based primarily upon relationships between persons rather than upon the substance of the action. As long as the relationship between persons is mutual, it is generally good. This presupposition has special application to sexual relationships, such as premarital sex, selective adultery, and steady-lover homosexual liaisons.[7]

2. THE POSITION OF CHARLES E. CURRAN

Turning now to major theological views that dissent from the official teaching of the Church, I begin with those authors who consider homosexual activity as not measuring up to Christian ideals of sexuality, but justifiable, given the homosexual's condition and the circumstances of one's life.

I begin with the theory of compromise of Father Charles E. Curran. While recognizing that homosexual acts do not measure up to the norms of sexual activity, Curran does not believe that all homosexual acts fall under total condemnation. Under certain circumstances, he claims, homosexual activity can be morally acceptable, because the person has no other alternative. Since Curran holds that there is an objective meaning in human sexuality that sin does not eradicate or neutralize and that the norm of human sexuality is the heterosexual relationship, he solves the dilemma of the homosexual person by his theory of compromise. This, he claims, opens up a viable way of living for the Christian homosexual. Curran uses homosexual behavior to illustrate the theory of compromise. In general, he accepts the experimental data proposed by the other mediating posi-

[6] Anthony Kosnik et al., *Human Sexuality*, ch. 3 (pp. 53–77), hold that empirical data, as such, do not change moral norms, but in ch. 5, the pastoral guidelines, empirical data are used as a decisive factor in justifying certain kinds of actions. See Kosnik's Special Questions, pp. 219ff.

[7] Gregory Baum, "Catholic Homosexuals" in *Commonweal*, Feb. 15, 1974, pp. 8–11. See also *Homosexuality and Ethics*, ed. Edward Batchelor, Jr., pp. 124–145, for several advocates of the relational point of view.

tions. The homosexual is generally not responsible for his condition. Heterosexual marital relations remain the norm. "Therapy, as an attempt to make the homosexual into a heterosexual, does not offer great promise for most homosexuals. Celibacy and sublimation are not always possible or even desirable for the homosexuals. There are many somewhat stable homosexual unions which afford their partners some human fulfillment and contentment. Obviously, such unions are better than homosexual promiscuity. . . . In many ways homosexuality exists as the result of sin. . . . Homosexuality can never become the norm of sexual activity."[8]

It is clear, then, that Curran applies his theory of compromise to the apparently confirmed homosexual who has little hope of change in sexual orientation through therapy and who has settled into a somewhat stable homosexual union. Such unions are a middle ground between celibacy and promiscuity. Curran continues to hold this view. Speaking to a symposium sponsored by New Ways Ministry in 1981, he said that "the normative ideal is heterosexuality, but because some people, through no fault of their own, are homosexual, homosexual actions in a committed relationship striving for permanency can be objectively good."[9]

In Curran's thinking, homosexual acts in a steady relationship are not objectively wrong, because in the presence of sin they are the only viable alternative for the person. Yet in another sense such actions are wrong, manifesting the power of sin. While man and woman must try to overcome sin, the Christian must realize that the struggle against sin is never completely successful in this world.

Critique of Curran[10]

Implicitly, Curran's theory of compromise denies the element of freedom in sin, because it holds that in certain situations one must perform the "sinful" act, which in one sense is good because it is the best one can do, and in another sense is bad because it is the expression of a sin-filled situation. Curran, then, holds that one *must* freely sin; but this is a contradiction in terms, since in the formal sense an act cannot be sinful unless it is truly free. In this analysis I am not concerned with the truly

[8] *Catholic Moral Theology in Dialogue* (Notre Dame, Ind.: University of Notre Dame Press, 1972), p. 217.

[9] "Homosexuals and Religious Life", *The Tablet*, Brooklyn, N.Y., Dec. 26, 1981, p. 19. See also Curran, *Issues in Sexual and Medical Ethics* (Notre Dame, Ind.: University of Notre Dame Press, 1979), p. 48.

[10] Curran has a critique of both my methodology and substantive conclusions in *Critical Concerns in Moral Theology* (Notre Dame, Ind.: University of Notre Dame Press, 1984), pp. 81–83. Unfortunately he bases his analysis of my thought on the article in the *New*

compulsive homosexual person, who is presumed to have suffered a significant diminution of freedom, but with a person possessing sufficient freedom either to act virtuously or to sin. Again, traditional moral theology has always recognized the difficult life situation, and pastoral programs have been offered to help the person do what ought to be done, even if this demands heroic courage. It must be assumed that God gives each one sufficient grace to fulfill the law of God in his life.[11] The principle of compromise is really a denial of the truth found in divine revelation that God gives to each person sufficient grace to avoid sin and to practice virtue.[12]

In his commendable effort to help persons in difficult situations Curran has posited an unacceptable principle which, when it is applied also to heterosexual persons who have been deprived of the fullness of genital pleasure for a variety of reasons, would allow them to indulge in some form of genital relationship. After all, in the thinking of the culture, everyone has to have genital sex, and "bad sex is better than no sex." Implicit also in Curran's position, although not enunciated, is the belief that complete abstinence is possible only to those who have the charism of celibacy through vow or promise. The homosexual, the divorced and unremarried, the unwilling singles, the deprived married, and various others, according to Curran's premise, should be allowed to have some genital indulgence as part of their intimate relationships with partners of the same or other sex.

Catholic Encyclopedia (1967). He did not take into consideration my updating of the encyclopedia article in *NCE*, vol. 17, 1977 Supplement, or in numerous other articles referenced in Chapter Six, where I develop the scriptural arguments, the argument based on the complementarity of man and woman, the dualistic nature of homosexual activity, and so on. Although valid, an argument based only on the inordinate use of the sexual faculty is incomplete. In Chapter Six I sum up arguments from Holy Scripture, philosophy, and psychology.

[11] In *Familiaris Consortio* John Paul II criticizes the view that the law may be viewed "as merely an ideal to be achieved in the future; they must consider it as a command of Christ the Lord to overcome difficulties with constancy. And so what is known as 'the law of gradualness' or step by step advance cannot be identified with 'gradualness of the law' as if there were different degrees or forms of precept in God's law for different individuals and situations" (Boston: St. Paul Publications, 1981), p. 65.

[12] Pius XII referred to the Sixth Session of the Council of Trent and to St. Augustine in support of the position that at times extended continence may be required of the married: "In confirmation of this argument we have the Council of Trent which, in its chapter on the observance, necessary and possible, of the commandments, teaches us that, as St. Augustine said, 'God does not command impossible things, but in commanding He admonishes you both to do what you can do, and to seek His grace to do what you cannot do.' " (Washington, D.C.: N.C.W.C., *Moral Questions Affecting Married Life*, 1951), ch. 2, p. 16, par. 40. The same principle applies to the homosexual person seeking to be chaste.

Another weakness in Curran's theology of homosexual activity is the inadequate treatment of the virtue of chastity. He says that celibacy and sublimation are not always possible or even desirable for the homosexual.[13] In short, in order to be happy the homosexual person must have physical sex. But the truth is that men and women do not need genital intimacy to be fully human. Yet they do need psychic intimacy in the form of deep friendships with at least one other person, and preferably more than one close friendship. Each person needs a community of friends. I shall say more about intimacy and chastity in the pastoral section.[14]

3. THE TEACHING OF PHILIP KEANE

Another moralist who seeks to remain within the traditional position on homosexuality but also wants to make allowances for homosexuals in steady relationships is Philip Keane, *Sexual Morality: A Catholic Perspective* (New York: Paulist Press, 1977). Keane is important because he bases his approach to sexual ethics on the theory of ontic evil and proportionalism, according to which there is no concrete historical act that is always immoral. The reason is that the morality of any human act cannot be determined until we consider not only the moral object but also a combination of other factors, the most important of which are the intended good consequences of the given act. If the intended good consequences of an action are greater than the "ontic" evil found in the action, then the action becomes morally good, according to this theory.

Thus, an action that traditional moral theology has regarded as morally evil, such as homosexual activity between persons in a steady relationship, would be considered in the new theory as not morally evil but only "ontic", or "premoral" or "nonmoral". Thus the decisive factor in the determination of moral behavior is not to be found primarily by analyzing individual human actions, but by noting the consequences of a series of actions over a period of time. In accepting this perspective Keane must

[13] See footnote 9. See also St. Augustine, *De natura et de gratia*, ch. 43, n. 50, Migne, *PL*, vol. 44, col. 271. This is the source of the quotation of Pius XII found in footnote 12. As noted, it was used by the Council of Trent.

[14] I have given critiques of Curran's position in "The Controversy Concerning the Psychology and Morality of Homosexuality", *The American Ecclesiastical Review*, Nov. 1973, pp. 613–624; "The Pastoral Implications of Church Teaching on Homosexuality", *Linacre Quarterly*, Aug. 1971, pp. 157–164; "The Morality Conference in St. Louis Revisited", *Homiletic and Pastoral Review*, Oct. 1968, pp. 35–42; "Law and Personalism", *Communio*, Spring 1975, pp. 70–71.

deny the official teaching of the Church that homosexual acts are morally evil in themselves.

Actions containing "ontic" evil become good under certain circumstances. This principle is applied across the board by Keane to a variety of situations, using a sliding scale of ontic evils and justifying proportional reasons. His fluid use of "ontic evil" is comparable to Joseph Fletcher's use of "love" in *Situation Ethics*, and just as elusive. (Readers may recall James Gustafson's critique of "love" in Fletcher. Love was like a greased pig running through the book and almost impossible to pin down in its variant meanings.) Keane's ontic evil, likewise, comes to mean whatever Keane wants it to mean. The ontic evil of masturbation becomes a moral good if it relieves tension in a separated spouse or in an engaged person. The ontic evil of homosexual activity becomes the moral good of stable friendship, and so on. In all these situations Keane stresses both the lack of something in the physical structure of the act and the intentionality justifying that lack or ontic evil. It is clear that intentionality is more important to Keane than the kind of act permitted. Keane skillfully draws out the implications of this theory for pastoral practice.[15]

At the same time Keane does not seriously consider the empirical data that militates against stable homosexual relationships and that would be important in evaluating consequences of an action (not that I accept this kind of argument). Again, there is little development of the intrapsychic difficulties that make stable relationships very difficult for most male homosexuals. (The subsequent studies of Moberly and van den Aardweg provide further data on the inability of most male homosexual persons to form lasting sexual-genital relationships.) The treatment of Holy Scripture on homosexuality is almost nonexistent. In brief, Keane's analysis is excessively dependent upon the theory of proportionalism.[16]

4. THE POSITION OF JOHN MCNEILL, S.J.

The dissenting theologian who has had the greatest influence on Catholic homosexual persons is probably John J. McNeill, S.J., in *The Church and the Homosexual*. His views are a radical departure from those of Curran and Keane and from the official teaching of the Church. This is a summary of his position. Genuine homosexuals are those whose

---

[15] *Sexual Morality: A Catholic Perspective*, pp. 84–91.

[16] Grisez, *op. cit.*, ch. 6: Critique of the Proportionalist Method of Moral Judgement, pp. 141–171. This is a thorough repudiation of the method used by Keane and many others, including Richard McCormick, S.J.

"permanent psychological condition" is erotic orientation toward the same sex. This condition can serve as a basis for constructive human love, involving genital relationships, which help each partner grow as a person. Genital expression becomes a form of human play in which the procreative value of sexuality is neglected; hence homosexual acts performed out of love by a "genuine" homosexual are good, whereas sexual acts performed by a heterosexual or by a homosexual out of lust would be immoral.

Father McNeill's effort to distinguish good and bad homosexual acts purely on the basis of motivation and intention leads him into dualism, which I shall explain. When homosexuals use their genital organs to express love, these actions *become* good because of their psychic disposition; but if the person performing the homosexual action is heterosexual, the action becomes evil because his psychic disposition is contrary to the homosexual meaning. Thus the physical action has no meaning in itself but derives its entire meaning from the psychic disposition and intention of the agent. Instead of confronting the meaning of the physical act, McNeill superimposes meaning. He says, for example, that love makes the physical act good. McNeill develops two major arguments to support the thesis that homosexual acts are good in themselves.

1. None of the texts in Holy Scripture concerning homosexuality contains a clear condemnation of faithful homosexual unions (see chapter one of *The Church and the Homosexual*).

2. Man's radical freedom enters into the formation of man's sexual orientation in such a way that biological givens, such as the sex in which one is born, should not be determinative of sexual activity.

First I shall consider McNeill's interpretation of Holy Scripture. Referring to the Genesis account of the creation of male and female, McNeill cautions that the Scriptures are historically and culturally determined. He questions whether the traditional view that genital human sexuality derives its meaning exclusively in terms of the relationship of male and female in a procreative union is really an expression of God's will or whether it is merely the reflection of the needs of the primitive human community. Thus the Genesis account represents various aspects of the then-monogamous family unit: (1) it reflects the need of a paternalistic society to show male superiority; and (2) like other accounts of sexuality in the Old Testament and New, it is fearful of Canaanite and other idolatrous sexual practices. Turning to the Code of Leviticus' condemnations of homosexual acts, McNeill sees it as an expression of the Jewish horror of the meaning of sodomy, for it was the common practice in the Middle East to submit a captured foe to sodomy. Homosexual activity was an expression of domination, contempt, and scorn. Since the Jewish male population had suffered this indignation and the male was of prime importance to this society, it would follow that any activity associated with the degradation of the male was a serious offense.

McNeill claims

that what is referred to in Scripture as homosexuality is either not the same reality at all, or that the Biblical author did not manifest the same understanding of that reality as we have today. Therefore it can be seriously questioned whether what is understood today as the true homosexual and his activity is ever the object of explicit moral condemnation in the Scriptures.[17]

After all, he continues, biblical writers were not familiar with the distinction between homosexual orientation and activity, and they could not have reasoned to the conclusion that a homosexually oriented person should be allowed to engage in homosexual activity. For this reason, even in the one passage that McNeill finds in the New Testament (Rom 1:26–27) as referring clearly to homosexual activity, he sees no condemnation of contemporary homosexual unions. He believes Paul understood the Greeks who indulged in homosexual activity to be heterosexuals involved in homosexual acts—probably as a form of sacred prostitution so often condemned in the Old Testament.

From his study of biblical scholars on human sexuality McNeill concludes that the primary message of the Old Testament is that love, including sexual love, requires respect for the other person as well. Thus the sin that one can commit in one's sexual conduct with another consists in dishonoring the person of a fellow human being. According to McNeill, the New Testament teaches a similar message of free, interpersonal love.

Critique of McNeill's views on homosexuality in Holy Scripture

While I believe that the Scriptures are not the only source of Church teaching on homosexuality, they are important for our understanding of sexuality in general and of homosexuality in particular. McNeill's use of Scripture presents many difficulties. It is significant that the biblical accounts are concerned with the man–woman relationship. The Genesis accounts in Chapters 1 and 2 have been regarded as both an ideal and norm of sexual behavior, and the sexual behavior is heterosexual. Matthew's reference to this norm strengthens the argument that Genesis taught a heterosexual norm of behavior in permanent marriage; in this passage (Mt 19:1–6) the author quotes both Genesis 1:27 and 2:24 when he says:

[17] "The Homosexual and the Church", *National Catholic Reporter*, Oct. 5, 1973, pp. 7–8, 13–14.

"He [Jesus] replied, 'Have you not read that at the beginning the Creator made them male and female and declared, "For this reason a man shall leave his father and mother and cling to his wife, and the two shall become as one"? Thus they are no longer two but one flesh. Therefore, let no man separate what God has joined.' "

Again, in the Genesis accounts it is said that man was created as male or female (Gen 1:27) and that it was not good that man should be alone. At this point, however, God did not create another man but a woman. Surely, the Genesis accounts, as well as the rest of Scripture, say something about the profound complementarity of man and woman—a point made most strongly by such scholars as John L. McKenzie, Pierre Grelot, Edward Schillebeeckx, and Helmut Thielicke.[18] The distinguished Protestant theologian Roger Shinn adds, "The Christian tradition over the centuries has affirmed the heterosexual, monogamous faithful marital union as normative for the divinely given meaning of the intimate sexual relationship."[19]

Another argument used by McNeill throughout his discussion of scriptural references is that sexual norms are determined exclusively by cultural factors: Jewish and Christian marriages were structured to assure male domination. Homosexual acts were condemned because they were forms of prostitution rites or unpleasant reminders of humiliation by the captors of the Israelites, and so forth. Against this kind of speculation it can be argued that the authors of the sacred books, beginning with the Genesis account of marriage, intended to affirm certain transcendental principles concerning human sexuality and marriage. If this were not so, why would the author of Matthew (19:1–9) refer back to the pristine purity of marriage? On another occasion why would Jesus say that divorce was not God's intention in the beginning but was a concession due to the hardness of men's hearts?

This is not to say that everything said about sexuality in the Old Testament is of permanent value, since one recognizes the prescriptions of Leviticus (15:19–30) concerning the menstruating woman as to some extent culturally conditioned. It is to affirm that in both Testaments we find perennial truths concerning the heterosexual norm of marriage, as is

[18] John L. McKenzie, *The Two-Edged Sword* (Milwaukee: Bruce, 1956), ch. 6, "Human Origins"; Pierre Grelot, *Man and Wife in Scripture* (New York: Herder and Herder, 1964); Edward Schillebeeckx, *Marriage, Human Reality, and Saving Mystery* (New York: Sheed and Ward, 1965), ch. 1; and Helmut Thielicke, *The Ethics of Sex*, trans. John W. Doberstein (New York: Fortress Press, 1964), pp. 3–13.

[19] "Homosexuality, Christian Conviction and Enquiry", *The Same Sex*, ed. Ralph Weltge (Philadelphia: Pilgrim Press, 1969), p. 26.

exemplified in the Vatican II statement on marriage in *The Church in the Modern World*, par. 47–52.[20]

As already mentioned, McNeill interprets all the specific texts referring to homosexual activity in terms of a relationship to prostitution cults. Prescinding from the Leviticus texts in the Old Testament and the other references in the New, one wonders how one can prove that in Romans 1:26–27 homosexual acts were condemned *only* because they happened in the background of deliberate repudiation of God or because it happened to be Greek heterosexuals performing homosexual activities. McNeill draws the conclusion that the men were heterosexuals because the author uses the active aorist participle, *aphentes*, men *giving up* their natural relations with women. But note that he does not explain St. Paul's reference to women making use of other women. His is hardly a convincing proof.

McNeill argues in one place that biblical authors condemn homosexual activity because of its association with prostitution rites and that in Romans such acts are wrong because they are performed by heterosexuals, drawing this conclusion on the basis of a grammatical phrase. Here he cannot have it both ways: on the one hand, St. Paul knew nothing about the homosexual condition; and yet he knew so much that he could discern the difference between homosexuals performing homosexual acts out of love, and heterosexuals performing the same acts out of lust. If St. Paul knew nothing of the homosexual condition, how could he make a distinction that is difficult for a competent psychiatrist?

In summing up McNeill's understanding of Scripture and homosexuality I would agree with his assertion of the primacy of love and mutual respect in both Testaments; but I find his attempts to justify faithful homosexuals theologically erroneous. The texts of Holy Scripture give no proof for his position. It remains to judge whether his argument for a homosexual lifestyle can be drawn from philosophy.

From the personal uniqueness of each person McNeill argues that the person, in relating to another unique person, is not bound by moral norms concerning human acts. A sexual act between two loving persons is an end in itself and an expression of radical freedom. It does not have to consider the procreative purpose of human sexuality. Indeed men and women can use their bodily organs in many creative ways; for example, one can use one's sexual organs, designed by nature for procreation, to

---

[20] The argument that sexual norms are determined exclusively by cultural factors is also found in Anthony Kosnik et al., *Human Sexuality*, in their discussion of sexual norms, particularly the morality of homosexual actions, pp. 186–218. See William E. May and my own criticism of such reductionism in *On Understanding Human Sexuality* (Chicago: Franciscan Herald Press, 1977), pp. 31–43.

give the most intimate personal expression of one's drive for union in love with a fellow human. The point is that man has the freedom to decide how he will use his powers.

McNeill goes on to explain how man's freedom enters into the formation of his sexual orientation. Biological givens, such as physical sexuality, do not determine human behavior precisely as it exists on the human level. What we are in our society is a free cultural creation. For each culture creates its own ideal identity images from the masculine and feminine roles. That is why the young undergo a process through which they adapt themselves to the prevailing cultural images and expectations that are in agreement with their biological identity. Although in the past theologians have mistakenly identified such cultural images as divinely given, in more recent times they, including John McNeill, have been able to identify such images as determined by particular cultures.

McNeill concludes that the sexual identity images that concretize heterosexual relationships are cultural creations and do not proceed from God's eternal and natural law. Humans need to develop an ideal human nature in the future. This will be seen in a free, mature person living in a mature relationship. In this way a homosexual relationship will be viewed as a truly constructive and mature expression of human love.

The theory that we create our cultural and moral values is often traced rightly (or, more probably, wrongly) to Maurice Blondel, who stated the principle "Nothing can impose itself on a man, nothing can demand the assent of his intellect or the consent of his will, which does not in some way find its source in man himself."[21]

Accepting this principle of immanence, McNeill draws the conclusion that whatever we are as humans in this present society is a free cultural creation. In the circumstances of his life and culture man creates his own freedom. In light of these premises it is not surprising that McNeill rejects the traditional position of the Church on objective standards of morality. Any sexual action by a loving person is a unique action not measurable by any *extrinsic* norm. Sharing in the radical freedom of man, this action derives its morality from the ideals that arise within the will of the person himself. Thus as long as a sexual act is free, loving, and creative, it is good. The biological and instinctive elements of the sexual act in no way determine its moral goodness or evil. But this is to ignore the meaning of bodily action. This is *dualism*.

All moral authority, then, according to McNeill, comes from within the person himself as he reaches out to grasp transcendental truth. This

[21] Taken from Blondel's *The Letter of Apologetics* (New York: Holt, Rinehart, and Winston, 1964), pp. 60–61. See also McNeill, "Freedom and the Future", *Theological Studies* 33 (1972):503–530. Also "Blondel on the Subjectivity of Moral Decision Making", *Proceedings of the Amer. Cath. Philo. Association* 48 (1974):208–217.

presupposes a process in all areas of development, including the sexual. McNeill sees this development beginning with promiscuous sex and advancing over a long time to a mature, loving relationship characterized by love and trust. Implicitly, however, contrary to his own theory of freedom, he presupposes that by myriad influences in early life, the homosexual person has been *determined* in his orientation toward the same sex, and he regards this learned inclination as connatural to him; so he seeks the same kind of fidelity from his chosen beloved as a man and woman in marriage. Just as sexual intimacy between two heterosexual persons is considered as an expression of union, so sexual actions between two homosexual lovers is meant to be an expression of their committed love. In contrast to Christian tradition, McNeill makes the homosexual union an alternative to marriage, meant only for those homosexually oriented.

From the above review of McNeill's thought it is glaringly evident how far away he is from the reality of the daily life of homosexual persons, both male and female. Only a small percentage of homosexual persons accept his proposed ideal of faithful homosexual union. There are other errors in his thinking as well, but I shall wait to discuss them until I have presented the thought of Gregory Baum, another theologian who is popular among homosexuals of Catholic upbringing and who also advocates a radical break with traditional Catholic teaching.

5. THE THOUGHT OF GREGORY BAUM

Baum holds that what a particular culture calls "human nature" is merely the self-understanding of the dominant class and that the perpetuation of that self-understanding tends to increase the power of the class. For this reason, "The theologian must try to discern in the inherited, historically conditioned human nature the possible structures of oppression, legitimating various forms of what Hegel has called master–slave relationships."[22]

The moral norm is mutuality: "What is normative for normal life is the human nature to which we are divinely summoned, which is defined in terms of mutuality. This, at least, is the promise of biblical religion."[23] Further in his discussion Baum describes mutuality as friendship. Thus the morality of homosexual activity is to be determined by mutuality. This means that a homosexual relationship is good if it is grounded on a

[22] Baum, op. cit., p. 9. In *Homosexuality and Ethics*, ed. Edward Batchelor, Jr., one finds a reprint of Baum's "Catholic Homosexuals", pp. 22–27.
[23] *Commonweal*, Feb. 15, 1974, p. 9.

friendship that enables the partners to grow and to become mutually more human. "For the structure of redeemed life is mutuality."[24]

Baum realizes that some forms of sexuality do not admit of mutuality: sadism, masochism, and pedophilia, but we should take seriously the witness of homosexual men and women who give evidence that their lives are based on mutuality. From the witness of those Christian homosexual men and women who have had lasting relationships theologians may conclude that constitutive homosexuals "must accept their orientation and live accordingly. Homosexual love, then, is not contrary to the human nature, defined in terms of mutuality, toward which mankind is summoned."[25]

Critique of Baum and McNeill

First one notes Baum's unproven assertions. When he speaks of a historically constituted human nature, he is asserting that human nature at any given time is constituted exclusively from the elements of a particular culture; he adds that human nature, as generally understood by scholastic philosophy, is so entangled with dehumanizing elements woven into our culture that it is no longer an operative moral norm. Yet the only example he gives of these dehumanizing elements is the tradition affirming the superiority of the male, or the master–slave relationship. He also asserts that the long-standing tradition against homosexuality is an example of the cruelty of the heterosexual culture that places a terrible burden of hostility upon the homosexual person, leading him or her to be filled with self-hatred.

Baum does not prove these assertions concerning human nature, the inadequacy of traditional moral norms, or the origins of self-hatred in homosexual persons. Dissatisfied with traditional objective norms, Baum invents a new one, mutuality. In so doing he ignores other varied and complex aspects of human sexuality, such as procreative longing, motherhood, fatherhood, and family stability. The norm of mutuality for sexual actions is not comprehensive enough to cover all the known elements of sexuality and does not take into account the scriptural teaching. To say, moreover, that society's attitude toward homosexuals is the major cause of whatever neurosis the person may have is contrary to sound psychiatric opinion.[26] This is not to deny that the self-hatred found in many homo-

[24] *Ibid.*, p. 10.

[25] *Ibid.*

[26] John F. Harvey, O.S.F.S., "Morality and Pastoral Treatment of Homosexuality", *Continuum*, Summer 1967, pp. 284–289; Harry Gershman, "Reflections on the Nature of Homosexuality", *Amer. J. of Psychoanalysis* 26 (1966):46–58. The author sees intrapsychic

sexuals is in *part* a reflection of the attitude of hatred found in society toward homosexual persons.

I would like to sum up the errors in the reasoning of McNeill and Baum:

1. If the norm is purely subjective and divorced from the history of man, it will not be able to see the full reality of man as he has learned from historical experience. Why should Baum's perception of morality as mutuality displace more nuanced norms that consider not only man's subjective condition but also the structure of human society, the structure of human acts, and one person in relationship to another person and to society?

2. Baum does not really treat the scriptural question, while McNeill interprets the pertinent passages condemning homosexual activity in such a way that he renders them all nonapplicable to the homosexual in a faithful union.

3. The concentration of both McNeill and Baum on the situation of the faithful homosexual couple is quite disproportionate when one considers that the vast majority of homosexuals do not desire and do not seek this kind of union. Moral theologians should pay more attention to the behavior of the typical homosexual person.

4. In psychiatry the concept of the person who is irreversibly oriented to homosexuality is not universally accepted by many researchers, including Lawrence Hatterer, Samuel Haddon, I. Bieber, Elizabeth Moberly, and Gerald van den Aardweg.[27]

In this lengthy treatment of McNeill and Baum I have endeavored to show their serious departure from the official teaching of the Church. Yet their teaching is very influential, particularly in the organization of Catholics called Dignity. In the *Commonweal* article already referenced, Baum encouraged the members of Dignity to remain in opposition to Church teaching. While I shall give further treatment to Dignity later, suffice it to say at this point that Dignity chapters—with few exceptions—encourage their members to enter into steady-lover relationships.

---

difficulties as more important than the perception of society's attitude toward the homosexual person—a position confirmed in the research of contemporary authors such as Moberly and van den Aardweg.

[27] Lawrence Hatterer, *Changing Homosexuality in the Male* (New York: Dell Publishing, 1971); Samuel Haddon, "Treatment of Male Homosexuals in Groups", *The Internat. J. of Group Psychotherapy* 16, no. 1 (Jan. 1966):13–22: "While there is little doubt that the homosexual is difficult to treat and is prone to break off treatment, this is not in itself sufficient reason to predict failure in the treatment of every homosexual" (p. 14). Haddon adds that he and Bieber and his associates have convincingly demonstrated the positive results of treatment conducted by therapists who neither anticipate nor accept failure in the treatment of homosexuals. The subsequent work of Hatterer, van den Aardweg, and others justifies the optimism of Haddon.

CHAPTER SIX

ARGUMENTS FROM REVELATION AND REASON IN FAVOR OF THE OFFICIAL TEACHING OF THE CHURCH

I. ARGUMENTS AGAINST HOMOSEXUALITY BASED ON SCRIPTURE

It should be noted that Church teaching is concerned primarily with homosexual acts, not the homosexual condition, which the person most probably did not will; furthermore, it is concerned primarily with free acts as opposed to compulsive acts, although the compulsive person does have responsibility to do something about his addiction. With these distinctions in mind, I turn to the Church's understanding of Holy Scripture in her condemnation of homosexual acts. I have already described how the opponents of Church teaching try to explain away the obvious meaning of the classical texts referring to homosexuality (on male homosexuality: Lev 18:22; 20:13; Rom 1:27; 1 Cor 6:9–10; 1 Tim 1:9–10; on female homosexuality: Rom 1:26).

But without denying the probative force of these specific texts, I think it better to begin with a scriptural argument against homosexual acts that is rooted in the Church's constant understanding of marriage in the Scriptures. As the October 1, 1986, document points out, homosexuality must be understood within the theology of creation described in Genesis, chapters 1 and 2: "He fashions mankind, male and female, in His own image and likeness. Human beings, therefore, are nothing less than the work of God Himself; and in the complementarity of the sexes, they are called to reflect the inner unity of the Creator. They do this in a striking way in their cooperation with Him in the transmission of life by a mutual donation of the self to the other."[1]

Thus only in marriage is found the proper place for genital sexual expression. From the first chapter of Genesis to the Book of Revelation the twofold meaning of sexual-genital expression—namely, procreation and union—is clearly manifest. In Genesis 1:27–28 it is said: "God created

---

[1] PCHP, 6. See also Ronald Lawler, O.F.M., Cap., Joseph Boyle, Jr., and William E. May, *Catholic Sexual Ethics* (Huntington, Ind.: Our Sunday Visitor, Inc., 1985), p. 197: "The Bible teaches that the sexual differentiation of the human race into male and female is divinely willed, that male and female complement each other, and that marriage, rooted in the irrevocable consent of man and woman to be 'one flesh', alone respects the goods of human sexuality."

man in the image of Himself, in the image of God He created him, male and female He created them. God blessed them, saying to them, 'Be fruitful, multiply, fill the earth and conquer it.' " In the second account of creation God presents Eve to Adam, and Adam exclaims, " 'This at last is bone from my bones, and flesh from my flesh. This is to be called woman, for this was taken from man.' This is why a man leaves his father and mother and joins himself to his wife, and they become one body" (Gen 2:23–24).

Despite deviations from the original norm of monogamous marriage, including polygamy and divorce, the norm for sexual activity remained a permanent heterosexual union. Yahweh is portrayed as the faithful bridegroom, and Israel, the faithless bride, indicating that heterosexual love can be the basis for expressing the mystery of God's loving the human race.[2] Throughout the Old Testament, however, the truth about persons being the image of God was obscured by original sin. Men and women lost their awareness of the covenantal character of the union these people had with God and with each other. Among other places, this is indicated in Genesis 3 and in Genesis 19:1–11.[3] Then in the New Testament Jesus Himself reaffirms the norm of Genesis.

The context is the Pharisees questioning Jesus whether a man may divorce his wife on any pretext whatever. Jesus answered: "Have you not read that the creator from the beginning *made them male and female* and that He said: '*This is why a man must leave father and mother and cling to his wife, and the two become one body?* They are no longer two, therefore, but one body. So then what God has united, man must not divide.' " When the Pharisees, then, asked Him why Moses allowed divorce, Jesus replied that it was "because you were so unteachable . . . but it was not like this from the beginning" (Mt 19:3–8).

Here Jesus reaffirms the monogamous, heterosexual norm of sexuality found in Genesis. Note that He quotes both Genesis 1:27 and 2:24, thereby repeating their teaching about the meaning of human sexuality.

The author of Ephesians, moreover, reiterates the same revealed truth about human sexuality in the context of the sublime comparison in which the husband is compared with Christ and the wife with the Church. When the author wishes to express the love that Christ has for His Church, he turns to the heterosexual love of husband and wife: "Husbands should love their wives just as Christ loved the Church and sacrificed Himself for

---

[2] Pierre Grelot, *Man and Wife in Scripture* (New York: Herder and Herder, 1965), pp. 34–37; Edward Schillebeeckx, *Marriage*, pp. 14–16, 20–21; John L. McKenzie, *The Two-Edged Sword* (New York: Doubleday, 1966). Grelot gives a full treatment of this question.

[3] PCHP, 6.

her to make her holy. . . . In the same way husbands must love their wives as they love their own bodies . . ." (Eph 5:25, 28). Then the author adds: "*For this reason a man must leave his father and mother and be joined to his wife and the two will become one body*" (Gen 2:24). Once again the Genesis norm of permanent heterosexual union is reaffirmed (Eph 5:30).

One could go on referencing other passages of Holy Scripture to demonstrate its teaching that sexual activity ought to be heterosexual and marital, but this has already been done by scholars throughout the centuries, as I have indicated.[4] Indeed the Second Vatican Council's document, *The Church in the Modern World*, 47–52 and *Humanae Vitae*, 11–14 sum up the teaching of Holy Scripture, of the Fathers of the Church, and of previous magisterial statements of popes and councils that the moral norm of sexual activity is a permanent union of husband and wife for the essentially inseparable purposes of love and union. This is the perennial teaching of the Church. Taken as a whole, it is at least authoritative; but the divine origin of marriage is a teaching of Faith.

In his July 25, 1986, letter to Father Charles Curran, Cardinal Ratzinger, Prefect of the Congregation for the Doctrine of the Faith, said that Father Curran had not given due consideration to the Church's position on the indissolubility of sacramental and consummated marriage. Father Curran had argued that the Church's position ought to be changed, but Cardinal Ratzinger points out that this "was in fact defined at the Council of Trent and so belongs to the patrimony of the faith".[5] It should be noted that Father Curran regards the Church's condemnation of homosexual activities as a non-infallible teaching, from which one has a right of responsible dissent. To this position Ratzinger replies that the teaching of Vatican II does not confine the infallible Magisterium "purely to matters of faith nor to solemn definitions". Quoting *Lumen Gentium*, 25, Ratzinger adds: "Besides this, the Church does not build its life upon its infallible magisterium alone but on the teaching of its authentic ordinary magisterium as well."[6]

From all this one may logically conclude that homosexual activity is objectively always seriously immoral, inasmuch as it in no way fulfills the essential purposes of human sexuality. The Catholic teaching flows *necessarily* from the *whole scriptural vision of the meaning of sexuality* and of the

---

[4] See previous references to Pierre Grelot, Edward Schillebeeckx, and John L. McKenzie (*The Two-Edged Sword*). The latter holds that Genesis 1 and 2—the story of the creation of mankind as male and female—is also the story of the creation of marriage. See also *Summa Theologiae*, II–II, q. 154, aa. 11–12.

[5] Excerpt from Cardinal Ratzinger's Letter in *The Philadelphia Catholic Standard and Times*, Thursday, Aug. 21, 1986, p. 2.

[6] *Ibid.*

complementarity of man and woman. Specific biblical texts, moreover, confirm this general thrust of Holy Scripture.

I have already discussed the way in which Kosnik et al., McNeill, and others attempt to explain away the specific texts of both the Old and New Testaments. Since the argument against homosexual activity would stand on the basis of the Church's teaching on sexual activity in general, I do not see the need to develop the argument from specific texts at great length. I shall begin with the Sodom story (Gen 19:4–11).[7]

In 1956 Derrick Sherwin Bailey argued in *Homosexuality and the Western Christian Tradition* that Sodom was destroyed for inhospitable treatment of the angel visitors sent by the Lord. In this interpretation the homosexual overtones of the story are minor, while the predominant meaning centers on the violation of hospitality.

His argument is not convincing. In my judgment the Genesis passage does refer to attempted homosexual rape, and the effort to interpret the passage primarily in terms of hospitality is forced, because taking the sexual element out renders the rest of the narrative nonsensical. As Ruth Tiffany Barnhouse observes, "If the men of Sodom had no sexual intentions toward Lot's visitors, why would Lot have replied, 'I beg you, my brothers, do no such wicked thing. Listen, I have two daughters who are virgins. I am ready to send them out to you, to treat as it pleases you. But as to the men, do nothing to them, for they have come under the shadow of my roof' " (Gen 19:7–9).[8]

John Mahoney, S.J., also believes that the effort to weaken the force of the Sodom narrative is unsuccessful, because "there can be little reasonable doubt that the story of Sodom and Gomorrah expresses a judgment, however dramatic, of divine displeasure upon the homosexual behavior of its inhabitants and in so doing only serves to echo the explicit condemnation of such behavior in The Holiness Code of Leviticus."[9]

John Boswell claims that numerous other references in Holy Scripture do not identify the sin of Sodom as homosexual activity, but it may be assumed that the readers of these passages knew what the sin was. Again, there is no reason why the sin of Sodom cannot denote homosexual behavior, inhospitality, and wickedness.[10] When Boswell attempts to reduce the explicit prohibitions of Leviticus (18:22; 20:13) to the level of ritual impurity, he is confronted by the objection of scriptural scholar

---

[7] The Vatican document of Oct. 1, 1986, stated that "the deterioration due to sin continues in the story of the men of Sodom. There can be no doubt of the moral judgment made there against homosexual relations" (PCHP, 6).

[8] *Homosexuality: A Symbolic Confusion*, p. 190.

[9] *The Month*, May 1977, p. 167.

[10] *Christianity, Social Tolerance, and Homosexuality*, pp. 93–98.

George Montague: "Sexual morality is often connected with the cult, but this does not prove that sexual sins, such as homosexual acts and bestiality, were condemned only because they were part of the Canaanite worship. While the book of Leviticus does have a cultic framework, the legislation of Leviticus does not give idolatry as the reason for avoiding the sexual practices of the Canaanites. Quite the contrary. The reason given why the Lord is driving the nations out of the land is not their worship of false gods, but their abominable sexual practices (Lev 18:24–30; 20:28). The strict prohibition of the sexual practices of the Canaanites indicates that more than the cult was at issue. . . . To say that the concern of Leviticus is not ethical, but cultic (or in Boswell 'ritual impurity') is a gross oversimplification and even more misleading is the statement: 'The condemnation of homosexual activity in Leviticus is not an ethical judgment.' "[11]

With regard to the classical text of the New Testament, Boswell does not deny that the text is concerned with homosexual activity, but he maintains that it is describing heterosexuals performing homosexual acts, and only this is immoral—the same position as that of McNeill, to which I have already responded. Without qualification St. Paul condemns homosexual acts, whether they are performed by heterosexual or homosexual persons; he does not attempt to analyze subjective dispositions, but only to condemn the act. Thus Boswell's efforts to do away with the meaning of Genesis 19, Leviticus 18 and 20, and Romans 1 is a failure. The first and obvious meaning of all three passages cannot be explained away.[12] In concluding my scriptural analysis I refer the reader to an overlooked verse in the Letter of Jude. "The fornication of Sodom and Gomorrah and the other nearby towns was equally unnatural, and it is a warning to us that they are paying for their crimes in eternal fire" (verse 7). In my judgment this indicates that the sin of Sodom and Gomorrah was unnatural and homosexual. It should be noted that whenever homosexual activity is described in Holy Scripture it is condemned, but nowhere is the homosexual person condemned.[13] I turn now to considerations of the nature of homosexual activity.

---

[11] "A Scriptural Response to the Report on Human Sexuality", *America*, Oct. 1977, pp. 284–285.

[12] See my review of Boswell's book in *The Linacre Quarterly*, Aug. 1981, pp. 265–275, particularly pp. 267–289, where I look at Boswell's use of Scripture.

[13] The Oct. 1, 1986, Vatican document also interprets Lev 18:22 and 20:13, 1 Cor 6:9, and 1 Tim 1:10 as condemning homosexual acts.

2. ARGUMENTS AGAINST HOMOSEXUAL ACTIVITY
BASED UPON ITS NATURE

From Church documents such as *The Church in the Modern World*, *Humanae Vitae*, *The Declaration concerning Certain Questions in Sexual Ethics*, and the *Letter on the Pastoral Care of Homosexual Persons* of October 1, 1986, we hold that sexual activity is both life-giving and person-uniting. We have seen that both these purposes of sexual-genital activity are found in the Scriptures. Sex is life-giving by its very nature. This does not mean that every genital act must lead to new life, but that it must not be structured in ways that rob it of its life-giving power. But homosexual activity can in no way fulfill this procreative power of human sexuality, which "transcends the activity itself and is essential for its human significance."[14]

Genital activity also has a life-uniting meaning: it joins two persons by a special kind of love. "This is marital love—a love that has an exclusive and enduring quality about it, precisely because it has reference to the life-giving end or meaning of genital sexuality. This is a love which opens those whom it unites to what is other than themselves, to a transcendent goal or good toward which they can commit themselves and their shared lives. But this sort of love is simply incapable of being expressed in homosexual activity."[15] Referring to this impoverished form of complementarity, André Guindon writes, "It is therefore easy to see how the homosexual relation fails as a totally human relationship. The authentic human sense of the other, as nourished by the enriching and complementary otherness of the other sex, is conspicuously absent. The other side of the bed is occupied, as it were, only by more of the same—the same half of humanity instead of the other half for whom each person is constitutionally seeking."[16]

It is useful to contrast the man–woman relationship in marriage with the steady-lover relationship of homosexual persons. The man–woman relationship is in accord with the aspirations and needs of both sexes. This is the way nature's God meant things to be. In his commentary on the two creation accounts, Helmut Thielicke describes beautifully the complementarity of man and woman. God did not want the man to be alone, so He created a partner for him. Then comes the poetic expression of the man upon seeing the woman: "Bone of my bone, and flesh of my flesh. For this reason a man shall leave father and mother, and cleave to his wife, and they shall be two in one flesh." These words are in harmony with present natural moral law reasoning. The complementarity between man and

[14] *Catholic Sexual Ethics*, p. 200.
[15] *Ibid.*
[16] *The Sexual Language* (Ottawa: The University of Ottawa Press, 1977), p. 339.

woman is physical (two in one flesh), psychological (the male's joy in the presence of the female), and spiritual (he leaves his own family to commit himself to her). Think of Jacob's love for Rachel; the Valiant Woman of Proverbs 31 or the two lovers in the Canticle of Canticles.

The kind of complementarity, however, between two homosexual persons in a steady relationship is much inferior in terms of its structure, strength of commitment, and consequences. To speak of the physical structure of the homosexual union is to raise the question of whether homosexuals can really achieve a true physical union. Consider the three common forms of sexual activity between homosexual persons. Mutual masturbation in no way constitutes a physical union. In the present AIDS crisis this is the practice recommended by the gay community. Among female homosexuals some form of genital massage is used to bring the partner to orgasm, but this is not a physical union. In anal or oral intercourse between males the intromission of the penis in an opening of the body not meant to be used for the genital expression of sexuality cannot be called a true physical union. It is also an unsanitary and pathological act, as Gene Antonio points out in *The AIDS Cover-up?*[17] It is really a vain attempt to imitate heterosexual intercourse—a form of bodily massage. By way of contrast, the heterosexual union aptly symbolizes the psychological and spiritual union that ought to exist between a man and a woman. To be sure, in many instances union on these levels is merely symbolized and not realized, but there is a congruency of the physical, psychological, and spiritual levels in the permanent commitment of the man to the woman, and vice versa.

It is not surprising, moreover, that the strength of commitment between a man and a woman in marriage is stronger than the steady homosexual relationship. The main reason for this stronger commitment is the pro-creational meaning of marriage. Even if the marriage is sterile on the biological level, nonetheless a yearning for children often causes such a couple to adopt children or to take care of relatives' children. There is also greater meaning in their sexual intercourse, as if the act were saying, "If we could have a child, we would have one." There is an affinity between husband and wife who complement each other's qualities on all levels. They see each other in terms of covenant. If they are bonded in Christ, the commitment should be that much stronger.

Thus even the best homosexual genital relationship is seriously flawed. It is "essentially disordered because it cannot be directed toward nor have a proper respect for the goods of human sexuality. Recall that the

[17] (San Francisco: Ignatius Press 1986). See also Chapter Eight, Section 3, below, where AIDS is considered.

lovemaking of spouses is either directed toward having children or is expressive of a love that essentially includes an orientation toward the fruitfulness of procreation. The love of spouses can and must be enduring, because it is essentially related to enduring goods; but homosexual love simply is not ordered to any transcendent good that requires of the partners utter self-giving and faithfulness until death. A marital kind of friendship cannot obtain among homosexuals; their sexual act cannot express a marital kind of love, for they cannot be what spouses are. . . ."[18]

As to consequences, consider two female homosexuals who bring in a guru from the East to witness their "holy union". They have a few witnesses. They go back to their domicile and live together. Presumably they love each other, but there are only the two of them, nothing more. In a sense, there is no past, no future—only the present. Now consider the ordinary wedding. Man and wife come from different families, each with its own history that gives identity to each spouse. At the wedding are the families of each spouse. They look forward to the new family that the bride and the bridegroom will form. In short, in this wedding there is meaning that transcends the two persons, a meaning relating to family and children and symbolizing the union of Christ with His Church. Obviously, the homosexual union lacks these transcendent meanings. It is closed in—just the same two persons with nothing beyond them.[19]

This fact leads many homosexual persons to admit the overwhelming sterility of such unions, very few of which are permanent, and even fewer, faithful. In working with homosexual persons in spiritual support groups in New York City I have discovered that the consideration of such frustrating sterility is a persuasive argument for giving up the active homosexual lifestyle.

The homosexual lifestyle finds a common focus in the "ultimate commitment to unrestricted personal sexual freedom. Whatever other values individual homosexuals may hold and pursue, this liberation conviction is at the heart of their common identity with other homosexuals. To accept homosexuality as a way of life is to call into question any attempt to enforce sexual standards of a more restrictive sort, whether based on political, social, or religious grounds."[20]

There is a reason for this commitment to sexual freedom and sexual pleasure. If one concentrates on achieving orgasm, usually with many partners, one deprives the act of achieving any genuinely and authentically satisfying human good. As one becomes hell-bent on such pleasure,

[18] Catholic Sexual Ethics, p. 201.

[19] See my reflections on complementarity: "Homosexuality" in The Supplement to the New Catholic Encyclopedia, vol. 17, pp. 271-273.

[20] Edward Malloy, Homosexuality and the Christian Way of Life, p. 181.

one also isolates oneself from any deep relationships with anyone. One becomes a loner, looking for intimacy but afraid of it and seeking it in the wrong way. This manner of life is characteristic of many male homosexuals. ". . . to organize one's life around the pleasure of orgasms in acts which separate sexual activity from its precious human goods is unreasonable and immoral."[21]

In *City of Night* (New York: Grove Press, 1963) John Rechy describes this lifestyle in all its alienation and loneliness; in *Numbers* (New York: Grove Press, 1967) he continues the description; and in *Sexual Outlaw* (New York: Dell Press, 1977) he further details the promiscuous lifestyle of many male homosexuals. Although Rechy's purpose is to show how an unfeeling society drives homosexual persons into compulsive and senseless copulation, he also demonstrates what happens when sexual activity is separated from its purposes. Were one to read the ads in the weekly homosexual newspaper the Los Angeles *Advocate*, one would gain deeper insight into the mentality of the promiscuous homosexual male—a frenetic search for new forms of genital pleasure. In short, *unrestricted personal sexual pleasure leads to loss of control over one's life*.

Throughout this work the reader may have noticed that I seldom use the term *gay* to describe the homosexual person: and this with good reason. In thirty-two years of counseling homosexual persons, I have yet to meet a practicing homosexual person who could be called "gay" in the sense of joyful.[22] In a penetrating article Samuel McCracken shows by a critical analysis of data in pro-homosexual books that the claim that homosexuals are as happy as other people has not been established; in particular, he points to data that show that suicide attempts are significantly higher among homosexuals than among others—for example, 3% for white non-homosexual males, 18% for white homosexual males.[23]

The unhappiness of so many so-called gay persons is rooted in their mania for sexual pleasure, coupled with their unwillingness to accept responsibility. Again, McCracken points out: "The fact is that homosexuality generally entails a renunciation of responsibility for the continuance of the human race and of a voice in the dialogue of the generations. This is a renunciation made also by some heterosexuals and indeed by

[21] *Catholic Sexual Ethics*, p. 201.

[22] Herbert F. Smith, S.J., and Joseph Dilenno, *Sexual Inversion* (Boston: Daughters of St. Paul, 1979), p. 63, point out that there is a touch of irony in the typology of gay, gaiety, gayety. "Although the first meaning is merriment, gay can also mean 'loving forbidden pleasure, wanton', as in Funk and Wagnalls *New Standard Dictionary* (rev. ed., 1919) or again 'dissipated; immoral' in the *World Book Dictionary* (1976 Edition). Thus, 'gay' contains an element of license and forbiddenness as well as merriment in its very conception."

[23] "Are Homosexuals Gay?" *Commentary*, Jan. 1979, pp. 20–22. See also *Catholic Sexual Ethics*, p. 269, nn. 65–67.

some married heterosexuals. There is, however, a still greater renunciation made by homosexuals, and that is of the intricate, complicated, and challenging process of adjusting one's life to someone so different from oneself as to be in a different sex completely."[24] One notes in McCracken's line of reasoning a similarity with Catholic teaching on the meaning of sexuality as a loving union of two persons for the purpose of progeny and family.

There is one final argument against homosexual acts: Some have held that for the sake of what is called psychic intimacy, feeling close to the beloved, one may violate the physical structures of heterosexual intercourse, as it is meant to be, a physical union of man and woman, through penetration of the vagina by the penis, and the pouring in of the seed of the man. On the plea that one can violate physical structures of the body for the sake of intimacy, it is proposed that one may ignore the due physical structure of the genital act between the sexes, to say nothing of the inherent meaning of such acts. This is *dualism*, i.e., the failure to recognize the essentially composite structure of the human person which makes the psychic and the physical inseparable. One will find in the writings of Pope John Paul II concerning the nuptial meaning of the human body a powerful repudiation of such dualism.[25]

Thus the arguments against homosexual activity proposed by cited Church documents are found to be rooted in Sacred Scripture as understood by the Church; in natural moral law reasoning; in psychological and sociological considerations; and in the experiences of many homosexuals whom I have counseled over the years, about which I shall say more in the pastoral section. There is no way one can justify homosexual acts. The homosexual lifestyle cannot be reconciled with a truly Christian way of life, as Edward Malloy points out in his book. Having established the *objective* immorality of homosexual activity, it is now necessary to consider the *subjective* responsibility of the homosexual person for his acts.

3. SUBJECTIVE RESPONSIBILITY OF HOMOSEXUAL ACTIVITY

The Vatican Declaration on Sexual Ethics, paragraph 8, reminds us that the culpability of the homosexual person must be judged with prudence, and the 1973 Pastoral Statement of the National Conference of Catholic Bishops (U.S.A.) states that in assessing the responsibility of the homo-

[24] *Ibid.*, p. 27.
[25] See *Original Unity of Man and Woman* (Boston: Daughters of St. Paul, 1981); *Reflections on Humanae Vitae* (Daughters of St. Paul, 1984).

sexual person "the confessor must avoid both harshness and permissiveness."[26] The subjective responsibility of the homosexual person may be considered under two aspects: (1) the origin of the tendency and (2) the manner in which the person controls it.

1. *Origin of the tendency:* As we have already seen (Chapter Three) in considering Moberly's and van den Aardweg's analyses of the origins of homosexual tendencies, it can be said safely that a man or woman does not will to become homosexual. At a certain point in his psychosexual development one discovers his homosexuality and usually suffers a certain amount of trauma in the discovery. Sometimes he is young and desires to find a program where he can have some hope of reorienting his sexual desires; sometimes, because he has allowed himself to be convinced by gay liberation propaganda, he has already given up hope of changing his sexual orientation; sometimes he has spent so many years in homosexual activity that he feels too old to benefit by such treatment, or he cannot afford to pay for it. In every case he *discovers* an already-existing condition.

Since in more recent years there is more evidence that persons can change their sexual orientation (though the evidence is by no means sufficient to constitute a probable argument in favor of any specific therapy), it seems that the spiritual counselor or confessor should at least keep his mind open to the possibility that the person, particularly the young person, can change sexual orientation and that counselors should encourage homosexual persons to look into the possibility of changing from a homosexual to a heterosexual orientation.[27] I shall say more about this important question in Chapter Seven; now I consider the manner in which the homosexual person controls his tendency.

2. *Controlling the tendency:* Admittedly, responsibility for controlling the homosexual tendency is a complex question. Persons vary in the degree of freedom they possess in controlling their sexual desires. At one extreme are homosexuals who have as much control over their tendencies as normal heterosexuals; at the other extreme are homosexuals who are as compulsive as alcoholics or drug addicts. Each person has the obligation to control his tendency by every means within his power, particularly by psychological and spiritual counsel; and, if his homosexual activity has become compulsive, he has an obligation to seek the means that are truly

---

[26] *Principles to Guide Confessors in Questions of Homosexuality* (Washington, D.C.: U.S. Catholic Conference, 1973), pp. 8–9.

[27] Irving Bieber et al., Samuel Haddon, Lawrence Hatterer, Colin Cook, Elizabeth Moberly, and Gerald van den Aardweg and others hold that sexual reorientation is possible in certain instances, provided the person stays with the program. With the exception of Moberly, the others present empirical evidence. Moberly's theory needs further verification which we hope will come.

adequate to control compulsive activity, namely, some form of group therapy that integrates the psychological and the spiritual, such as A.A. or Courage (the latter is a spiritual support group for homosexual men and women).

Since I have already treated compulsion in homosexuals,[28] I should like to add the caution that the counselor, or the confessor, however compassionate one may want to be, should not convey to the compulsive person the impression that he is not responsible for his actions. Nothing is more devastating to the dignity and freedom of the homosexual person than the feeling that he has not only lost control of his life but is unable to regain it. The assessment of responsibility for past actions done apparently under the force of compulsion is often almost impossible and is usually a purely academic exercise. The best the confessor can do is to point out that the compulsive person does have a modicum of freedom left and that he should use that freedom to become involved in a spiritual support group system.

The assessment of responsibility, however, in the non-compulsive homosexual is similar to the responsibility of the heterosexual person in sexual matters, with some differences. It is more difficult for the homosexual person to remain chaste in his environment—one in which, generally speaking, he is unable to share his difficulties and temptations with others for fear of ridicule; there is loneliness as well as the attraction of homosexual companions; and, unlike the heterosexual person who usually can look forward to marriage, the homosexual person cannot do so as long as his orientation continues. In many homosexual persons there is also a terrible sense of inferiority.[29]

Thus, while the non-compulsive homosexual person is morally responsible for his actions, his freedom is nonetheless very often diminished, more in some situations than in others. One may speak of a weakened will, but at the same time one must be careful not to excuse the homosexual person's past activity. As already observed, the chief responsibility of the homosexual person is to discover ways of strengthening the power of the will through renewed vision and fresh motivation, particularly through group-support systems. The accent should be on the future and on the need to develop an ascetical plan of life so as to be able to lead a celibate

[28] See Chapter Two, Section 3: distinction between compulsive and non-compulsive activity.

[29] *To Live in Christ Jesus* (Washington, D.C.: National Conference of Catholic Bishops, Nov. 11, 1976), asks that the homosexual person be provided with a special grace of pastoral understanding and care. Van den Aardweg (*On the Origins and Treatment of Homosexuality*) sees the sense of inferiority linked to the origin of homosexual orientation. See our Chapter Three, Section 2, on van den Aardweg's thought.

Christian life. The person with homosexual orientation, however, should be made aware that, despite the resolution to begin a new way of living, very probably there will be relapses because of the psychosomatic effects of long-standing sexual indulgence, but this must not be allowed to be the occasion of sterile self-pity.[30]

4. CIVIL LAW, MORAL LAW, AND THE RIGHTS OF HOMOSEXUAL PERSONS

Readers are familiar with the media's frequent coverage of homosexual-rights issues in various parts of the country, particularly in New York City. Questions arise concerning what are the rights that numerous homosexual organizations are fighting for. Are their rights, like those of heterosexual persons, not already adequately protected by the Constitution? Do their claims to unrestricted housing and employment come in conflict with the rights of other citizens, and if so, how are these conflicts to be resolved? These are some of the questions one needs to discuss. Before getting into any specific issues it will be profitable to review recent history on the civil law concerning homosexual acts.

In 1957 *The Wolfenden Report* in England suggested that homosexual acts taking place in private between consenting adults should no longer be subject to the criminal law.[31] Previously (1955) the Model Penal Code had made a similar proposal. Both proposals precipitated widespread discussion of the merits of such a revision of civil law, and the controversy continues to the present. In 1967 after considerable debate the main features of *The Wolfenden Report* became law in the *Sex Offenses Act*. While decriminalizing consensual acts done in private by adult males, the *Report* made three types of situations punishable by the law: (1) offenses against minors; (2) offenses against public decency; and (3) exploitation of vice for the purposes of gain. In the United States only a few states have followed the example of England, although the Gay Liberation Task Force continues to seek the repeal of state laws that make punishable by law homosexual acts freely done by adults in private.[32] What are usually illegal are acts of oral or anal intercourse, but in many states these acts were also forbidden to heterosexuals.

[30] *Principles to Guide Confessors in Questions of Homosexuality*, p. 9.

[31] (London: Scottish Home Department, 1957). An excerpt from the Roman Catholic Archbishop of Westminster's comment on *The Wolfenden Report* appears in *Homosexuality and Ethics*, ed. Edward J. Batchelor, Jr., appendix, pp. 239–240. It draws the distinction between moral and civil law and states the issues but does not draw any conclusions.

[32] See Edward Malloy, *op. cit.*, ch. 6, "Homosexuals and the Civil Law", pp. 145–162, for a brief history of the civil-rights controversy and his personal view.

Although the United States is considered to have the most severe anti-homosexual laws, nevertheless in the vast majority of cases homosexuals are not prosecuted under these explicit statutes. Instead, a number of vaguely worded misdemeanor statutes that apply to behavior in public places are invoked. Most arrests are made in regard to solicitation in restrooms or parks. The proof employed is the testimony of one or two police officers, the second usually standing in the wings and ready to enter the picture upon a signal from the officer who entraps the homosexual person. From speaking with persons involved in such encounters with the police, I discern that the worst thing that happens in many cases is that the person suffers a *severe* loss of reputation. The penalty may be slight in the sense that the person is placed on probation or spends a month in jail, but the damage to his good name is incomparably worse. Again, the penalties, when rarely inflicted, are often arbitrary and disproportionate, ranging from a month in jail to life imprisonment.[33]

In discussions concerning a change in civil law, many have come to the conclusion that on utilitarian grounds the laws regulating homosexual conduct among adults should be repealed. The argument goes thus: Whatever one's personal convictions about homosexuality in general, the social harm that derives from trying to make this a matter of prohibitory legislation far outweighs the social good. The evidence for this claim is based on a series of factors of an empirical nature that can be summed up under the following headings: (1) The laws are ineffective. In most states the laws are not enforced, and active homosexuals are not deterred by such laws. (2) The laws are capricious. Even when there is a felony arrest situation the judiciary is reluctant to impose even the slightest of penalties. In Los Angeles, 457 homosexuals were convicted on felony charges, but only 3 went to prison.[34] (3) The laws can be enforced only when police use illegal tactics. The usual method is to ferret out homosexuals in restrooms or parks. (4) The laws create a condition where wealthy or influential homosexuals can be victimized by extortion or blackmail. I may add that the not-so-wealthy or influential are also subject to such blackmail.[35]

For all these reasons Malloy argues for a change in the law, so that the civil law does not apply to acts done in private by consenting adults. But he adds certain qualifications to his position that the law should not deal with private homosexual acts done freely by adults.

[33] An example of the way in which publicity can shatter the career of a public figure is found in the autobiography of former Representative Robert Bauman, *The Gentleman from Maryland* (New York: Arbor House, 1986).

[34] Malloy, *op. cit.*, p. 154.

[35] *Ibid.*, p. 155.

Malloy holds that certain kinds of conduct should not be protected, such as offenses aganst minors, particularly pedophilia. It is not merely a question of seduction and innocence, inasmuch as the child or the youth may make explicit overtures. The law insists that the adult is responsible in such situations and that mandated therapy and sometimes imprisonment are just penalties. A disputed point is the legal age of minors in this context. Many authorities favor the age of eighteen, because this is generally when a young person leaves home for college or for work. Again, the law should prohibit offenses against public decency, whether by heterosexual or homosexual activity. Thirdly, homosexual prostitution should be regulated by confining it to certain sections of a city and by periodic health checks of male prostitutes similar to those made of female prostitutes. Fourthly, the laws against homosexual rape should be rigorously enforced, particularly in prisons, where among men it is known to be rampant.[36]

In addition to the many problems in the regulation of any kind of prostitution, there is even more difficulty when it comes to health regulations. Despite the fear of AIDS, homosexual organizations in San Francisco blocked the closing of bathhouses which were known to encourage promiscuity. While I agree with Father Malloy that homosexual rape in prisons should be brought under control, I note also the shortage of prison personnel to keep vigil over young new arrivals. In the practical order, it can be hoped that in certain cases a prison term for the offender can be changed into probation and some form of public service.

Malloy states that his position in no way authorizes homosexual conduct. It is merely a realistic appraisal of the present practical impossibility of enforcing the anti-sodomy laws where the offenses take place in private between consenting adults. Then Malloy adds that this policy of non-interference "should *not* be extended to the question of empowerment in other areas."[37] He does not approve of homosexual "marriages" nor the right of homosexual couples to adopt children, because the societal values at stake are too basic. Yet he is curiously inconsistent when he implicitly approves of homosexual couples' filing joint income-tax returns, having rights of inheritance, and sharing property. If the law extends special status in the financial realm to homosexual couples, it is giving them practically the same legal protection as married couples.

Malloy also generally supports the efforts of homosexual organizations for protection against discrimination in housing and employment. But he expresses reservations when it comes to certain occupations, such

[36] *Ibid.*, pp. 155–158.
[37] *Ibid.*, p. 158.

as teaching and counseling, where homosexual men and women deal regularly with young children and adolescents. He is aware that we do not have evidence that the rate of solicitation by homosexual teachers is any higher than it is for heterosexual teachers. But Malloy is worried about what kind of impact self-proclaimed homosexual teachers can have as role models for their students. After all, students need role models at critical stages in their development, and "the public proclamation of a counter-cultural identity by a significant-other, such as a teacher, can have a profound effect on the interpretation of the world that is available to impressionable youngsters."[38]

I believe we should presume that such impact will be harmful and should take appropriate measures to prevent *proclaimed* homosexuals from teaching in elementary or secondary schools. I shall come back to this point later. I agree with Malloy that, beyond the danger of seduction of students or the inculcation of a promiscuous pattern of behavior, there is the question of role models for the young—with the only two acceptable role models, the married state or the chaste single state. In no way is a steady-lover relationship an acceptable role model for the young. On the practical level we should be able to uphold this Church position in our Catholic schools. In conclusion, Malloy hopes that in advocating a moderate policy of legal reform, society will be able to retain a Judaeo-Christian sexual ethic.

In *theory*, I can agree with Malloy that greater evils can issue from the attempt to enforce laws forbidding anal and oral intercourse for consenting adults, but in the present reality of the gay liberation movement one may rightly wonder whether in the wake of a victory on this issue the homosexual movement will not want to go much farther with new demands upon society for advocacy of the homosexual way of life as good and as an alternative to marriage—indeed, as a kind of marriage. If acts between consenting adults are legal, they are also regarded as good. Why not, then, teach this lifestyle to our children? I say "rightly wonder" because this is what is happening.

In *The Homosexual Network* Father Enrique Rueda documents the homosexual movement up to 1982. He treats the acceptability of homo-sexuality in America, the nature of the homosexual subculture, the ideology of the homosexual movement (with insightful discussion of the difference between gay and homosexual), and the ideological and political goals of the homosexual movement. He details the nature of networking among homosexual organizations and their links with other liberal organizations. After treating the relationships between homosexu-

[38] *Ibid.*, p. 159.

ality and religion, he shows the networking between various religious bodies and the homosexual movement. His thesis here is that the homosexual movement has penetrated the leadership of many religious bodies, including the Roman Catholic Church in America, to which he devotes a special case study (pp. 299–382). Another chapter is devoted to the way liberal politicians have supported the homosexual movement. The last chapter uncovers the sources of funding for the movement, particularly the federal government. The book contains twelve appendices dealing with a variety of aspects, including homosexual marriage rituals and an analysis of Gay Pride parades. When one reads this book one finds abundant evidence for the thesis that the homosexual leadership will not be satisfied until the active homosexual lifestyle is completely accepted by society.[39]

The issue that the Church in America faces is whether our society can allow this sexual libertarianism. Joseph Sobran reinforces Rueda's thesis when he describes the current campaign for gay rights in New York City and elsewhere:

> What the militants sought and seek to legitimize, even in the face of the AIDS epidemic, is the most extravagant expressions of homosexuality, as their own publications and statements make clear. While it would certainly be wrong to say that most promiscuous homosexuals are serious activists, most of the activists endorse the promiscuous lifestyle; much of gay activism has as its goal the promotion of that lifestyle. Most people have only a dim idea of the lifestyle under discussion. The general press is singularly uninformative, . . . preferring to keep discussion of gay issues at the level of abstraction chosen by the gay activists themselves. . . . But a glance at the *New York Native*, the city's leading gay newspaper, does a lot to fill in the information gap. Even after the advent of AIDS, the *Native* serves as a dating service for lonely homosexuals. The personal ads tell the story the general press glosses over. . . . In a typical issue the *Native* carries two tabloid-sized pages of personal ads. They are accompanied by a boxed list of abbreviations for standard—repeat, standard—homosexual practices and partner specifications. . . . Many of the ads are bluntly graphic—too graphic to quote here. Suffice it to say their authors are not seeking romance. . . . Sordid and desperate, the ads make it impossible to idealize gay life. . . . Such is the behavior gay-rights legislation protects or, rather, such is the behavior gay-rights legislation forbids normal citizens to disapprove. Gay-rights laws

---

[39] (Old Greenwich, Conn.: Devin Adair); regretfully, some overstatements and inaccuracies have hurt the credibility of the research and were exploited by some of the critics of the volume. In discussing Archbishop May of St. Louis, for example, the author failed to point out that the prelate had given to the Dignity chapter in that city a talk in which he urged all the members to the practice of chastity. On the whole, though, the book is both accurate and invaluable.

don't establish equal rights. They redistribute rights from straights to those gays willing to use the power of the state to compel social acceptance. . . . Though it may be amended, as it stands the New York City law directs the city's Human Rights Commission to prepare school curricula aimed at teaching 'non-discriminatory', i.e., amoral attitudes toward homosexuality. Gays gain the right to have the city proselytize on their behalf to . . . children; parents lose the right to form their children's morals.[40]

Sobran focuses our attention on the real goals of the homosexual movement that can be gleaned from reading the gay press. He also makes us realize what kinds of activity the New York City law and other laws like it in San Francisco and Washington, D.C., protect. But it must be stressed that what is being protected is behavior, not status, as in the case of blacks. The New York Archdiocese and the Diocese of Brooklyn objected to the law because it would without precedent treat morally controversial behavior as a civil right, with penalties of up to a year in jail for those who violated that "right". This is really positive privilege for sodomy. "What the bill primarily and ultimately seeks to achieve is the legal approval of homosexual conduct and activity."[41]

Although homosexual writers were accusing the archdiocese of exaggeration in holding that this bill was an opening wedge for further homosexual legislation, yet other homosexual writers were saying exactly what the Church in New York had asserted. Said a *Village Voice* columnist: "In the end the gay alternative means a departure not just from heterosexuality, but from social orthodoxy. . . . In its most moderate politics— the enactment of civil-rights legislation—it has radical potential, because civil-rights legislation opens the way to acceptance, and acceptance opens the way to dissolution of the norm."[42]

The homosexual community has argued often that homosexuals are a minority just like blacks, but this is not true. Blacks have been a minority because of their race and the color of their skin, not because of their freely chosen behavior. Blacks want to be recognized as equal in dignity to whites and to prove their moral worth by their free choices. Homosexual activists have made their deviant behavior central to their self-identification, and they insist that society give it centrality too by giving it immunity from effective moral judgment. "No other kind of citizen is specified by a personal taste, let alone a deviant one. Militant gays have chosen to make *themselves* a 'minority' ".[43] Sobran sums up his view of the

[40] "The Politics of A.I.D.S.", *National Review*, May 23, 1986, pp. 22, 24, 26, 51.

[41] Joint Statement of Position on Intro. 2 by John Cardinal O'Connor, Archbishop of New York, and Bishop Francis J. Mugavero, Bishop of Brooklyn.

[42] Quoted by Sobran, *op. cit.*, p. 24.

[43] Sobran, *op. cit.* p. 26.

homosexual activist by pointing out that he is obsessed with his homo-sexuality: "That too is what 'gay' means. Gays are therefore specified by their ideology—which, like all ideology, largely consists in systematically blaming the world for their woes."[44]

Having considered the views of Malloy and Sobran on the homosexual rights issue, I shall now set down my own views. Going back to the question of the toleration of homosexual acts between consenting adults in private, I distinguish between moral law and civil law. Civil law has regard primarily to public acts; private acts are ordinarily outside its scope. Yet there are private acts that have public consequences insofar as they affect the common good, and these may rightly be subject to civil law. It may be that the civil law cannot effectively control such acts without doing more harm to the common good than the acts themselves would do. In that case it may be necessary in the interest of the common good to tolerate without approving such acts.

In my judgment, attempts to ferret out persons performing homo-sexual acts in private places does more harm than good, and therefore the law should tolerate such acts. In holding this view I would find it necessary to let the public know that such toleration is not approval of homosexual activity, which must be shown to be clearly immoral. Still, in the minds of many the decriminalization of such acts transforms them into morally good acts. The law, even criminal law, has educative effects, and that is why others may not agree with my position. But this is almost an academic issue; the current moral problem is whether society should give full approval to a homosexual lifestyle. That many active homosexuals in their organizations are seeking such freedom has already been documented by Rueda, and others.[45] First, then, I shall deal with the rights of the homosexual person and then our attitude toward the gay-rights movement.

The rights of homosexual persons

In 1976 the U.S. Catholic Bishops said that homosexuals should not suffer from prejudice against their basic human rights. They have a right to respect, friendship, and justice, and they should have an active role in the Christian community.[46] Archbishop Hickey adds that homosexuals "deserve good pastoral care based on the teaching of the Church. Our parishes need to be signs of Christ's love, forgiveness, and truth. We need

[44] Ibid.
[45] Rueda, op. cit.
[46] To Live in Christ Jesus (Washington, D.C.: U.S.C.C., 1976), p. 21.

to examine our attitudes and practices to dispel ignorance, discrimination, or insensitivity."[47] From this one may draw the conclusion that, in general, the homosexual may have the same rights to employment, housing, and public accommodations as the heterosexual person, and if he keeps his sexual orientation to himself and a few trusted others, he will have no difficulty exercising these and other civil rights. "Unlike racial minorities whose physical characteristics distinguish them from the majority population, and unlike members of some religious communities whose garb, practices, and surnames often identify them as such, there is no inherent way to identify any given person as a homosexual. This being the case, how can one deny employment or otherwise discriminate against an undeclared homosexual? Indeed homosexuals occupy positions at all levels of the economy, in every industry, and in the most staid environments."[48]

Where, then, is the difficulty? It is the fact that homosexual activists want both unrestricted sexual freedom and the right to teach their way of life to the world. They are not requesting merely the right to live their lifestyle in private, to be left alone; to use their own words, they want to convince all elements of society—even children—that "gay is as acceptable as straight."

But this aim brings them into direct conflict with heterosexual society in certain sensitive areas, especially the education and guidance of the young. In such a situation of a conflict of rights one must ask who has the prior rights. I am of the opinion that the parents have the right *not* to have their children exposed to the teaching that the homosexual lifestyle is both morally good and an acceptable alternative to marriage. Therefore parents should oppose any educational programs on the grade-school or the high-school level that present the homosexual lifestyle as morally acceptable. Consequently, educational authorities on these levels may refuse to hire or may fire any teacher who makes a point of living the homosexual lifestyle. It is not a question of seduction of the young—there is no evidence that such seduction is not found equally among heterosexual teachers on these levels. It is rather that the declared homosexual teacher becomes a role model to impressionable youth.

Catholic teaching, on the one hand, respects the dignity and moral worth of each person, no matter what his sexual orientation, but it also points out that his rights to educate the young are limited by the prior rights of parents. Another argument against allowing homosexuals to promote their way of life is that it would lead to a moral normlessness that

[47] *Letter on Homosexuality* (Washington, D.C.: U.S.C.C., 1984).

[48] Dr. Bernard Fryshman, *Societal Rights and Homosexual Rights: Analysis of a Conflict*. Agudath of Israel of America. May 28, 1985. Paper presented to the New York City Council in opposition to Homosexual Rights Bill, Intro. 2, p. 2.

would seriously injure the health of family life and indirectly injure the common good of society. Rabbi Fryshman reinforces our position when he writes:

> The Constitution guarantees everyone freedom of speech and expression. It doesn't guarantee that a declared homosexual be allowed to occupy a job that would force children to be exposed to beliefs and ideas destructive of the values instilled by their parents. There is, after all, a public interest in protecting children. Thus, while the courts have been extremely reluctant to curtail the publishing activities of certain pornographers, they have supported laws which force newsstands selling certain material to display them in a manner unavailable to children. No doubt, there is a clash of interests. Freedom of speech is, after all, one of our most cherished rights. But the need to protect children is no less a societal imperative. So that it is perfectly in order for society to ensure that sensitive positions not be filled by an individual who would use his/her job as a vehicle to advocate behavior that conflicts with the interests of society. For the homosexual there is a way out of this impasse. A homosexual who does not declare his propensity has access to every available position. Discrimination simply does not take place for the undeclared homosexual.[49]

Fryshman is correct in holding that homosexuals have all the rights they are entitled to as citizens of the United States. For the undeclared homosexual there is no discrimination, and a gay-rights bill would induce no changes. Thus it is less than honest for advocates of a gay-rights bill to characterize it as needed to help the undeclared homosexual. The difficulty is that society has moved to the point where publicly declared homosexuals have unfettered freedom of speech and access to any job. The only limitation that society has maintained for the protection of children is restricted access to certain kinds of employment for declared homosexuals.[50]

I think that gay-rights legislation would harm children at an impressionable, malleable, and gullible age. There is plenty of evidence for the position that homosexual propaganda can sway young people into homosexual activity and, perhaps, permanent orientation in that direction.[51] For this reason both the Church and the state ought to take a serious interest in defending the rights of children not to be subject to such influences in their educational institutions.[52]

---

[49] *Ibid.*, p. 6.

[50] *Ibid.*, p. 8.

[51] See my article, "The Impact of Gay Propaganda upon Adolescent Boys and Girls", *The Priest*, March 1980, pp. 15–16, 19–24.

[52] *Ibid.*, pp. 9–13. Fryshman refers to Dr. Laurence Hatterer, Drs. William Masters and Virginia Johnson, Drs. Edith Gromberg, Violet Franks, and Lillian H. Robinson as all holding to the thesis that homosexual orientation can be induced in some children.

Before concluding this section on the moral aspects of homosexual civil rights it is necessary to discuss homophobia. There is no doubt that society has traditionally attached a stigma to the condition of homosexuality. This has led writers to coin the term *homophobia* to describe this fear and related fears, such as a person's fear that he is homosexual, or the feeling of self-loathing that a homosexual may have for himself.[53] I am using the term in the sense of the unreasonable fear that the majority of Americans have for the homosexual person and his lifestyle. This fear is rooted in a series of common myths about homosexual persons: (1) All homosexual persons are attracted to children and adolescents and wish to have contact with them. (2) All male homosexuals are effeminate and lack the typical male characteristics of courage, aggressiveness, and strength. (3) All homosexuals are sexually active. (4) All homosexuals can change their sexual orientation merely by willing to do so and by cultivating friendships of the other sex.[54]

These myths or stereotypes produce in the minds of many an unfair image of the homosexual person. It is no wonder that many homosexual persons do not reveal their orientation. It will do no good to say that you are a chaste homosexual, because many of your friends will not believe you. Even the phrase "coming out of the closet", meaning publicly revealing one's sexual orientation, indicates that homosexuals experience a kind of imprisonment because of the myths surrounding them. In this psychological sense homosexual persons constitute a minority, because they so often feel like strangers at the gate. Heterosexuals seldom experience the alienation that homosexuals endure. It is not easy to hide one's identity in a mixed society where one feels he will not be accepted if he reveals his identity. He listens to jokes about "queers" while suffering deep loneliness and lack of self-respect. He may assimilate the horror that he perceives society has for homosexuals and consciously or unconsciously hate himself. With good reason, then, Archbishop Hickey asked his people to examine their own attitudes toward the homosexual person. The stigma that society has attached to homosexual persons is really an immoral response to a deeply troubled minority.[55] Hence the need for all the teachers in the Church—parents, bishops, priests, lay professors of theology, catechists, religious women, and brothers—to present a fair

[53] Anthony Kosnik et al., *Human Sexuality*, p. 270, n. 146.
[54] Donald McCarthy and Edward Bayer, eds., *Critical Sexual Issues* (Garden City, N.Y.: Doubleday Image Books, 1984), pp. 183–184.
[55] *Catholic Sexual Ethics*, p. 184. See also Harvey, "Morality and Pastoral Treatment of Homosexuality", *Continuum* 5, no. 2 (Summer 1967):279–297 at 285.

image of the homosexual in his struggle for virtue.

From my long experience in counseling homosexual persons I know that even the most virtuous suffer from the knowledge that they cannot really reveal themselves to family and friends without danger of losing a relationship they want to keep. I shall come back to this fear in the pastoral section. Suffice it to say that homosexual persons as a group suffer unjustly from society's attitudes toward them. There is urgent need for education by the Church on this issue.[56]

To sum up our reflections on homosexual rights, one may hold that, while homosexual activity is always immoral, one should respect the homosexual person, allowing him all the rights of any other citizen, but denying him unrestricted sexual freedom and rejecting his claim to the right to teach the young that such a lifestyle is morally acceptable.

---

[56] "The Prejudice against Homosexuals and the Ministry of the Church", Washington State Conference of Catholic Bishops (Seattle, Spokane, and Yakima, Wash., April 28, 1983).

CHAPTER SEVEN

PASTORAL PERSPECTIVES AND PROGRAMS

1. GENERAL ATTITUDE OF THE PUBLIC TOWARD THE PASTORAL CARE OF HOMOSEXUALS

The phenomenon of AIDS has complicated an already-complex situation. Before the onslaught of this fatally destructive disease, many communities had become tolerant of the homosexual lifestyle, while many others, usually not publicly, continued to oppose any relaxation of the existing laws concerning homosexual behavior.[1] But in the atmosphere of fear generated by AIDS, great polarization has taken place between homosexual leaders and the general public. One hears persons saying that if the homosexual person gets AIDS, he gets what he deserves. While reserving complete comment on this cruel attitude until I treat the subject in Chapter Eight, I must point out that the prejudice against the AIDS patient is often extended to all homosexual persons without distinction.

Another factor in the public image of the homosexual person is the identification of homosexual orientation with pedophilia, particularly if the person who is known to be homosexual is also a cleric. Only a minority of pedophilics are homosexual, and only a very small percentage of Roman Catholic priests and religious brothers are known to be pedophilics, but in the public imagination every priest or brother who is friendly with boys is suspect of secret sins with them. Conversely, teenage boys may interpret a priest's or brother's genuine concern for their difficult home situation as a form of seduction. Thus, as soon as one mentions pastoral care for the homosexual, one is frequently met with silent hostility. "Why special pastoral care for the homosexual? He's no worse off than most heterosexuals. Let him exercise his free will."

---

[1] It is interesting that twenty-four states and the District of Columbia still have laws on the books outlawing homosexual sodomy (*New York Times*, July 5, 1986, p. 32). The article by Robert Lindsey described the efforts of homosexual community leaders to abolish anti-sodomy laws in the wake of the Supreme Court decision of June 30, 1986, which upheld the right of states to ban sodomy, whether homosexual or heterosexual. The Georgia law makes it a crime for anyone, whether heterosexual or homosexual, to participate in oral or anal intercourse. See *Philadelphia Inquirer*, July 1, 1986, 1 A.

2. SPECIFIC ATTITUDES OF CHURCHMEN TOWARD PASTORAL CARE OF HOMOSEXUAL PERSONS

One can understand why many priests and male religious are reluctant to be involved in any kind of ministry to homosexual persons. They are happy that someone else is doing it, and they will be glad to refer homosexual persons to someone else, but the matter is something they prefer not to deal with. In one archdiocese it was agreed that priests would try to be informed on the subject so that they could give spiritual direction to homosexuals on an individual basis and that only in more difficult cases would they have to resort to psychotherapy. It was their carefully considered decision that there was no need for the kind of group that I have been working with in New York City since October 1980. But the plan failed, because many priests do not feel they have the background and training to give spiritual guidance to homosexual persons, and there was no center to help these homosexuals who wanted guidance from the Church. Happily, two years later the ordinary decided that a Courage group was needed in his archdiocese. The point of the story is the reluctance of many priests and religious to work out either individual guidance programs or group spiritual support systems because of a variety of fears. Besides the fear of being inadequate in providing spiritual direction to the homosexual person, many priests also fear that they themselves will be regarded as homosexuals or as approving of the homosexual lifestyle. This reluctance makes it difficult for those priests and religious who volunteer to begin a Courage group. That is why a *team* in charge of a Courage group will make it easier for the members of the team to be effective. They will be able to encourage one another and to learn from one another.

Still another factor is the very meaning of the term *pastoral care* with regard to the homosexual person. Among many spiritual guides and confessors there is tacit acceptance of the opinion that a homosexual person has a right to a steady-lover relationship because he has no charism of celibacy. They have drawn such a conclusion from the dissenting theologians already considered in the previous chapter. "Yes, it may be true that homosexual acts are always wrong, but we must consider the person in his difficult situation; one must exercise sensitivity by offering a 'pastoral' solution that allows the homosexual person to have a love partner." Such a "solution" is contrary to Catholic teaching, yet it is used by many priests and counselors throughout the United States and in other parts of the Western world.

Frequently, representatives of the Catholic press ask: What are the bishops doing about the pastoral situation of homosexual persons? This question has become more pressing with the AIDS crisis and with the October 1, 1986, Vatican Document. Indeed, the question includes three questions: (1) What should the diocese do to help AIDS patients? (I will address that question in Chapter Eight.) (2) What programs should the diocese provide for those homosexual persons who want to lead a life of sexual abstinence? (3) Should the diocese take a clear stand on organizations of Catholics which do not accept the teaching of the Church that homosexual activity is always immoral and yet claim to be a source of guidance for homosexuals seeking understanding and support? Allow me first to address the question of pastoral programs designed to help the homosexual person to lead a chaste life.

The beginning of Courage

In 1978 the late Terence Cardinal Cooke requested a committee, of which I was a member—together with Father Benedict Groeschel, O.F.M. Cap., Monsignor Edwin O'Brien, and Dr. Kenneth Wapnik—to plan a spiritual support group for homosexual persons in the archdiocese of New York. After four workshops for priests and professionals in archdiocesan agencies, the first meeting took place in Manhattan during the last week of September 1980. This spiritual support group eventually named itself Courage and drew up a statement of goals and purposes, which I shall describe later in this chapter.

Later in 1983 I established an office where two days every week I counsel not only homosexual persons but also their parents, wives, or family. Over the past six years our office has become an information center for other dioceses across the country who are interested in how and how well Courage works. The archdioceses of Los Angeles, St. Louis, Boston, and Toronto have established Courage groups. La Crosse, Wisconsin, San Diego, and Vancouver, B.C. are beginning Courage units. In short, the idea has caught on and is progressing slowly in spite of opposition in other dioceses where Dignity has a strong foothold. This is not to say that Dignity is the only source of opposition, but many of its priest-chaplains are so committed to promoting steady-lover relationships as an alternative to promiscuity that they do not want a Catholic group promoting sexual abstinence as a way of life for homosexual persons. Perhaps the October 1, 1986, document will lead to a change of heart on the part of many priests.

In regard to the question of what stance a diocese should take toward Dignity, several opinions were found among priests prior to the release of the above document:

1. Inasmuch as Dignity has been viewed as the only organization

helping Catholic homosexuals (before Courage) and since it discourages promiscuity while advocating a kind of faithful relationship, many priests believed that such relationships were the lesser of two evils. Priest-chaplains should celebrate Mass for Dignity members. It would do no good, the opinion stressed, to ban Dignity meetings from church property, because this would merely drive the organization underground and alienate many homosexual persons who are leading chaste lives on their own and who find some measure of companionship in attending Dignity functions.

2. A second view held that as long as the diocese does not give official approval to Dignity with its permissive teaching it can be tolerated, but no priests will be assigned to offer Mass at their meetings, and it will not be allowed to meet on church property. This view includes awareness of the fact that some priests will continue to minister sacramentally to Dignity groups or that Catholic colleges or religious order parishes will continue to have Masses on Sundays for the Dignity group. This position dis-associates itself from Dignity more clearly than the first view—indeed in some instances a Courage group has been set up as an alternative for Catholic homosexuals—but it still tolerates meetings of Dignity in the diocese and for the same reason: not alienating the Catholic homosexual population. This view still prevails in many dioceses.

3. Since the present teachings of Dignity are contrary to the magisterial position on homosexual activity, it should be requested either to change its positions, bringing them into harmony with Catholic teaching, or to be declared a dissenting group, to which homosexual Catholics should not belong.[2] This view is implicit in the decisions of several bishops and archbishops in the United States and Canada. At this writing the arch-dioceses of New York, Atlanta, Minneapolis-St. Paul, Philadelphia, and Vancouver, B.C., as well as the dioceses of Buffalo, Brooklyn, and LaCrosse, Wisconsin, have banned Dignity from the use of church facilities. In some archdioceses Courage and Dignity exist side by side—with Courage having the approbation of the ordinary (e.g., Boston, St. Louis, Los Angeles, Washington, D.C. and Toronto, Canada). In Chicago Courage has become dormant for lack of clerical support.

I believe, however, that ordinaries should call the local chapters of Dignity to task as did Archbishop John Roach. He asked the local chapter of Dignity to respond to the following statement: "Dignity/Twin Cities

[2] As I mention in my analysis of the October 1, 1986, document on homosexuality by the Congregation for the Doctrine of the Faith, Dignity fits the description of Catholic homosexual groups that ignore or undermine the teaching of the Church with no intention of giving up homosexual activity. At most only a few Dignity chapters accept the Church's official teaching.

as an organization is in accordance with the Catholic Church teaching on homosexuality." The local chapter voted to make no response, and Archbishop Roach then requested that Dignity no longer use archdiocesan facilities after their lease expired (*St. Paul Pioneer Press*, March 25, 1987). The implicit message of this banning is that Catholics should not join Dignity. I agree with this position for these reasons:

1. The scandal that many Catholics, both heterosexual and homosexual, have experienced by the American church's non-condemnation of Dignity was far greater than the anticipated hostile reaction of many homosexuals on the occasion of episcopal bannings of Dignity meetings on church property. Whenever Dignity is not requested to leave church property the faithful are given the impression that Dignity and Courage are two legitimate options for the Catholic homosexual person. It is as if the local church were saying, "You may belong to Dignity or Courage. Now Courage is the conservative group which holds that sexual abstinence is mandatory for homosexual persons, but one does not have to go that route. Celibacy is only optional for the homosexual person." I have heard the equivalent of this many times from members of Dignity and even a few members of Courage because, while seeking to live a celibate life themselves, a few Courage members feel that other homosexuals who are in steady-lover relationships should be allowed to receive the Holy Eucharist. This is moral confusion or scandal.

2. As long as Dignity is openly tolerated in a diocese, the ordinary homosexual Catholic will not be encouraged to join an organization such as Courage. As long as he is not convinced that sexual abstinence is the only moral option, it is not likely that he will take the more difficult route, particularly when he knows that priests and religious support the dissenting position of Dignity and that prominent theologians such as Gregory Baum and Charles Curran provide theological arguments in favor of it. One must keep in mind that Dignity has over a hundred chapters in the United States and has strong support from many members of the clergy.[3] Courage, on the other hand, was relatively unknown to many Catholics until the publicity which followed the banning of Dignity in several large dioceses.

Apparently, many ordinaries either remain unconvinced of the need for a spiritual support system for homosexual Catholics or believe that Dignity is the lesser of two evils or they think that having both Dignity and Courage groups in the diocese would create tensions. I am aware that

---

[3] Enrique Rueda, *The Homosexual Network*, pp. 327–339 *et passim*, contains a wealth of information on many Dignity chapters. Rueda refers to a number of priests who act as chaplains for Dignity, "which has access to Catholic churches in many dioceses where homosexual-oriented religious rituals are celebrated" (p. 327).

several American dioceses have requested that Dignity affirm the Church's teaching on homosexuality.[4] I am also aware that other dioceses (such as Baltimore, Seattle, and Montreal) had given the equivalent of official approval to Dignity.[5]

The letter of the Congregation for the Faith on October 1, 1986, has made it clear that an organization such as Dignity has no place in the Church because its members "either ignore the teaching of the Church or seek somehow to undermine it. It brings together under the aegis of Catholicism homosexual persons who have no intention of abandoning their homosexual behavior."[6] It is true that Dignity is not mentioned by name, but, as I indicated earlier in this chapter, Dignity fits perfectly into the category described by the Vatican document. Yet the option of establishing spiritual support groups such as Courage remains open to our bishops, and I believe that in the near future more will sponsor Courage or a group with the same principles.

3. THE HISTORICAL APPROACH TOWARD THE HOMOSEXUAL PERSON: ONE-TO-ONE COUNSELING, AND ITS RELATIONSHIP TO GROUP THERAPY AND GROUP SPIRITUAL DIRECTION

When I first gave spiritual direction to homosexual persons in 1954, I was not aware that there was any other approach than the classical one-to-one method, but during the last part of the sixties I became aware of the group therapy methods of Dr. Samuel Hadden in Philadelphia. Without rejecting the value of individual therapy, Hadden had found group therapy superior. For those sufficiently motivated to come twice a

---

[4] I received this information from the ordinary in one diocese and from a theologian in another.

[5] See Paul K. Thomas, *Homosexuality: A Positive Catholic Perspective*; published by the Baltimore Archdiocesan Gay/Lesbian Outreach, 1985, for a pro-homosexual position that carefully avoids acceptance of the teaching that homosexual activity is always objectively immoral. Father Thomas informs us that "all nine chapters of this booklet originally appeared in *The Catholic Review*, the weekly newspaper of the Archdiocese of Baltimore. The articles . . . represent the positive vision of the Aglo Team Ministry, an official Catholic outreach. . . ." Father Thomas is also a chaplain of the Baltimore Dignity chapter. Archbishop Raymond Hunthausen's hosting of the National Dignity Convention in 1983 is a matter of record. Auxiliary Bishop Crowley of Montreal spoke at Mass during the Montreal Dignity workshop (May 16–19, 1986), stating the Church's teaching, but also saying that the Church was not in a position to evaluate the private lives of the individual members of Dignity. In 1986 Archbishop Borders of Baltimore ordered the withdrawal of Paul Thomas' booklet.

[6] PCHP, 9.

week for ninety minutes over several years, good results were obtained. Of thirty-two patients reported, twelve had progressed to an exclusively heterosexual pattern of adjustment and had shown considerable improvement in solving other emotional difficulties. Most of the participants benefited from other homosexual persons in therapy.[7] From a study of Hadden's works and personal contact with him I began to see the value of group *therapy* for homosexual persons, but it did not occur to me then that religious counselors could also use group spiritual *direction* in guiding homosexual persons. A few years later a newly ordained priest challenged me in pastoral theology class when he asked why I did not do something to help priests and brothers with homosexual difficulties by giving group retreats. Within a few years that challenge led to the establishment of Renewal, Rest, and Re-Creation, a group-retreat movement for priests and perpetually professed brothers, which we shall describe later.

The point to be made is that just as the advent of group therapy methods did not do away with the need for individual (one-to-one) therapy, so also the employment of methods of group spiritual direction does not eliminate the continued need for individual spiritual direction. In New York City, persons who join Courage are asked to get an individual spiritual director whose guidance will complement the work taking place at the weekly group meetings.

Personal experience in directing Courage meetings during the past six years in New York City has taught me that not everyone is able to benefit from group meetings. Moreover, some who are excessively immature tend to disrupt the group, and, even if the group says that it is willing to tolerate them, the group is not really able to cope with this kind of situation. In these circumstances the person who cannot take part effectively or who is overly dependent and attention-seeking should stay with individual spiritual direction until he attains enough maturity to be part of a group without disrupting it. In practice this is not easy to do, but the director of the group must be firm, making it clear that the person will be able to come back to the group as soon as the director feels he is ready.

[7] Samuel Hadden, "Treatment of Male Homosexuals in Groups", *Internat. J. of Group Psychotherapy* 16, no. 1 (Jan. 1966):13–22. See also "Group Therapy for Sexual Maladjustments", *American J. of Psychiatry* 125 (1968):327–332; "Group Psychotherapy of Male Homosexuals", *Current Psychiatric Therapies* 6 (1966):177–186; "A Way out for Homosexuals", *Harper's*, March 1967. The last is recommended for laypersons.

4. GROUP SPIRITUAL SUPPORT SYSTEMS, PROTESTANT AND CATHOLIC

Group spiritual support systems have spread among Protestants more rapidly than among Catholics, if we exclude Dignity as a spiritual support system, because it is not based on the necessity of sexual abstinence as the first step toward full integration of one's sexuality into the Christian way of life. There are several examples of Protestant spiritual support systems: Exodus International, Metanoia Ministries, Outpost, Homosexuals Anonymous, and Regeneration, all of which are in communication with one another, meeting annually in different parts of the country. Tapes from the annual conventions are available from Exodus International.[8] The Protestant support systems differ from the Catholic form (Courage) in that they demand sexual abstinence from same-sex relationships only as a step toward the formation of heterosexual relationships and, they hope, marriage. Again, as I have already pointed out in Chapter Three, Colin Cook identifies homosexuality with our sinful nature, and many Protestants would concur. Nonetheless, the Protestant support systems and Courage agree that homosexual acts are always immoral and that we all need to develop spiritual support systems to help the person live a full Christian and chaste life.

While Courage asks only that the homosexual person live chastely, it encourages anyone who is willing to undergo the kinds of therapy proposed by Moberly or Aardweg to seek a heterosexual orientation with or without the hope of marriage. At the same time it cautions the person not to be discouraged if, after such therapy, he is not able to change his sexual orientation. He can still live a full Christian life as a celibate. As a moral theologian, I hold that the homosexual person is bound to celibacy, but I cannot bind him to seek a heterosexual orientation, because he may not have the financial resources to undertake a therapy program that will last at least eighteen months and will give him no certitude that it will bring about sexual reorientation. Besides, there is the danger that one who has been promised that he will attain heterosexuality if he follows a certain program will relapse into a promiscuous lifestyle if he believes that the therapy has not worked. Even if a homosexual person who undertakes therapy does not attain a heterosexual orientation, he will still be much better off, both psychologically in terms of self-acceptance and spiritually

---

[8] Exodus International, P.O. Box 2121, San Rafael, CA 94912, is a kind of umbrella organization for the others: Metanoia Ministries, P.O. Box 33039, Seattle, WA 98133; Outpost, 1821 University Ave., S. #296, St. Paul, MN 55104; Regeneration, P.O. Box 10574, Baltimore, MD 21285. See footnote 22 in this chapter on Homosexuals Anonymous.

in terms of full acceptance of God's will in his life. For this reason I do encourage persons who are able to begin such therapy to do so.[9]

Among Protestant support groups, the fastest growing is Homosexuals Anonymous (H.A.). This is a Christian fellowship of men and women who have chosen to help one another overcome homosexuality.

> Begun in November of 1980, Homosexuals Anonymous was the result of Cook and a former school principal, Doug, pooling their ideas on how to pass on to others what they had experienced in recovery from homosexuality. H.A., a non-sectarian organization working inter- and non-denominationally, helps people to find that freedom from homosexuality through the support and guidance available to them at weekly group meetings. At present there are approximately fifty H.A. chapters throughout the United States and Canada, with one chapter in Auckland, New Zealand. While similar to Alcoholics Anonymous, H.A. is unique in its Christian emphasis, to bring people to an awareness of the love of God for the fallen, the victory of Christ which leads to freedom from obsessive-compulsive disorders, and the identity of our personhood in Christ that leads to the completing of needs which homosexual behavior inappropriately attempts to complete.[10]

Comparison of H.A., A.A., and Courage

In the above citation Roberts points out that H.A. is similar to A.A. but unique in its Christian emphasis. The same may be said of Courage. Both H.A. and Courage make generous use of the wisdom and insights of A.A., the father of all other spiritual support groups. Since I shall detail Courage's program later, I should like at this point to comment on the Fourteen Steps of H.A. The first thing to be kept in mind is that these steps are not lectures, not abstract principles, but a way of living.

Step One says: *"We admitted that we were powerless over our homosexuality and that our emotional lives were unmanageable."*

In a deeply personal way one admits his powerlessness over homosexuality. This does not take place easily, but only after much suffering and prayer and the powerful influence of the group into which one has come. Many fear that they have lost control over their homosexual impulses, but they will not admit this to themselves, let alone anyone else. Others engage in endless rationalizations that there is no harm in their private sexual activity; or, if they admit promiscuous activity is wrong,

---

[9] Van den Aardweg mentions non-therapeutically-cured cases of homosexuality in *On the Origins and Treatment of Homosexuality*, pp. 201–204.

[10] Daniel Roberts, "Freedom from Homosexuality: The Third Option", *Interaction*, newsletter of the Association for Religious and Value Issues in Counseling, Winter 1986, p. 6.

they still believe that they have it under reasonable control. "After all, an occasional fling doesn't harm anyone." Thus it takes a particular grace of God, equivalent to conversion, really to admit that one is, left to himself, powerless over his homosexual tendencies. This is a *real* assent to personal powerlessness and the full admission that one has uncontrollable tendencies which he cannot control by mere acts of the will.

Step One of H.A., however, speaks of "our emotional lives" being unmanageable, where A.A. speaks merely of being powerless over the condition of alcohol. A.A. passes no judgment over the causes of alcoholism, regarding it as a disease. But Cook sees homosexuality as a disorder in the emotional life of the person, following Moberly's theory that a major disposing factor is a child's unsatisfactory relationship with a same-sex parent. The basic insight of A.A., then, that one must admit utter helplessness before one can begin to regain control over one's life, is utilized by H.A. and by Courage.

Step Two of H.A. is different from that of A.A., stating: "*We came to believe the love of God, who forgives us and accepts us in spite of all that we are and have done.*" (Step Two of A.A. reads: "*We came to believe that a Power greater than ourselves could restore us to sanity.*") In this second step Cook is addressing the depths of self-hatred in the heart of the homosexual person, something all experienced counselors of homosexual persons are aware of. Until one comes to accept oneself and one's condition of homosexuality as a starting point, one will not be able to relate properly to God or to others. Cook speaks of believing in the love of God, who forgives all our sins and accepts us in spite of our inadequacies. In a profound essay on self-acceptance, Peter van Breemen says there are very few people who can really accept themselves. "Indeed it is rare to meet a person who can cope with the problem 'Why me?' Self-acceptance can never be based on my own self, my own qualities. Such a foundation would collapse. Self-acceptance is an act of faith. When God loves me (which I believe by faith), I must accept myself as well. I cannot be more demanding than God, can I?"[11]

While counselors stress this need for the counselee to accept himself, they leave open the manner of doing so. Cook stresses the perception by the homosexual person of God's overwhelming love which God has for him. So does van Breemen, who says it is far more important that one believe that God loves him *personally* than it is for him to love God. "It is far more important that God loves us. Our love for God is secondary. . . . 'This is the love I mean: not our love for God, God's love for us' "

---

[11] *As Bread That Is Broken* (Denville, N.J.: Dimension Books, Inc., 1974), p. 15. Taken from the first chapter, "The Courage to Accept Acceptance", pp. 9–15.

(1 Jn 4:10).[12] Van Breemen wants the person to feel that God loves him, just as he is, not as he *should* be; otherwise, one can go through life feeling that God does not love him.

A.A.'s Step Two, on the other hand, puts the emphasis on the necessity of the person's turning to a Power greater than himself to restore him to sanity. The Power greater than oneself may be variously interpreted: the A.A. group, several friends who keep close tabs on the recovering alcoholic in the first critical days of recovery, or God Himself. As two recovering alcoholics who had been sober for some years said to me, "Even if the immediate and visible power greater than oneself is the A.A. group, ultimately in our experience it is God Himself." I agree. I believe that God works through the group, which then becomes the power greater than oneself. Cook does not really omit A.A.'s Step Two, but in my understanding subsumes it under Steps Nine and Twelve, which I shall describe later.

Personally, I believe that in H.A. A.A.'s Step Two should follow immediately after Step One, because it makes it easier for me to convince the homosexual person that he cannot go it alone. The vast majority of the homosexual persons I have worked with over the years have been loners even when they gave their acquaintances the impression that they were gregarious. For many, their confiding in me was the first time they had revealed their homosexual orientation to anyone. To the homosexual person, the counselor oftentimes becomes the first expression of the power greater than oneself. The counselor should persuade such a person to seek other friends with whom he can learn to share. If he can find an H.A. group or a Courage meeting, he should go regularly to the meetings.

In Step Three, Cook provides H.A. members with a theology of suffering: "*We learned to see purpose in our suffering, that our failed lives were under the control of God, who is able to bring good out of trouble.*" Here Cook presents a scriptural view of suffering, applying it to the difficulties of homosexual persons. He is really responding to a question most homosexual persons ask of the Lord: "Why me, Lord?" He responds that God will help the person to realize that he has imprisoned himself in a false identity, but that is Step Six, to which we shall come in due order. It is noteworthy that Cook cuts off self-pity, or at least the reasons for self-pity, by showing that all our sufferings have a supernatural purpose:

. . . God does not threaten you, self is powerless to threaten you, and the world cannot threaten you. Everything that appears to be against you is actually in your favor. This at least makes sense of those otherwise insane words of Paul, "We also rejoice in our sufferings" (Rom 5:3). Suffering, trial,

[12] *Ibid.*, p. 13.

pain do not speak to us of the abandonment or punishment of God. Whenever Satan attempts to hinder the progress of someone struggling with homosexuality who knows by faith how to turn every negative into an advantage, the devil's hindrances will only lead to that person's advancement.[13]

Step Four states: *"We came to believe that God had already broken the power of homosexuality and that He could restore our true personhood."* Step Four of H.A. flows out of Step Three. If God allows homosexual persons to suffer to manifest His divine purposes, He will help them. In "Homosexuality and the Power to Change", a series of twenty talks by Cook, he develops the theme that Christ's redemption of the human race atones for our sinful nature, including the tendency to homosexual activity of any sort and that one is already freed from the bondage of homosexuality. Cook goes on to stress that heterosexuality is an attribute of one's true personhood, even as homosexuality is part of one's sinful nature.[14]

Step Five of H.A. is concerned with one's illusory concept of oneself: *"We came to see that we have accepted a lie about ourselves, an illusion that has trapped us in false identity."* It is interesting that in Step Five, where Cook is concerned with the false identity the homosexual person has accepted because of the ignorance of sin and the darkness of mind that comes as a result of indulging in homosexual acts, one finds a similarity with the chief tenet of Aesthetic Realism: that the homosexual condition is the result of a false interpretation of the meaning of life and of human sexuality.[15]

Aesthetic Realism, however, sees the homosexual condition in a purely philosophic perspective, while Cook sees the source of the false identity in terms of spiritual blindness and the lust of the flesh. He illustrates his point by using Genesis 3, where Satan convinced Eve that it was good for her to eat the forbidden fruit. He tampered with her mind, so that she began to think that the fruit could not possibly be dangerous. She would not die from it; it would be very good for her and Adam; it would make them wise and godlike.

Evil, you see, had now become good. And if evil was now good, what would that make good to be? God, who is good, was now seen to be evil. They hid

[13] *Homosexuality: An Open Door?* (Boise, Idaho: Pacific Press, 1985), p. 29.

[14] Colin Cook, cassette no. 12, "That Puzzling Past Tense", from *Homosexuality and the Power to Change* (American Cassette Ministry, P.O. Box 922, Harrisburg, PA 17108).

[15] Aesthetic Realism Foundation, Inc., 141 Greene St., New York, NY 10012. The organization publishes a series of position papers under the general heading: *The Right of Aesthetic Realism to Be Known*. Some members of this group claim to have changed their sexual orientation to heterosexuality through the philosophical process of the late Eli Siegel, the founder of the group.

themselves from Him as He came toward them, for fear that He would kill them. This inversion of good and evil lies at the core of every defeating temptation[16]

St. Augustine would agree with Cook, since he describes sin as a *lie*, blaming his own covetousness for wanting to possess both God and his sin; consequently, he lost God, who refused to be possessed by a lie. That is, God suffered no compromise with sin. Sin is a lie inasmuch as it always involves the choice of an object that is not in accord with the due and true order of things; and, as a lie, it brings punishment upon the very one who commits it, shutting him off from the truth, and perverting his nature.[17]

Once one realizes that he is trapped in a false identity, homosexuality, one wants to seek his true identity, and that is Step Six of H.A.: "*We learn to claim our true identity that as mankind, we are part of God's heterosexual creation and that God calls us to rediscover that identity in Him through Jesus Christ, as our faith perceives Him.*" In its statement on marriage Vatican II supplies an argument in favor of Cook's position that men and women are "part of God's heterosexual creation". It refers to the fact that "the married state has been established by the Creator and endowed by Him with its own proper laws: it is rooted in the contract of its partners, that is, in their irrevocable personal consent. It is an institution confirmed by the divine law. . . ."[18]

Cook sees the redemption of mankind as restoring men and women to the due order of creation, which includes the heterosexual relationship. Vatican II, likewise, states that

> Christ our Lord has abundantly blessed this love, which is rich in its various features, coming, as it does, from the spring of divine love and modeled on Christ's own union with the Church. . . . Authentic married love is caught up into divine love and is directed and enriched by the redemptive power of Christ and the salvific action of the Church.[19]

Through Faith in Jesus Christ as Redeemer the homosexual person can rediscover his true identity as part of the heterosexual creation now restored by the act of redemption.

In Step Seven Cook formulates a resolution on the basis of the *learning* process that takes place in the first six steps. Note the language of

[16] *Homosexuality: An Open Door?* p. 30.

[17] *Confessions of St. Augustine*, trans. Frank Sheed (London: Sheed and Ward, 1949), bk. 10, ch. 49, p. 205.

[18] *The Church in the Modern World*, 48, *Vatican II: The Conciliar and Post Conciliar Documents* and *Vatican II: More Post Conciliar Documents*, Austin Flannery, O.P., ed. (Dublin: Costello Publishing Co., 1975).

[19] *Ibid.*, 48, p. 951.

the previous steps: "We admitted", "came to believe", "learned to see purpose", "came to see", "learn to claim". In this way Cook shows that it is a long and struggling process. Accordingly, Step Seven states: "*We resolve to entrust our lives to our loving God and to live by faith, praising Him for our new unseen reality, confident that it will become visible to us in God's good time.*"

Cook cautions his listeners in the tape series *Homosexuality and the Power to Change* not to be disturbed if the old habits of homosexual fantasy die hard. He stresses that one does not pray that God *will* take away one's homosexual tendencies, but rather that one praises the Lord for *having taken* away this condition through the act of redemption. At the same time one has much work to do on oneself, as he indicates on tapes 13 to 20. One must learn to form chaste friendships with members of both sexes; after a time one should date persons of the other sex; during this period one should not go about claiming that he has been transformed into a heterosexual. One should reveal one's inner self only to close friends. One must be patient, as one daily pursues a life of mental prayer, biblical reading, and journal keeping, with weekly group meetings in H.A. One must trust that one's "unseen identity" will become "visible to us in God's good time".

If we compare Step Seven of H.A. with Step Three of A.A., we find in both steps a resolution to turn oneself over to the care of a loving God. Step Three of A.A. reads: "*Made a decision to turn our will and our lives over to the care of God as we understood Him.*" Step Seven of H.A., on the other hand, specifies God as *loving*, and indeed Steps Two, Three, Four, and Six of H.A. help to complete the biblical image of the *Father* of Jesus Christ.

Step Eight of H.A. states: "*As forgiven people, free from condemnation, we made a searching and fearless moral inventory of ourselves, determined to root out fear, hidden hostility, and contempt for the world.*" This step is similar to Step Four of A.A.: "*Made a searching and fearless moral inventory of ourselves.*" Both steps acknowledge that it is necessary to make frequent examinations of the state of our soul to search out hidden faults. Rooting out "contempt for the world" may be interpreted to mean the avoidance of an attitude of superiority. One should undertake this inventory, however, with the firm belief that one's sins are forgiven and that one is free from condemnation.

Step Nine of H.A. reads: "*We admitted to God, to ourselves, and to another human being the exact nature of our wrongs and humbly asked God to remove the defects of character.*" This is equivalent to Steps Five and Six of A.A. Step Five of A.A. states: "*Admitted to God, to ourselves, and to another human being the exact nature of our wrongs.*" Step Six of A.A. reads: "*Were entirely ready to have God remove all these defects of character.*"

Among A.A. members Step Five is crucial, since it enables the person to break out of the cell of isolation by opening up completely to another human being. It is the power greater than oneself at work. I have seen one compulsive homosexual person open up more completely to his therapist and to me after he was able to speak to a third party with whom he worked. In fact, I have noted other persons working faithfully on Step Four (the fearless moral inventory of A.A.) and then go on to Step Five with the contents of the inventory. As the recipient of the confidence of the person making Step Five in regard to homosexuality in his life, I have seen radical improvement in the person's behavior. For the first time in his life he was willing to confide deeply in another human being. I have witnessed this transformation many times in the last eight years.[20]

Step Ten of H.A. states: *"We willingly made direct amends wherever wise and possible to all people we have harmed."* This is equivalent to Steps Eight and Nine of A.A. Step Eight says: *"Made a list of all persons we had harmed, and became willing to make amends to them all."* Step Nine says: *"Made direct amends to such persons, wherever possible, except when to do so would injure them or others."* In both programs the desire of the recovering person to make amends is satisfied within the bounds of prudence. In the recovering alcoholic this can be done more easily, since the effects of alcoholism are so manifest to all those near the alcoholic, but in the case of the homosexual person the preservation of a good reputation may dictate that he not reveal his identity to persons whom he may have injured or manipulated. Much homosexual activity is promiscuous: the persons do not know, and do not wish to know, one another. Very often such a person can make only indirect reparation by acts of charity such as volunteering to work with AIDS patients.

Step Eleven of H.A. has no parallel in A.A., addressing itself to the specific fears of the homosexual person as he seeks to develop a hetero-sexual identity: *"We determined to live no longer in fear of the world, believing that God's victorious control turns all that is against us into our favor, bringing advantage out of sorrow and order from disaster."* In tape 9 of the series *Homosexuality and the Power to Change* Cook encourages the homosexual person to realize that in and by the power of God's grace he can overcome the various erotic desires that come upon him and live as an equal to the heterosexual persons around him. Aware of the feelings of inferiority and timidity that many homosexual persons have, Cook points out that God will help them bring good out of evil and turn their sorrows into joy. They must not be afraid to take their place as equals wherever they are.

---

[20] One must be aware that there are persons incapable of such self-revelation, particularly psychopaths.

Nothing is going to separate them from the love of Christ (Rom 8). Appropriately, tape 9 is entitled "Everything against You Is in Your Favor".

Again, Step Twelve of H.A. has no equivalent in A.A.'s steps: "*We determined to mature in our relationships with men and women, learning the meaning of a partnership of equals, seeking neither dominance over people nor servile dependency on them.*" This step is meant as a guideline for those who are dating with the hope of marriage. One finds in any group of homosexual persons both those who are excessively assertive, tending to dominate the discussion, and those who are overly dependent upon the favor of their peers. Frequently, the dominant suffer from the same feelings of inferiority as the submissive, but they are not consciously aware of them. Aardweg writes: "The 'boy' in the homosexual frequently plays the role of being superiorly sensitive, artistic, handsome, well dressed. The choice of the field of overcompensation depends on the 'child's' point of view. . . . When he is good at sports or learning, he is likely to choose these respective fields for affirming himself. All this can make a person tyrannical."[21]

Step Thirteen of H.A. is the equivalent of Step Eleven of A.A. Step Thirteen states: "*We sought through confident praying and the wisdom of Scripture for an ongoing growth in our relationship with God and a humble acceptance of His guidance for our lives.*" Step Eleven of A.A. reads: "*Sought through prayer and meditation to improve our conscious contact with God as we understood Him, praying only for knowledge of His will for us and the power to carry that out.*" The difference between the two steps is that the God of H.A. is the God of Holy Scripture, whereas the God of A.A. could be conceived not only in a Judaeo-Christian system of belief but in a Moslem or other perspective. But both steps emphasize the fundamental need for the practice of prayer of the heart. No program of recovery can omit this step. However impractical it may seem at first sight, the first thing I teach the compulsive homosexual person is the art of meditation, or prayer of the heart. It has to become a daily practice. It will lead the person to a knowledge of God's will for him and the power to carry it out.

Step Fourteen of H.A. parallels Step Twelve of A.A. They are the final steps in each program. Step Fourteen of H.A. reads: "*Having had a spiritual awakening, we try to carry this out to people in homosexuality with a love that demands nothing and to practice these steps in all our life's activities, as far as lies within us.*" Step Twelve of A.A. reads: "*Having had a spiritual experience, as the result of these steps, we tried to carry this message to alcoholics,*

---

[21] *On the Origins and Treatment of Homosexuality*, p. 53.

and to practice these principles in all our affairs." Both steps ask the person who has had a spiritual awakening to share it with others in the same difficulties.

There is great wisdom in these last steps. Both the alcoholic and the homosexual person have tended to be egocentric, preoccupied with their own inner troubles; now they are urged to center their psychic energies on the needs of others whom they can understand. In practice, such persons deepen their own life of virtue by their constant care for other homosexual persons. I know individuals in the Courage group who live this step daily. Obviously, those associated with Cook in H.A. also live this step.[22]

From comparing the steps of A.A. and H.A. one notes certain general similarities. Both programs stress that a step is not a lecture, but a way of life. In both programs one must work the steps. As H.A. says, "If you want the steps to work, you've got to work the steps." The *H.A. Newsletter* (July-August 1986) gives specific directions on working the steps. First, one determines what the step means to him; then he seeks help from a counselor or step-coach; he commits himself to work the step for one week, one day at a time. But he never works a step without admitting to God the truth of Step One, that we are powerless to do anything without His help. One also uses a journal on a daily basis to "talk to oneself" about how one is using the step. Then when one goes to the H.A. weekly meeting, one expresses to the group what the step meant to him. After some weeks one should rest from conscious concentration on the step, allowing it to work subconsciously. Meanwhile one goes on to another step, later coming back to the same step. In this way—by making the steps a way of life—one will find freedom from homosexuality.[23]

H.A.'s support group of parents, spouses, and friends

Just as A.A. has its Al-Anon, which is composed of spouses, parents, and friends of the alcoholic person, so H.A. has a corresponding support group of parents, spouses, and friends of the homosexual person. From working with parents of homosexual persons in New York on an individual basis during the past six years I have perceived the need for a support group for those close to the homosexual person, but so far I have

[22] For more information on H.A., see *H.A. News*, the Official Newsletter of Homosexuals Anonymous Fellowship Services, P.O. Box 7881, Reading, PA 19603. Colin Cook also has help for counselors in H.A. in a new series of tapes entitled "The Healing of Homosexuality", American Cassette Ministries, P.O. Box 922, Harrisburg, PA 17108.

[23] Colin Cook, H.A. tape album: "The Fourteen Steps", P.O. Box 7881, Reading, PA 19603.

not been able to establish one. We Catholics can learn from our Protestant brethren. The Newsletter of the Philadelphia H.A. Support Group describes the value of such meetings. When parents discover or are told that one of their children is homosexual, they experience shock, anger, disappointment, bewilderment, and guilt. As I have heard so often in New York and in Philadelphia, and indeed everywhere, parents ask, "What did we do wrong? Where did we go wrong? What can we do about it? Do you know any doctor who can 'cure' him?"

It is helpful in our response to parents to stress the family dynamics. One should consider first of all the homosexuality of the son or daughter and its related problems; then one should observe the reaction and response of the parents to the disclosure that one of their children is homosexual; finally, one needs to see the whole family in its brokenness. Generally speaking, the young man or woman is in the late teens or twenties before the disclosure of homosexual orientation occurs. Often he or she is not willing to talk to a religious counselor or will come on one occasion only to placate parents. The parents need to realize that the orientation and behavior of their grown-up children is beyond their control. They may suggest that their son or daughter talk to a religious counselor or priest, but they should not put pressure on him or her to do so. No matter what the son or daughter does, it is wise for the parents to join a support group such as one associated with H.A. They need to express their inner feelings about this new knowledge in a group of people who have suffered in the same way. They will find a greater measure of peace at these meetings. Particularly, at such gatherings they benefit from the presence of individuals from a homosexual background who have found healing and freedom from this disorder. They can pray together for their homosexual loved ones. The mother of a homosexual son says it all:

> When your child reveals a piece of his own life to you, this is an expression of deep trust. Making this disclosure to you is probably one of the major decisions of his life. Your reaction will be long remembered. What a terrific opportunity for all parents to show their loyalty and allegiance to their child, when they are first aware he is caught in this dilemma. Does the knowledge of it somehow cripple our ability to show our allegiance to him? Get across to him that you love him no matter what. This unconditional love is what you must communicate to him. You love him, but you must hate his sin because it hurts him. . . . If he is caught deep in sin, willing to change, unwilling to change, or even if he is too uptight to talk about it with you, make him aware that your love does not depend upon his behavior. You can love because of his struggle, not in spite of it. Keep your love flowing to your child in every possible way you can demonstrate it. This will prevent stagnation and

bitterness from settling in your heart. It will assure him of this unconditional love you are showing him which will remind him of God's love for him.[24]

The real issue in dealing with parents of homosexuals is to help them develop their own relationship with the Lord. They must turn over stewardship of their child to the Lord, allowing Him to bring healing to their own hearts and to the hearts of all the family.[25]

Catholic spiritual support systems

There are actually four spiritual support systems that minister to Catholics: Dignity; New Ways Ministry; Renewal, Rest, and Re-Creation; and Courage. I shall comment on Dignity and New Ways Ministry later in this chapter; now I shall consider the two spiritual support systems in which I have been involved since 1978: Renewal, Rest, and Re-Creation and Courage.

1. Group retreats for priests and brothers known as Renewal, Rest, and Re-Creation came into existence in 1977. With the approval of Bishop Thomas Welsh, then bishop of Arlington, Virginia, I prepared for the first retreat in February 1978. It was agreed that only priests and brothers who were perpetually professed would be invited to these retreats, but provision was made for some clerics not yet ordained or brothers not perpetually professed to make the retreats for good reasons. In the last eight years two hundred priests and brothers have made twenty-two retreats. The purpose of the retreat is to help the person regain control over homosexual desires and to live the life of consecrated celibacy. While psychological insight enters into the week-long discussion sessions, particularly stimulated by a three-hour session with Dr. John Kinnane (a Catholic University clinical psychologist who has two decades of practical experience in working with

[24] Barbara Johnson, *Where Does a Mother Go to Resign?* (Minneapolis: Bethany Fellowship Press, 1979), quoted in *Harvest News* 1, no. 2 (Spring 1986):2, ed. John Freeman. This is a quarterly devoted to an interdenominational ministry of hope and healing to those struggling with a homosexual problem.

25 *Harvest News*, p. 2. See also Robert Nugent, "Homosexuality and the Hurting Family", *America*, Feb. 28, 1981, which counsels parents how to deal with the filial revelation that their son or daughter is homosexual. He suggests that homosexuals themselves be more perceptive of their families' lack of understanding. Trust and openness are needed in every attempt at reconciliation. But Nugent weakens the force of the Church's position against homosexual acts by speaking of the "present" pastoral ministry of the Church to help homosexual persons to live in chaste celibacy, while immediately adding that a growing number of theologians allow on the pastoral level for the formation of stable, faithful homosexual relationships for certain individuals. The accent on "present" pastoral ministry implies that the Church will change its moral stance under the influence of theologians.

priests and religious), nonetheless the primary accent is *spiritual conversion*. The only sermons given are those at the daily liturgies, and these are given in dialogue form by the priest participants.[26]

Reflection on and discussion of the Twelve Steps as applied to homosexual priests and religious provides an opportunity for all to reveal their personal difficulties in an atmosphere of trust and acceptance. Generally, no more than nine persons are accepted for a retreat. Anonymity and confidentiality are preserved. It is as if each participant had a confessional stole around his neck. Some individuals dread the thought of their superiors knowing they are homosexual. Others who have made known their difficulties to superiors come with their support. Still others involved in situations that have come to the attention of civil authorities or the ordinary of the diocese come under mandate. Contrary to ordinary expectations, these latter do very well in the retreats.

From leading most of these retreats, I have noticed how at the beginning most of the participants are reserved, in some instances tense, but as each day passes, the level of trust increases. By Thursday morning the retreatants request that a list be made of their addresses and telephone numbers so they can continue to communicate with one another after the retreat is over. The mutual sharing, the sense of relief that "here I can express my innermost feelings and not be condemned," the hope that one can make it in his mission, school, or parish when he returns there, because now he knows that others understand and support him—all these dynamics occurring in every retreat—convince me that there is no substitute for a spiritual group support system for persons with such difficulties. This does not mean that there is not a great deal of spiritual homework to be done by each retreatant in the solitude of his heart.

Time is provided for prayer. Indeed, in the most recent retreats Thursday becomes a day of contemplative prayer. But the support of the group actually motivates each individual to accept himself as he is before God and to make the spiritual surrender necessary for conversion of heart. Although we use the Twelve Steps as a working model, we never get past Step Five (revealing to God and to another human being the exact nature of our wrongs) during the five days. We tell the retreatants that they have only begun the work of reconstruction of their spiritual lives during the brief period of the retreat, and we urge them to continue the task under the direction of a reliable spiritual guide. Again, group support does not replace an individual spiritual director.

---

[26] I gave some reflections on the first retreat of R.R. and R. in "Reflections on a Retreat for Clerics with Homosexual Tendencies", *The Linacre Quarterly*, May 1979, pp. 136–140. In using the Kinsey scale I absentmindedly gave the rating 0 to the extreme homosexual, and 6 to the extreme heterosexual. It should be the opposite. The message is clear enough.

It needs to be reiterated that the retreats do not aim to change sexual orientation or to provide an apologetic on the Church's teaching concerning the immorality of homosexual activity or the necessity of celibacy for the Roman clergy. They are meant to plant a seed of hope in the hearts of the participants that by God's grace and the support of friends—and in some instances, with the additional help of a competent therapist—the individual may be able to live chastely.

When one considers the confidentiality and anonymity promised the participants, one realizes the difficulties of follow-up studies to evaluate the effectiveness of such retreats. To be sure, with the exception of one retreat, the participants expressed in writing great enthusiasm for the benefits of the retreat, desiring to come back again because it was the best retreat of their lives, and saying they would never be the same again. But we have no real way of knowing the long-term effects of the retreat on the majority of the participants. From personal correspondence with many, particularly at Christmas time, I know they are doing well. About six have come back for another retreat. However, I know of several who relapsed into their former way of promiscuity.

Nevertheless, I believe on the basis of personal communications that the retreats have been immensely beneficial. In late October 1986 I received a letter from a retreatant who wrote:

> It was one of the most significant experiences of my life and I can't adequately express how much I appreciate the opportunity to participate in such a fine program. . . . It was a powerful and positive program and it has helped me to integrate the one area of my life that has been so out of kilter for so many years. Celibacy has taken on a new dimension in my life and I have new insights into my own sexuality. I felt the program was well developed and realistic.

The greatest weakness of the retreats has been the inability to form a strong spiritual support system afterward. Often great distances separate the participants.

There is, however, one happy exception to this shortcoming. In the New York metropolitan area an experienced priest spiritual director and professional therapist, Father Benedict Groeschel, O.F.M. Cap., has supplemented the work of R.R. and R. by biweekly meetings during the last five years.[27] Regularly, he has a group of seven or eight. He and I have discussed the objection raised against R.R. and R. when the idea of group spiritual support was first presented to three Washington psychiatrists in

[27] Father Benedict dedicates his book, *The Courage to Be Chaste* (New York: Paulist Press, 1984) "to the men and women of Courage and to all who have the courage to try" (p. vii). He goes on to say that he wrote the book at the express request of several members of Courage.

1974. Their conclusion was that it was imprudent to bring a group of homosexual priests and male religious together because it could lead to manipulation of the group leader and seduction of one another. Of course, there is risk in any such gathering, but we have honestly faced up to this danger, warning the retreatants about it at the very beginning of the retreat and pointing out that any attempt at seduction would negate the very purposes of the retreat. Thank God, this has not been a problem. Such a risk can be justified by the argument that the great good of experiencing group support for the practice of virtue is in proportion to the danger of seduction, which is rendered remote by the high motivation of the participants and the guidance of the retreat master.

While the program of R.R. and R. is not meant to be formally therapeutic, and always makes referrals to professionals, the effect of the program is indirectly therapeutic in the sense that the openness and trust that develops during the retreat cause the participants to discuss emotional factors of anger and self-hatred and to benefit by the insights of the group. Again, the faithful practice of the Twelve Steps, spotlighted during the retreat, has helped compulsive homosexuals regain control over their sexual actions. This does not mean that the compulsive person does not need professional therapy as well. Indeed, subsequent therapy complements the work of R.R. and R. It seems that whenever one is involved in any form of compulsive activity he needs a program such as A.A. Compulsive sexual activity, then, demands both a spiritual support system and a rigorous plan of life, which are provided by the Twelve Steps.

One compulsively homosexual priest has turned his life around by adapting the Twelve Steps to his own difficulty. He has written a commentary on the steps for use in our retreats; he has also organized a Sexaholics Anonymous (S.A.) unit in his diocese. Since then I have become acquainted with a member of this group, and I am deeply impressed by the good effects I see. From reading their literature it is clear that they insist upon both a strictly spiritual living of the Twelve Steps and complete abstinence, even for married persons, until such time as they are able to regard their need for heterosexual intercourse as optional, or no longer compulsive. It leaves no room for homosexual steady-lover relationships.[28]

2. Spiritual support groups for Catholic homosexual persons known as Courage, as already mentioned, began in New York City in September 1980 with five men. All the little group knew was that they would meet

[28] For further information concerning S.A., an interdenominational group, write to Sexaholics Anonymous, P.O. Box 300, Simi Valley, CA 93062.

weekly and listen to the spiritual director with the hope of finding encouragement to live a life of sexual abstinence. From the beginning I sought to get each one involved in the discussions that were then too academic because I had not yet learned how to center whatever topic was discussed on their lives as homosexual persons. During the first two years the group expanded to ten members but not beyond that number until Anne Buckley wrote a column about Courage in the *Catholic New York* (March 28, 1982). Her article brought many inquiries and led to an increase in membership.

Fortunately, during the first eighteen months the original members were encouraged to reflect on the goals and purposes of the group and to seek an appropriate name. The priests who worked with me at the beginning and I were deliberately not present when the members were formulating their goals and purposes; we wanted them to be responsible for their organization. They arrived at the following:

The goals of Courage

1. To live chaste lives in accordance with the Roman Catholic Church's teaching on homosexuality.

2. To dedicate our entire lives to Christ through service to others, spiritual reading, prayer, meditation, individual spiritual direction, frequent attendance at Mass, and the frequent reception of the sacraments of Penance and of the Holy Eucharist.

3. To foster a spirit of fellowship in which we may share with one another our thoughts and experiences and so ensure that none of us will have to face the problems of homosexuality alone.

4. To be mindful of the truth that chaste friendships are not only possible but necessary in celibate Christian life and to encourage one another in forming and sustaining them.

5. To live lives that may serve as good examples to other homosexuals.

After the goals had been formulated one member proposed the name Courage, and it was accepted. This young man died of AIDS two years later after an illness during which he came as often as he could to the weekly meetings. His life exemplified well what Courage is all about: it is meant for the homosexual person who desires to regain control over his life and who realizes that he cannot do it alone. He senses that he needs the support of others who share his condition and ideals. He hopes to find support in the group to live a chaste life. As each prospective member is interviewed, he is asked whether he accepts those purposes. Sometimes he will say he is not able to live the five goals of Courage. Usually this is his fear speaking. He needs reassurance that Courage is not a society of the perfect, but of persons like himself struggling to be chaste. If he tries to live the purposes but fails, the sacrament of Confession is available.

Format of meetings

In view of the fact that Courage is primarily a spiritual support group we give ample time during weekly meetings for prayer, which takes place at the beginning and the end of the formal session. Several members prepare the prayers, which usually are of a meditative character. After the opening prayer the director (or in his absence, the president of the group) presents some topic relating to the spiritual life or to a deeper understanding of homosexual orientation and activity. From our experimentation with various ways of conducting a meeting we have come to prefer discussions of issues that are related to our personal lives and to our spiritual goals. Usually I provide a handout on a specific point, such as the effects of repressed anger on one's life or the nature of compulsive cruising. The group spends some time reading the handout, then discusses it for fifty minutes or so. We try to give everyone the opportunity to share in the discussion. If there are more than ten members at a meeting, two groups are formed. The discussion and prayer periods total about two hours.

Afterward there is a social period during which light refreshments (coffee, tea, cookies) are served. The social hour is very important, particularly for newcomers, because it gives participants a better chance to know one another and to form personal friendships that enable them to be supportive of one another should difficulties arise. By organizing group parties to attend entertainment or social events, such as public lecture series by prominent speakers, religious and secular, in New York City, Courage also encourages its members to share a full and healthy social life.

While I prefer to see new or veteran members privately at another time than the hours of meeting, the contingencies of work and travel often necessitate that I schedule some interviews during the half hour before the meeting or during and even after the social hour. (I sense the need for the spiritual director to see newcomers as soon as possible and regular members periodically.) I stress the need for each member to find a spiritual director whom he should see at least every other week. Experience has shown that it may take some time to find a qualified and competent confessor or advisor.

Our meetings are so structured that they remain open to a variation in the format whenever necessary. Once a month, for example, Mass can be offered for all the members, and on that occasion the subsequent discussion period can be shortened. Periodically, guest speakers, religious or professionals, are invited to address the members on topics related to the lives of the members. Doctors and social workers have made presentations on AIDS; clinical psychologists have discussed passive-aggressive behavior; theologians have discussed moral questions. These departures from routine schedule add interest and zest to the meetings.

Content of discussion periods

At the beginning of the Courage experience in 1980 I thought the best way to proceed was to give a systematic presentation of Catholic teaching on the truths of Faith, on the moral law, and on the sacraments. But as time went on, the members made it clear to me that Courage needed more informal discussions of those elements of the Faith that bore more directly upon their personal lives. They wanted to participate in the discussions— indeed *to share experiences* with the other members. The above format is the result of the ongoing dialogue between the members and me. They want me (or anyone who assumes the role of director) to prepare handouts, preferably even a week or more before the discussion. They desire their leader to show how the topic is pertinent to their lives; they complain of guest speakers who make no effort to relate their topic to the lives of homosexual persons. In all this there is a danger of confining discussion at meetings only to the topic of homosexuality. As I have pointed out, it would be a mistake to exclude other questions pertinent to Christian living. A person is more than a homosexual tendency; as a Christian, one has more to think about than temptations to homosexual acts. Hence the topics discussed, while relating to homosexuality, should go beyond them.

The director of Courage meetings should be willing to interrupt any logical sequence to deal with questions emerging during the discussion period. Very often these questions provide the leader with future discussion topics. Members are appreciative whenever the leader has been sensitive to their questions by at least attempting to answer them. At the same time he should not allow the meetings to deteriorate into sterile speculations or disguised rationalizations of homosexual activity. While one is willing to present the opinions of dissenting theologians objectively, one should also show the flaws in their arguments so that the members may become more rooted in their Faith position. The principal purpose of our meetings, however, is not intellectual formation, but schooling in the practice of Christian virtue, which is indeed based upon the *truth* of Catholic teaching. Accordingly, I have felt the need to present several specific topics, not once but at regular intervals, simply because members raise these issues.

One such topic is the practice of meditation, or the prayer of the heart. Although this method of prayer has long been regarded as the best preservative of chastity, relatively few persons actually engage in it regularly. The director should teach the group a method of prayer, indicating that there are other methods, but insisting that everyone adopt a method and use it daily. Without repeated emphasis on the importance of prayer and the practice of an ascetical plan of life, Courage can easily deteriorate into just another social club. That is why it is good that several of the members prepare a brief meditation for the beginning and the end of each meeting.[29]

Another topic worthy of serious examination is the responsibility of the person who either freely or compulsively engages in homosexual activity. How imputable are these habitual or compulsive acts? More important still are the pastoral guidelines that the director can offer to a person who seems driven by persistent and uncontrollable sexual desires. While such a person needs group support and an ascetical plan of life, he usually requires in addition the help of a professional therapist who can work with his director. It is generally unwise for the director of a Courage group to try to aid a compulsive homosexual without help either from a therapist or from participation in groups dealing with the compulsion.[30]

An element for consideration, often overlooked, is the person's fantasy life and the manner in which one endeavors to control it. Sometimes a person who has been doing very well suddenly finds himself beset with erotic fantasy whenever alone. He is filled with fear that he may go back to the bars, restrooms, and porno shops. He feels so lonely. This is real temptation. The first rule he should follow is to turn to the Lord and talk to Him about these fantasies. Truly turn them over. As Colin Cook said at a conference in August 1985, one makes the temptation much stronger by becoming tense and fearful. It is better to look the fantasy in the eye, seeing how ridiculous it is. "What, give up the interior peace I have acquired over six months by cruising the bars? No, Lord, I can find something better to do to fill up my loneliness. I can go visit a sick relative or attend a lecture", and so on.

One breaks the spell of fantasy by reaching out in love to people in the *real* world. All of us have had the experience of daydreams rudely interrupted by the phone ringing. As we answer it, the fantasy world disappears, and we confront the real world. Likewise, the *attractiveness*

---

[29] I have suggested various readings to help the neophyte in his meditations. In *Introduction to the Devout Life*, St. Francis de Sales provides ten model meditations (pt. I, chs. 9–18). The New Testament is a good place to begin the art of meditation, since it is centered around Christ.

[30] Patrick Carnes, *The Sexual Addiction* (Minneapolis: Compcare, 1983). See chapter six: "Twelve Steps to Recovery", pp. 141–167. The following groups deal with sexual addictions, heterosexual and homosexual, male and female: Sexaholics Anonymous: S.A., Box 300, Simi Valley, CA 93062; New York Founders Group of S.A., Box 1542, New York, NY 10185; Sex Addicts Anonymous: S.A.A., Box 3038, Minneapolis, MN 55403; and Sex and Love Addicts Anonymous: S.L.A.A., Box 529, New Town Branch, Boston, MA 02258.

of sin is a fantasy: the unreal world of Satan. We must confront real persons and real things. That is why I recommend those obsessed by fantasy to learn how to live constantly in the real world, which includes the reality of prayer. This obviously demands the practice of self-discipline from morning to night, constantly pulling self from negative fantasy back into reality.

A third topic that bears repetition is the necessity of celibacy for the homosexual person. Even if one were following a program like H.A. with the hope of learning to live as a heterosexual person, one is still bound to celibacy until such time as he enters marriage. Whatever the reasons, the vast majority of those who come to Courage, however, are not interested in changing their sexual tendencies. Yet they do see the necessity of celibacy for themselves. Again, one must understand the erotic surroundings in which most homosexual persons live—indeed, in which heterosexuals live as well—and the prevailing propaganda in the Catholic homosexual community in New York City favoring *optional* celibacy. Courage members are told by members of Dignity that there is no need to live the celibate life and that one can have his steady lover and at the same time receive the Holy Eucharist regularly.

One former Courage member who had left the group to take a lover berated me in a letter for unnecessarily binding the members of Courage to celibacy when it was his understanding that celibacy was only optional for the homosexual person. When I replied that this obligation of celibacy for the homosexual person was based upon the teaching of the Church, he countered with the objection that priests in Dignity quoted theologians in favor of the opinion that homosexual persons are not bound to celibacy, and that he felt free to follow their opinion. Recently, with the clear stand of the Congregation for the Doctrine of the Faith in the Father Charles Curran case, as well as the October 1, 1986, CDF Document, it is hoped that some of this confusion in the minds of Catholic homosexual persons will be dispelled. Meanwhile, leaders of Courage must try to understand the pressure under which many members live.

It would be a mistake, however, to present celibacy as a burden the homosexual person must carry across the lonely desert of life under the burning sun—something imposed from without against his will. Such an approach I have found in clerics and laity alike. I remember a disgruntled priest during one of the retreats who kept muttering, "This goddam celibacy." What the leader should do is to show the members that celibacy can be interiorly accepted and joyfully lived out. Only by accepting the graces the Holy Spirit sends to the person can one learn to make celibacy his own, to see it as a gift and not a burden, to live it as an act of love for Christ.

Furthermore, celibacy should be shown to be another way of expressing our sexuality. We are body persons, and therefore our expression of celibate living must not be a denial of our bodily reality. That is why the expression used so often in the past, "angelic chastity", was so misleading. Without bodies, the angels have no problem with the practice of chastity. We need to talk about fantasy, emotions, affections, sexual attractions, and nonsexual attractions as humans experience them. We need to discuss how one can bring them into line with our desire to love God first of all and to love friends and relatives with well-ordered affection. Two excellent books can help the Courage group to understand the full meaning and beauty of Christian chastity. *The Courage to Be Chaste*, by Father Benedict Groeschel, O.F.M., Cap., and *Celibacy, Prayer and Friendship*, by Father Christopher Kiesling, O.P., are both down-to-earth approaches to celibacy for the single person and for members of Courage.[31]

Friendship's many faces

A fourth topic to be explored in depth by Courage members is friendship. Since one of the goals of Courage is the formation of chaste friendships, it is crucial to describe the different forms of friendship and to distinguish between virtuous and dangerous friendships. Everyone needs deep or intimate friendships with a few persons. Humans can do without genital relationships, but they cannot fully develop as humans without some measure of human friendship. It is useful to explore the meaning of intimacy and friendship more thoroughly, inasmuch as Courage members find it difficult to achieve.

In today's culture the frenetic pace of life militates against the formation of close friendships. Caught up in competition for advancement in careers, many are not aware of their need for intimacy, not even in marriage, with consequent harm to the quality of marital and family life. The same flight from intimacy is found among priests and religious of both sexes. Many become workaholics, and usually very productive in their pastoral ministry and teaching. They acquire many acquaintances but few, if any, friends. Recently I was speaking to a twenty-year-old hairdresser who had become involved in drugs and promiscuity. I said to her, "You are a lonely person." She responded that she had many friends. I replied that she had many acquaintances but no real friends. She had never thought of it that way, and in this she is typical.

Perhaps one of the best explanations of this phenomenon is found in Henri Nouwen's essay on the desirability and possibility of love. Nouwen

---

[31] See *The Courage to Be Chaste*, pp. 109–114, for additional references on chastity. See also my article "Chastity and The Homosexual", *The Priest*, July-August 1977.

first describes two forms of existence, the *taking* form and the *forgiving* form. Persons experience the feeling that they are no good and that if others knew them just the way they are, they would no longer love them. So they do not reveal who they are to others for fear of being taken. This is part of the all-pervasive *taking* form. The same is true of every student who fills out an application for graduate school or of every professor who writes letters of recommendation. One is obedient to the taking form of life: "We are judged, evaluated, tested, graded, diagnosed, and classified from the time our parents compared our first walk with a little neighbor's. . . . The main concern then becomes not who I am but who I am considered to be, not what I think, but what others think of me."[32]

Nouwen proposes as a remedy the *forgiving* form of existence, which includes a willingness on my part to trust another person, to let him know exactly where I stand, to be willing to share with him my most intimate thoughts and dispositions. When two persons do this, friendship is born. In the fellowship of the weak, strength is born, to use Nouwen's insightful language. Indeed love "asks for a total *disarmament*. . . . Can we ever meet a fellow man without any protection? Reveal ourselves to him in our total vulnerability?"[33]

In short, true friendship demands mutual sharing, and many homosexual persons are generally not prepared to share their intimate feelings and thoughts with others because of the fear that Nouwen describes so well, the fear of being *taken*, and also because of the childhood-learned hostile detachment from a parental figure of the same sex that seems to recur in later adult relationships with persons of the same sex. Aardweg's theory that the homosexual person feels inferior to other men, precisely as *masculine*, would also explain why some homosexual men are loath to share on a deep level with another man, heterosexual or homosexual.

Whatever the explanation, homosexual men generally have difficulty in forming friendships with other men. This I know from many years of pastoral counseling. I am not able to say the same about friendships among female homosexuals, who in my experience do not seem to have the same degree of difficulty. Homosexual women tend to shun promiscuity in favor of a stable relationship, while homosexual men tend to avoid psychological intimacy even as they pursue physical intimacy in promiscuity. It is not surprising, then, that Courage discussions frequently come back to the topic of friendship. What can be done to help homosexual persons form virtuous friendships within a spiritual support group?

[32] "The Challenge to Love", in *Intimacy* (Notre Dame, Ind.: Fides Publishers, 1969), p. 26.
[33] *Ibid.*, p. 31.

Guidelines for virtuous friendships

First, one must be convinced that true human intimacy can be achieved without genital intercourse. Secondly, he should seek a wide variety of relationships at work, in his family, or among members of Courage. As he does so, he will come to realize that he is attracted more to certain persons than to others. The attraction may be nonsexual or sexual. If it is sexual, he should seek the guidance of his confessor to ascertain whether it is too great a risk for him. As he continues his various relationships, he will be able to discern further who are his real friends. One does not go looking for friends; one discovers them as one is pursuing goals. It dawns on one that this other person is a real friend with whom one can share celibately.

A little introspection will reveal to each one of us that our personhood is like a many-faceted jewel. One has friendships on different levels of personal history: friendships with professionals in one's field; friendships with certain members of one's own family that go beyond the ties of blood; friendships with former classmates at college, or with faculty at a university; friendships with students or patients, and so on. Again, one reveals different portions of one's self to different individuals. This is the richness of our mysterious personhood, and the homosexual person must be encouraged to come out of the prison of self-alienation to begin relating to persons in his own history who will be pleased to have him as a friend.

Homosexual persons often complain that they have not been able to find any friends, although they go to many social events. They form a relationship, and later drop it, complaining that the other person did not return their call or in some other way did not measure up to their expectations. Herein one detects passive aggressivity. Father Groeschel says it well: "If you think you should be loved just because you are you, you missed your vocation. You should have been God."[34]

Thirdly, in his quest for virtuous friendship the homosexual person should prefer those persons with whom he can truly share ideals. As he tries to live out an ascetical plan of life or to follow the Twelve Steps adapted from A.A. he will meet certain persons who are equally interested in developing their inner life. With such persons he can go to lectures and retreats. He feels that he belongs with these friends. As Father Groeschel quotes Morton Kelsey, the other person becomes a "companion on the inner way".[35] I have seen such friendships among some members of

---

[34] *The Courage to Be Chaste*, p. 39.

[35] *Ibid.*, p. 40. Groeschel refers to Kelsey's *Companions on the Inner Way* (New York: Crossroad, 1983).

Courage. It is recommended that one have more than one "spiritual" companion lest the relationship become *exclusive*, with the consequent danger of emotional overdependency. In real adult life each one of us has more than one intimate friend; we share with others on different levels of our personhood, unless one has neurotically withdrawn into oneself.

Fourthly, as St. Augustine says in his *Confessions*, "There is no true friendship unless You [God] weld it between souls that cleave together through that charity which is shed in our hearts by the Holy Ghost."[36] The Saint had arrived at this conclusion after experiencing the death of a young man to whom he as a youth had been closely attached. His grief was so shattering because he had loved someone mortal as if he were immortal. This leads him to exclaim: "O madness that knows not how to love men as men."[37] Augustine further enlarges upon the truth of God as the bond of human friendship when he writes: "Blessed is the man who loves Thee, O God, and his friends in Thee, and his enemy for Thee. For he alone loses no one who is dear to him, if we are all dear in God, who is never lost."[38]

Friendship and group support

The need for close friends is closely related to the need for group support. While one's relationship to all the members of the support group is not as intimate as that to a chosen few inside or outside the group, it is nevertheless important, inasmuch as the group makes the person realize that he can no longer go it alone and that one must constantly turn to a power greater than oneself for help. Out of group support flows a sense of belonging, of being interdependent, of giving to the group and receiving from the group. If all this sounds like an echo of A.A. principles, it is, but it should be kept in mind that the Twelve Steps have universal application. They can be used by anyone who is struggling to overcome a bad habit or a compulsion and who feels hopeless because of repeated failures. All Twelve Steps are concerned with a spiritual situation. One person may feel helpless with regard to alcohol, whereas another may feel helpless with regard to homosexual activity.

Finally, while excluding the genital expression of sexuality, which is proper to marriage, celibate friendships should have an appropriate expression of sexuality, whether this is between man and woman, man and man, or woman and woman. Each person must be aware of his own

[36] Bk. 4, ch. 4, Frank Sheed transl. (London: Sheed and Ward, 1949), p. 48.

[37] *Ibid.*, bk. 4, ch. 7.

[38] *Ibid.*, bk. 4, ch. 9. For further analysis of friendship in Augustine, see my thesis, *Moral Theology of the Confessions of St. Augustine* (Washington, D.C.: Catholic University Press, 1951), pp. 35–38.

motives and rigorously honest in avoiding any external expression of sexuality that could be construed as seductively erotic. Needless to say, he should also exercise control over fantasies that could lead to masturbation and the further temptation to change the very nature of the relationship one has with another person. In these questions the person should be completely honest with his confessor or spiritual director.

Experience of Courage members

In recounting and in a human way evaluating the diversified experiences of Courage members, the goals of Courage should be kept in mind. Unlike H.A. and similar groups, Courage does not try to change the sexual attractions of its members, although it does not discourage anyone who seeks to become heterosexual. Courage seeks to help its members free themselves from homosexual activity and fantasy in the pursuit of a full Christian life. In six years of directing New York Courage units I have observed that those who persevere in living out the goals of Courage and attend meetings regularly gain much spiritual benefit from the program. They are like the good seed in the Gospel parable. Others, however, come and go, and there is no human instrument to evaluate the effect the program has had on them. Still others have made it clear that they no longer accept the teaching of the Church concerning the obligatory nature of celibacy for homosexual persons and have left the group. That, of course, was the honest thing to do.

Since our New York groups are small (Manhattan group: 40; average weekly attendance: 15; one-year-old Westchester, N.Y., group: 9; average weekly attendance: 6), statistical analysis makes no sense. Instead I shall recount autobiographical responses: positive, mixed, and negative. I shall add observations from representatives of the Los Angeles and Boston groups. I shall have to be selective, but at the same time I shall try through these personal letters to give you a sampling of both positive and negative responses so that those considering the formation of a Courage unit can learn from the experience of the New York groups. I shall protect the anonymity of each person by using fictitious names, with one exception, that of my secretary and assistant, Vera, a homosexual woman, who has given me permission to use her name. Already she has given public witness on television to leading a celibate life.

Al, in his early fifties, came to Courage four years ago as a result of meeting someone at an A.A. meeting who was also a homosexual and who recommended Courage. Al has been sober for seven years, and chaste since he joined Courage, thanks to "these support groups and their loving concern". Al had been aware of his homosexual tendencies before puberty, cruising public places when he was only nine or ten years old. When the Protestant parents who adopted him as a little child discovered that he was homosexual when he was arrested in a movie theatre, they told him he was no good, just like his mother, who was a prostitute. Al at one time hated his adoptive father, but after his adoptive mother died he became reconciled with him. At the age of twenty he became a Catholic. Despite alcoholism and obsession with sex, Al retained a burning desire for spiritual fulfillment. Finally, after almost forty years Al was able, with the help of God, to turn his life around through A.A. and Courage. He is very active in his parish and attends Mass and receives Holy Communion almost daily.

Ben in his fifties also joined Courage four years ago at the suggestion of a confessor. The very first night he told me he was not sure that he would be back the following week. But he keeps coming. In his early days in the group he received a great deal of help from a young man who later went to a seminary. Ben loves to participate in the weekly discussions. To him they are "a great benefit". He adds: "I have come a long way, but there is so much more to go. The main thing is spiritual." Finally, he believes he could have gotten more out of Courage than he has, but he does not blame Courage for that.

Bill relates that "there is no doubt that Courage has helped me a great deal." Although he suffered disappointment when some members did not support him in a special project, he goes on to say: "I did, however, make two very good friends from having the group and for that I'm very grateful." Lest one think that Courage persons have no difficulties, Bill tells how hard it was for him after he had fallen to pull himself back together again, "but with God's grace I managed to. I found it difficult to return to the group when that would happen, but thank God I got over it." Bill has learned from experience that "if one wants to be celibate, one must completely break away from any active friends he has. It isn't always so easy to do that, . . . but after my experience I realized I had to. Even just little dinner parties with other gay couples only confused me. . . . It has been best for me to be friendly with people from the group or people who share the same morals as the group." During the past two and a half years of celibacy, Bill has avoided gay bars, discos, and alcohol.

In terms of worldly pleasures Bill has paid a dear price for celibacy. He wishes that the members, including himself, could share their experiences with one another "without becoming *judgmental*". He confesses he finds it difficult to open up in a group, and he hopes he will improve. He concludes that "the main reason one belongs to Courage should be because we love God and want to do His will."

Danny was a young loner who was afraid of intimacy, afraid it would lead to homosexual activity. At Courage he would say: "This is the first time I could have friends and be chaste." During his three years in Courage he became a dynamic leader. At the same time he received regular spiritual direction, learned to tone down his enthusiasms, and decided to study for the priesthood.[39]

Vera was the first woman member of Courage. She came to the group after reading Anne Buckley's column in *Catholic New York*, "The Word Is Courage" (March 28, 1982). Eighteen months later Anne Buckley wrote an account of Vera's conversion entitled "Vera's Choice". Vera had an eight-year struggle that she describes as a conversion experience. Previously, Vera had been involved with one woman for ten years. Vera observed one of the differences between the homosexual man and the woman: "It's the whole psychological makeup of a woman. I was with one person for ten years. It was an emotional attachment. It is harder to make that leap out of it. The men tend to be promiscuous, the women attached."

Vera remains a member of a lay community that truly prepared her for her work in Courage. In September 1983, Vera began to work with me two days a week in a newly-set-up office at St. Michael's rectory in Manhattan. Our immediate goal was to reach out to homosexual women with the hope of forming a women's Courage unit. By February 1984, Vera and I began such a group. But it never grew beyond four members, and when two left in May 1985, the group ceased to meet. Vera and I hope that with new inquiries we can revitalize the women's group. Meanwhile for three days a week we will continue to counsel both men and women at St. Michael's rectory.

Vera, who has dedicated herself to the work of Courage, is working for a Master's Degree in Counseling at Iona College. She is a living witness to the truth that a homosexual woman can live a chaste and happy Christian life.[40]

Before Courage ever had its first meeting it already owed a debt to Stuart.

---

[39] In *Lay Witness*, the monthly periodical of Catholics United for the Faith, a Courage member, writing under the pseudonym Dan Mettrie, says that "the homosexual stands in need of healing rather than catechesis. The pastoral care given him must help him fully realize his great worth. He must first see himself as a person redeemed by Christ. This form of care cannot be merely intellectual; it must touch the heart" (*A Homosexual Tells His Story*, Oct. 1985, pp. 6–8).

[40] In the Aug. 11, 1984, *National Catholic Register* Vera gives some valuable insights into the experience of Courage.

Stuart and I met in the Capuchin rectory on 31st Street in Manhattan in late February 1980 and began planning the future support group. His crucial organizational work from October 1980 to 1986 has helped to make Courage known throughout the country. During the first few years he was the center of communication for new members, inasmuch as I was in New York only on Friday night. Stuart joined such abilities to a deep prayer life, indeed a contemplative life in the world. Years before, he had undergone a conversion experience in San Francisco. Thereafter he took his spiritual life seriously, reading the works of St. Teresa of Avila and St. John of the Cross. He has also devoted many of his Saturdays to visiting homosexual persons in prison. To know Stuart, now in his middle years, is to realize that here is a homosexual person who holds a high position in the secular world and yet has time for a profound prayer-life and service to his fellow men.

Courage is not only for the single person, but also for the married experiencing homosexual difficulties. In the Westchester group there are several married men and one divorced woman. Middle-aged Mike has come to realize through prayer that he had to turn his life around. He saw homosexual acts as adultery toward his wife, and during the last three years he has attended meetings in both Manhattan and Westchester. He has come to respect his wife "for her sanctity". Since his conversion he has expressed his commitment to God through devotion to his family. He finds in Courage an avenue for discussing his problems and working them out in accordance with his Faith. He has been an inspiration for the three young members of the Westchester group.

Nancy, divorced and with one child, sought help in Courage after psychiatric therapy some years ago failed. The psychiatrist told her she was a homosexual, so "admit it, and go with it, and be one". To this she replied: "No, I'm Catholic. I can't be one. The whole time I lived it, I felt guilty." Then she added, "You can't do it on your own. You need someone there. It's the idea that you're not alone. You can't do anything about your past, but you can about the future."

Nancy and the other married members of the Westchester group desire anonymity, for they fear that their families may learn of their past. Most of the members of Courage in Manhattan as well fear any disclosure to friends or family. There are exceptions such as Vera and several men who were willing to appear on a Catholic TV program to explain what Courage was all about. For this reason the location and exact time of weekly meetings is given only to those who are in telephone communication with our New York office (212-421-0426).

Many other accounts of positive benefits from participation in Courage meetings could be detailed, but space will not allow it. In both Manhattan and Westchester we have members coming from over two hours' distance regularly and getting home very late at night. Suffice it to say that Courage has helped many to lead a chaste life in accord with the Gospel and the teaching of the Church. So far three former members of New York Courage are studying for the priesthood. But let us now consider what the founders of Los Angeles and Boston groups have found in Courage.

From Los Angeles Joe writes that Courage was what the founders of Dignity and other gay organizations were looking for in their beginnings. He sees Courage as the "type of support group needed for the person in homosexual conflict". He goes on to say that since some support groups tend to become political, they tend to neglect personal goals. Courage, on the other hand, has the format needed for spiritual growth. The goals are all spiritual. With proper spiritual guidance and group support one can fulfill the goals of Courage and adhere to the Plan of Life found in *How to Redirect Your Spiritual Life*.[41]

The unofficial founder of the Boston group, however, found the last half of 1986 very difficult. In the summer of 1985 he had come to New York to several Courage meetings, and he went back to Boston determined to get approval of the Archdiocese of Boston for a Courage unit. But since the Boston group has come into existence, there have been difficulties of structuring meetings, of individuals monopolizing the meetings, and so on. I wrote back to him, pointing out that such difficulties are found in the beginnings of most organizations. We had them at Courage in New York, and Joe reports that he and his little group of leaders have experienced similar difficulties in L.A. Joe sees in these difficulties a challenge to lead the group out of apathy. While discussing theological disagreements, one must lead the group to the fulfillment of spiritual goals.

The process of self-evaluation of Courage

It comes as no surprise, then, that there are problems in Courage meetings. In 1984–1985 a survey was made to ascertain the strengths and weaknesses of Courage. There was a good response from both members and former members. Among the weaknesses pointed out were the following: (1) failure by the lay officers of Courage to formulate and apply a policy

---

[41] This is the Daughters of St. Paul (Boston) pamphlet I wrote in 1979.

of follow-up of new members and failure to inquire into prolonged absences of veteran members; (2) some of the meetings tended to be too much like an academic discussion in which relatively few felt free to participate or there was not sufficient opportunity for sharing by the members; (3) many members are not willing to share of themselves; they come to listen almost passively; (4) the prayers prepared for the beginning and end of meetings were often too "heavy"; (5) lay leadership was considered too autocratic in choosing suitable liturgies and conducting meetings; and (6) the Spiritual Director, Father John Harvey, was considered too academic in presenting materials for each week's meeting.

The strong points of Courage meetings include: (1) lasting friendships formed, for some the first time they ever felt they could speak freely about themselves without rejection; (2) improved format of meetings and good liturgies; (3) stimulating outside speakers; and (4) sound spiritual direction by Fathers Harvey and Shelley.

Since the spring of 1985 the officers of Manhattan Courage and I have worked to respond to constructive criticism. We have striven to prepare materials that will stimulate greater participation; members have offered more attractive prayer selections; without accepting the allegation that previous leadership was too autocratic, the new group of officers has been able to maintain a welcoming atmosphere at the meetings. In taking my place for six months, Brother Stephen Olert has brought a new and fresh approach to both Westchester and Manhattan meetings, as I know from letters received from members. But there remains one area we need to address in the near future, and that is the quality of our follow-up.

In a letter written to me in mid-July 1986, an elderly and veteran member says: "Your dedication was obvious at all times. However, the quite equal handmaiden to a spiritual leadership is the management and administrative machinery which must be in place and operating sensibly before your work can produce the results you are after. This latter is, in my view, the basic flaw: there was no attempt by your lay leadership to follow up on men who came once or twice and then did not reappear; the newsletter was an "on and off" thing. . . . Some men were invited by phone (to anniversary meetings, days of recollection, etc.); others were not. Your part—the spiritual leadership—is well formulated, but Courage will never begin to fulfill its potential until reasonable administrative machinery is formulated."

We hope to profit by this criticism, and I must accept my share of responsibility for this weakness. The author also adverts to a difficulty not addressed by the comprehensive questionnaire of 1985. Some members, not convinced of the truth of Catholic teaching that all homosexual activity is immoral, "relentlessly brought the 'gay world' values into group relationships." My response to this observation is that, although that did happen, it did not have the approval of the majority of Courage members. I attribute this in part to a few persons who believe they can be members of both Dignity and Courage despite the fact that the principles of Courage are diametrically opposed to the positions advocated in Dignity newsletters over the years. It is very difficult to deal with persons who at meetings accept the stated goals of Courage but in private conversations with other members claim that celibacy is only optional for the homosexual person. We need to reaffirm *constantly* the teaching of the Church, while showing the *seductive* nature of dissenting opinions not supportive of the goals of Courage.

In comparing my initial experiences with Courage in Manhattan and Courage in Westchester County I noticed that from the very beginning of the latter group there was no difficulty getting people to share with one another. Perhaps part of the reason seems to be the comparative youth of the Westchester group. Of the nine members four are under thirty, and five under forty. Another reason may be that I have learned from working with the Manhattan group how to get a discussion moving. From the very beginning of the Westchester experience I have used the first three steps of A.A., and the group took to them. As Bob, one of the married members said, "I got an A.A. booklet and ran it parallel. It's the same principle. An alcoholic cannot have another drink, and I cannot have another sexual encounter." Then Bob quoted the Courage Handbook: "Members should be encouraged to translate the first three steps of the A.A. program into their own situaton. For example: I am a homosexual, and I am powerless over this condition. I believe that a Power greater than myself can restore me to sanity. I wish to surrender my will and my life to the care of an all loving God."

Are the Twelve Steps appropriate to Courage meetings?

From Bob's account one has to consider the question whether A.A. and the Twelve Steps are appropriate for Courage meetings. At the beginning of the Courage experience in 1980 I ran into resistance when I proposed the Twelve Steps as a framework within which to work. The first members insisted they were not alcoholic or compulsive. As time went on, however, I began to use the Twelve Steps. In April 1986 I invited an eighteen-year A.A. man who was also a newspaper columnist to attend one of our meetings. After the meeting he pointed out some of the differences between A.A. and Courage. A.A. stresses that it is a spiritual organization but not religious in the sense of a particular creed. At an A.A. meeting one is first of all an alcoholic, a person who has truly lost control over his drinking, and one is secondarily a follower of some religion or of no religion. At Courage one is first of all a Roman Catholic who hopes with God's grace to be sexually abstinent. Because Courage is primarily a religious organization it will not have as wide an appeal as A.A., which reaches out to persons of all creeds. I would add that the appeal of Courage will not be to all Roman Catholics, because many Catholic homosexual persons are not willing to accept celibacy. Perhaps the biggest difference between Courage and A.A. is that every alcoholic is compulsive, but not every homosexual is compulsive. A.A. Steps apply strictly to the compulsive homosexual, but they apply only analogously to the non-compulsive homosexual person.

Granting the differences between A.A. and Courage, I wish to stress the positive similarities. Both cultivate a sense of being helpless to fulfill God's law by one's unaided power. Both find their virtue by appealing to a power greater than oneself. Both believe that one must surrender oneself completely to God and learn to accept oneself as lovable just as one *is*. Both believe in making a fearless moral inventory periodically. Both believe in the necessity of some true friends to whom one reveals oneself. Both believe in the necessity of daily mental prayer. Both believe in being sponsors to those who need our affection. These similarities have been noted by many other spiritual support groups, including H.A., which, as I have shown, modifies them by adding several other steps.

From careful reflection upon the Twelve Steps I believe that any Christian can benefit from their practice. One must get beyond the particular problem to which the Twelve Steps are applied and discern the universal spiritual principles upon which they are based.[42]

There is one more value in having a Courage unit in a diocese. It is a sign of hope to many homosexual Catholics, and to their relatives, that the Catholic Church is not merely explaining the law of God but providing the kind of concrete help that people need to remain chaste. During two days every week I counsel homosexual persons who, for a variety of reasons, cannot attend Courage meetings. Although lacking group support, they have the benefit of both guidance and support in leading a Christian life. Again, because Courage has received national publicity for the last three years, we have received many letters whose principal theme is gratitude that Courage exists. The writers may not be able to set up a Courage unit where they are, but they are happy that Courage exists, and they can receive guidance through correspondence. But how much better it would be were each diocese to set up its own Courage unit!

[42] Philip St. Romain, *Becoming a New Person: Twelve Steps to Spiritual Growth* (Liguori, Mo.: Liguori Publications, 1984). The author adapts the steps to help persons overcome their "addiction" to selfishness and lead a life of healthy self-love.

Finally, with regard to the experience of Courage, people often ask: "Why are most of the men in your Manhattan group pushing or over 40?" From listening to these men and to Vera, as well as to other members of the women's group, I believe that young active homosexuals in New York City have not yet begun to reflect on the meaning of their lifestyle. In a sense they feel they have the best of two worlds: sexual indulgence and no responsibility for a spouse and children (although AIDS has put a damper on indiscriminate sexual indulgence). But at a certain point in their lives—often the late thirties—many homosexual persons begin to wonder about the meaning of their whole life. What have they contributed to life, to the community, to the Church, to the family? Scripturally speaking, like the prodigal son, they are ready for conversion, ready for a chaste lifestyle, and Courage becomes attractive. This explanation, however, does not apply to all younger men, as the Westchester experience indicates.

Without minimizing the value of group experience it must be said that not every one is fit for it or benefits from it. Members who manifest signs of excessive emotional dependency upon one individual in the group do not belong at meetings until they have received professional therapy, which we hope will help them to behave in a more mature fashion. This may be a painful decision for the president of the group, but the spiritual director should urge him to be firm for the good order and peace of the group.

Present status of Courage units in the United States

During the past three years Courage in New York has received many inquiries from other dioceses who are considering a spiritual support group. At this time Boston, Los Angeles, and St. Louis have functioning groups, while La Crosse, Wisconsin, Washington, D.C., and San Diego are in the process of forming them. Philadelphia has revitalized its Courage unit after a two-year lapse. In Canada, Toronto has a new and functioning group, and a new unit is planned in Vancouver, B.C.

5. SPECIFIC ELEMENTS OF A SPIRITUAL PLAN OF LIFE FOR CATHOLIC HOMOSEXUALS

While spiritual group support is all-important, it is not enough; in addition, each member should develop for himself a spiritual plan of life in conjunction with his spiritual director and the director of the Courage unit. Indeed many who are not in any support system have developed such a plan of life. The content of such a plan of life I have outlined in previous writings, and most recently in two pamphlets: "Pastoral Care and the Homosexual" (1979) and "A Spiritual Plan to Redirect One's Life" (1979).[43]

In Christianity, spiritual plans of life are as common as monastic codes of living, but with this difference. The plan of life is meant to be tailored to the individual person. The one herein described makes a series of suggestions for homosexual persons, most of which would also apply to heterosexuals. The general purpose of a plan of life is to give direction to one's life within the context of Christian Faith. A plan of life is not a series of external activities to fill one's day or week, not a rule of thumb to happiness, but a *radical rethinking* of an inadequate view of life, with the profound resolution to redirect the will in the pursuit of God. It leads to the gradual formation of systematic practices designed to help the homosexual fulfill these thought-out objectives. In more recent years a great help in working out these objectives has been the practice of journal keeping. It takes real discipline to set down regularly in writing the state of one's soul. On the basis, then, of prayerful reflection and with the help of a spiritual director the homosexual person develops his plan of life.

As I have already said, the most important element in the plan of life is meditation, which is best described as the prayer of the heart. No matter how weak a person thinks he is, he still must learn how to engage in this type of prayer. As I have already mentioned, St. Francis de Sales gives explicit instructions on the art of prayer in his *Introduction to the Devout Life*. But many contemporary writers can help the beginner to pray. Each generation has its favorites. The important point is to begin now, not merely talk about it. Usually the beginner uses Holy Scripture, choosing those books that have a particular attraction for him.

The following items are given by way of example as elements in a plan of life. They can be changed for other elements except for meditation:

> Morning prayer with at least fifteen minutes of meditation
> Mass as often as possible during the week
> Examination of conscience at least once a day
> Ten minutes of spiritual reading every day
> Carefully chosen regular confessor
> Some form of devotion to the Virgin Mary and to the saints
> Some work of charity to one's neighbor

[43] "Pastoral Care", Knights of Columbus, no. 85, Catholic Information Service, P.O. Box 1971, New Haven, CT 06521—with four-page bibliography; "Spiritual Plan", Daughters of St. Paul, 50 St. Paul's Ave., Boston, MA 02130.

I should like to comment briefly on making a specific contribution of time, for example, on one's free day, to the service of the poor, handicapped, or aged. This work of love helps the homosexual person to give *meaning* to his life. It takes him out of the world of fantasy. Instead of draining his vitality in bitter complaints about society's lack of acceptance of homosexuals, he learns to go out of himself to care for others. I have in mind one homosexual man who for years has spent his free day in the service of the poor. In New York City many homosexuals are giving of their free time to visit the sick, particularly those with AIDS.

This work of service to the Lord gives one a sense of achievement and of self-acceptance that everyone needs. It really does not matter what kind of work one does. Whether visiting the sick or ministering to the other members of Courage by maintaining a system of communication with all the members as a work of love, all such activities make one feel that he belongs to the Church, and to a community of faith.

Morning prayer should include some kind of general direction of all the day's actions to God and a brief exercise of preparing the day. As the shrewd businessman prepares his day, so also the person desirous of the love of God must make an effort to foresee the important events of the coming day. He will think seriously of the contingencies that may occur, of the places where he may be required to go, and the like. In this way, with the help of God he will be able to face the difficulties and dangerous occasions that otherwise might surprise and overwhelm him. By planning his strategy to overcome or circumvent difficulties, he will do more than anticipate them. For example, during his noon–hour break, he will attend Mass nearby instead of loitering around the park that has been his downfall many times. Experience has proven this exercise of preparation to be helpful in guiding homosexual persons beset with a habitual or even compulsive tendency to homosexual acts.

Like the recovering alcoholic, the homosexual person must take one day at a time and make it a day of activity combined with trust in the grace of God: "I am a homosexual, and I am powerless over this condition. But the Lord can get me through it." This sense of our own helplessness should be part of every morning prayer. If one is under great pressures and cannot find time for an extended period of prayer, he can at least turn the movements of his heart to God in brief aspirations, says St. Francis de Sales. Yet in the normal day time should be found for prayer.

The examination of conscience is adapted to the homosexual propensity for introspection. It is directed, not to a sterile self-examination of maladjustment, but to an analysis of personal motivation in the practice of Christian virtue. Because of the human tendency to self-deception, this is a difficult exercise. St. Augustine is on target when he writes, "Man is a great deep, O Lord. You number his very hairs and they are not lost in your sight, but the hairs of his head are easier to number than his affections and the movements of his heart."[44] In another place Augustine says, "If by an abyss we understand a depth profound, is not man's heart an abyss? Man may speak, may be seen by the operation of his members, may be heard speaking, but whose thought is penetrated? Whose heart is seen into?. . . Do you not believe there is in man a depth so deep as to be hidden in him in whom it is?" (Ennaratio in Psalmum XLI, sect. 13, in Migne, vol. 36, col. 475).

St. Francis de Sales sees the basic motive for the examen as the desire to please Christ. One examines one's conscience because one desires to be free of sin only to be more pleasing to the Savior. One is not concerned with a sterile arithmetic of exact faults committed, but with the inner motivation of the faults, and with the affections of the heart vis à vis the person's determination to love God. The question one asks daily is: "How stands my heart before God?"

6. CONTROVERSY CONCERNING THE KINDS OF FRIENDSHIPS THE HOMOSEXUAL PERSON NEEDS

It is agreed that the homosexual person should develop chaste friendships with at least a few persons. This is part of his spiritual plan of life. It is also one of the goals of Courage: "To be mindful of the truth that chaste friendships are not only possible but necessary in celibate Christian life and to encourage one another in forming and sustaining them." In practice, some who have spent many years of their life holding everyone at a distance find difficulty learning how to cultivate chaste friendship and intimacy with a few persons. Nevertheless, the spiritual director should insist that the homosexual not become a loner, but instead find someone with whom he can relate, someone to whom he can turn whenever moods of loneliness, anger, and moral despair overwhelm him. If the spiritual director can send the person to a Courage unit, the person will have a better chance of finding friends. But controversy arises as soon as you ask whether the first friends such a person makes should be of one's own sex or the other sex.

a. *Moberly's view*: As one can discern from her theory concerning the etiology of homosexuality, the individual should first cultivate friendships with members of his own sex in order to compensate for same-sex

---

[44] *Confessions*, Bk. 4, ch. 14, p. 57, Sheed transl.

developmental deficits, to become more masculine or feminine; then, having fulfilled one's true homosexual needs, one can be heterosexual and find friends of the other sex, probably marrying as the desire for heterosexual intimacy leads one to the right person.

b. *Aardweg's view*: Linking the origin of homosexuality with *feeling inferior as a masculine person*, Aardweg sees the cultivation of friends of both sexes as a means of building self-confidence and overcoming feelings of inferiority and of self-pity. The dangers he sees in Moberly's position are several. Since very often one's pattern of self-pity is addictive, one may relapse into a steady-lover relationship, giving up on celibacy and a spiritual plan of life. If one remains chaste but does not make the effort to relate to the other sex, he may continue to form immature and dependent relationships with persons of his own sex. Same-sex intimate relationships become a kind of crutch for him.

c. *Harvey's view*: Since we do not have certitude concerning the origins of homosexuality, however much one may favor Moberly's or Aardweg's understanding of the relationship of the homosexual condition to friendship, we should take an eclectic attitude in helping persons to cultivate friendships. In a given instance, Moberly's theory seems worthy of pursuit, because the individual resonates well with it and believes it is the best approach for him. In another person's situation, feelings of self-pity are most marked, and he may find the anti-complaining therapy of Aardweg very helpful. In still another person, who agrees with Colin Cook's analysis of homosexuality as part of man's sinful nature, his faith that God intends him to be heterosexual may provide the motivation to seek to change. While admitting that both Moberly and Aardweg have contributed to our understanding of our sinful nature, Cook and others will seek to develop for the homosexual person a truly spiritual plan of life. Cook would have the person who has given up a homosexual lifestyle learn how to associate with persons of the other sex, even if at the beginning he feels no attraction to them. Cook believes that for many it will eventually come.

If it is agreed, moreover, by all parties to this controversy that the aim of therapy is the *healing* of the person of the homosexual and if it is the common experience that good friendships are part of the healing process, then the question whether one begins with same-sex friends or other-sex friends becomes secondary, albeit still important. If one follows Moberly's theory, one should bear in mind the dangers that Aardweg points out, making due allowance for them and taking effective means to counteract them.

Summary of the one-to-one approach to the homosexual person

To move from the realm of theory to pastoral practice, one can sum up the three principal elements of the one-to-one approach to the homosexual person thus: (1) Cultivation of a habit of prayer. This is indispensable. (2) Faithfully living out a self-constructed plan of life, like that of Courage or of H.A. This involves asceticism and self-discipline, something he had previously lacked. With the help of grace one no longer *drifts* from day to day, but regains *control* over his life. (3) Cultivation of virtuous friendships. This can be done more easily within a spiritual support group, but if a group is not available, one must find at least one person to whom one reveals himself completely. Oftentimes in places where no spiritual support group exists, the spiritual counselor or director becomes the homosexual person's best friend, but other friends must also be cultivated.

Thirty years ago when I was not aware of the value of group spiritual support, I became one homosexual's best friend as well as counselor, and I have had the joy of witnessing his life of virtue and dedication to the aged. Often in public conferences on the care of the homosexual person I am asked whether I use any special techniques in my counseling. I reply that I believe that I should treat homosexual persons like any other human person with a difficulty. I respond to the person, and the more I respond to the person, the more I forget he is homosexual. That is the paradox. Furthermore, I treat homosexuals as my equals, sharing their difficulties. I fully agree with the advice Bishop Mugavero gave to homosexual men and women in a pastoral letter on human sexuality, following the Vatican's *Declaration on Certain Questions concerning Sexual Ethics*. "We urge homosexual men and women to avoid identifying their personhood with their sexual orientation. They are so much more as persons than this single aspect of their personality. That richness must not be lost."[45]

7. SOME LINES OF CONVERGENCE IN PASTORAL PROGRAMS, AND THEIR COMMON DEBT TO A.A.

In this lengthy chapter I have treated both Catholic and Protestant support groups, and I have indicated in different places the influence A.A. has had on both Catholic and Protestant support groups, between whom there

[45] Diocese of Brooklyn, pastoral letter on human sexuality, Feb. 1, 1976. The letter concludes: "We respect you in your struggle."

is increasing communication and cooperation. We need to continue integrating insights from psychology, such as those of Aardweg and Moberly into our spiritual and biblical theologies. Work like that of Colin Cook needs to be nourished by the great spiritual writers of the Church, such as St. Francis de Sales, Cardinal Newman, and St. Augustine. The process of integrating new insights in both psychology and theology has only begun. In the past, pastoral theology did little to make use of the deep spirituality inherent in the doctrines of creation and redemption to fashion an approach to the homosexual person as a redeemed child of God and as heterosexual in nature. Those insights, in turn, need to use the research of both Moberly and Aardweg in working out a concrete pastoral program.

8. DIGNITY AS AN ORGANIZATION OF CATHOLICS, BUT NOT A CATHOLIC ORGANIZATION

Earlier in this chapter I outlined the pastoral problem facing American bishops with Dignity chapters in their dioceses (and there are over a hundred). Now I intend to examine the stated purposes of Dignity, together with some of its newsletters, activities, and writings supporting this movement. In April 1976 the *National Catholic Reporter* referred to Dignity as a fishbone lodged in the throat of the Catholic Church in America: "The institution can't swallow it; and it just won't go away."[46] It is a serious question that I shall endeavor to treat fairly.

In a 1985 statement of Dignity International, Inc., the organization is described as "an opportunity to express one's faith within a community, an affirmation of one's sexual orientation, a resource for education within the gay/lesbian community and the Church, a celebration of God's love for all persons. As Dignity we believe that gay men and lesbian women can express their sexuality in a manner consonant with Christ's teaching. We believe further that all sexuality should be exercised in an ethically responsible and unselfish way."[47]

The statement also says: "Dignity is an organization of gay and lesbian Catholics and their friends who believe that through Baptism we all share in the death and resurrection of Christ. As a result, we have an inherent dignity that is preserved and strengthened through the sacramental life of the Church, a life we rightfully share with all Catholics."

In that statement of Dignity one may note that the expression of

[46] Richard Rashke, "Dignity 'Like a Fishbone Lodged in Church's Throat' ", *National Catholic Reporter*, Kansas City, Mo., April 9, 1976, p. 28.

[47] Dignity, Inc., Washington, D.C. This is the national headquarters. Dignity/New York, in a single page handout, adds that it also "accepts heterosexuals who are concerned enough to aid lesbian and gay people in correcting social and religious prejudices".

sexuality can be "consonant with Christ's teaching". But nowhere is this consonance defined. Significantly omitted is any mention of Church teaching on sexuality. The reference to the sacramental life of the Church that they "rightfully share with all Catholics" seems like a veiled rebuke of the accepted theological teaching that the person who freely engages in homosexuality activity may not receive the Holy Eucharist unless he has first sought forgiveness in the sacrament of Penance or, where no priest is available, has made an act of perfect contrition.

It is not, however, from a study of Dignity's stated purposes, which are couched in vague language, that one can discern the true nature of Dignity; rather, this is found in the national office's monthly publication called *Dignity* and in the publications of the various local chapters throughout the United States. Since I am more familiar with the publication of the New York chapter, *Calendar*, I shall present a sample of its teachings over the past several years. Others have made studies of Dignity, most notably Father Enrique T. Rueda in *The Homosexual Network*, to which we have already referred.[48] I shall begin with an article from *Calendar*, June 1984, entitled "What Is Dignity All About?"

One person said that Dignity should be the prophetic voice of the Church. One of the first things a "gay Christian" should do is to reconcile his religious convictions with his homosexuality. "In doing that, the homosexual comes to realize that the 'answers' of society and the Church, with regard to sexuality, are not adequate, and, in fact, false. To use a hackneyed phrase—Gay is good—despite what society and the Church say. However, once realizing that society and the Church were in error on the question of sexuality, this propels the gay Christian to go one step further. If society and the Church were wrong on sexuality, could they also be wrong in other ways and concerning other issues, including the most fundamental of these—the meaning of life, of the human person, of Christianity itself?" He goes on to say that Dignity can be the place for the development of a new theology.

This respondent denies the truth of the Church's teaching and wonders whether one can accept her teaching on more fundamental issues of Christianity. Another writer in the same issue, John Rash, asks whether Dignity could find ways of "improving the Church's sexual teaching".[49] Then he submits a few ideas about sexual ethics, examining what he calls

---

[48] See also John F. Russell, J.D., "Hate the Sin, But Love the Sinner. Sin? What Sin?" *Linacre Quarterly*, Aug. 1976, pp. 179–195, at 189–195. Rueda gives over a hundred references to activities of Dignity on the national level and on the local chapter levels. See Indices, particularly pp. 637–639, in his book. There are organizations similar to Dignity in their rejection of Church teaching in Great Britain (Quest), in Australia (Acceptance), and in New Zealand (Accent).

[49] "All's Fair in Love and War?" p. 2.

the "economics" of sex. Adverting to the fact that many homosexual persons have not learned how to love themselves properly, he says: "Gay men, when they go into a bar or other gay meeting place (perhaps the Dignity social after Mass) *in the hope of finding a companion for the night* [italics added] or whatever range of time seems suitable to them, treat sex as an economic resource in the sense that they treat it as a scarce commodity for which they must compete." As the author rambles on, he invokes no appropriate moral principle. He describes the promiscuous dating game as part of the mating behavior of the species in which so many shy homosexual persons lose out to the more enterprising: ". . . having made the contact [for sex], someone else may come along and simply attempt to appropriate for himself all one's hard work, and one winds up going home alone."

The value of this article is that it reveals not only the way the author thinks, but the way the persons he describes feel and act. He accurately adds that "loneliness, alcoholism, and suicide are frequent companions in the gay community, the last two frequently arising from the former." The only suggestion that could be called pragmatically "moral" is that the more successful homosexual lovers should not steal prospects from the lonely. Referring to the fear of AIDS, he believes that "some lonely men are so desperate for a little love and affection that they will tumble into bed with anyone who says yea, and I suspect that not a few AIDS cases have resulted from such encounters." In short, the author reveals volumes about the attitudes of New York/Dignity, without showing us how to "improve" the Church's teaching.

The next document is from the national office (May 1985). It is a series of statements by members of *The Task Force on Sexual Ethics* established by Dignity's House of Delegates at Seattle in August 1983. The aim of the Task Force is to present a statement to the Twentieth Anniversary Convention in 1989. A priest member asks to whom the document is being addressed. That will determine the issues, the language, and the tone. Then he reveals how he feels about the Magisterium: "To continue efforts at dialogue with the Magisterium, at this time, seems futile." He goes on to say that the hierarchy ignores evidence, repeats its previous position, and imposes silence. He suggests instead that gay and lesbian Christians begin their adult role of living according to an informed conscience: "The individual conscience remains the ultimate authority under God." In his personal life he has been beset with feelings of guilt because of Church teaching, so he hopes the Task Force will free the members to form their own consciences in their daily lives. "Waiting for the hierarchy to endorse genitality in order to feel right about it reveals an interior slavishness which stifles spiritual growth."

This is really a position contrary to Catholicism: the ultimate authority is personal conscience, with the Magisterium being simply advisory to conscience. Obedience to the pope and bishops throughout the world stifles spiritual growth. These are the views of a priest in Dignity. It does not take much imagination to understand how many lay members of Dignity are influenced by him and by hundreds of other priests of like convictions.

A woman religious of the Task Force agrees with the priest just mentioned when she writes that a major responsibility is to address "the issue of the formation of conscience, the development of one's *own* code of sexual ethics, moral education for adults, and methods for adult decision making" (italics added). Another priest-theologian believes that "the Church has often neglected its proper vocation as moral prophet to society in favor of defining moral rules for its members." Instead of official declarations, the Church should join Dignity in a process of discernment and discovery. A woman member hopes that the Task Force will give Dignity the opportunity to evaluate its code of sexual behavior *independent* of the Magisterium, "to give our brothers and sisters an instrument that hopefully will be useful in the formation of their individual consciences".

While in agreement with the previous positions, the longest statement of a Task-Force member shows uncertainty as to how Dignity comes to the positions already described. "All of us believe that we can be Christian, and all of us believe that we can express our sexuality at the same time. But have we really combined the two ideas in such a way as to make it clear to ourselves what that means as I interrelate with the many people I meet. . . ? There are so many people within our community who sadly, firmly believe that what they are doing in their sexual interactions is wrong and sinful because the Church has told them so. And when they come to a Dignity gathering they are seeking answers, comfort, and some kind of assurance that they are good people. But, seldom have I heard anyone give them *a clear concept of how we believe this*" (italics added). At meetings when questions concerning sexual acts get down to specific situations, the answer is often given, "I can't tell you what's right or wrong for you. You have to determine that for yourself."

While resisting the authority of the Church, the above writer hopes that Dignity will come up with a rationale in favor of genital activity that can be reconciled with the teaching of Christ. He is not satisfied with individual conscience alone, as is clear from his dissatisfaction with the answer "I can't tell you what's right or wrong for you." Tragically, he separates the Church from Christ, while he does not realize that Scripture and divine Tradition are the source of the Church's teaching on human sexuality.

Unfortunately, he has not examined the reasons for the Church's position, assuming it to be in error. From speaking to Courage members who used to be members of Dignity I learned that an important difference between the two groups is that one receives direction at Courage meetings. By sharp contrast, Father Robert Carter, S.J., from the Dignity/New York chapter, said in the Gay Synagogue that "Dignity, as such, takes no moral position on the morality of homosexual activity."[50]

Commenting on the annual Gay Pride march in New York City, Joe Akus, a Dignity member, writes that Dignity can help the gay community realize its potential for uniting gays and lesbians through depth, care, healing, honesty, commitment, self-sacrifice, and self-effacement. He realizes that these are ideals difficult to achieve. But they can be achieved through the Spirit who brings them together and forms them into something new, the *koinonia*, the fellowship. He asks Dignity members to accept the challenge of becoming holy and to be willing to suffer for these ideals in the presence of the gay world and of the rest of the world. They are asked to follow Christ and to die to themselves for the sake of others. This is a beautiful statement of ideals, but it makes no mention of the need for celibacy or for the Church. Yet I believe that if one were to take these ideals seriously, he would end up living a life of sexual abstinence within the Church.[51]

From the previous statements found in Dignity newsletters it is clear that Dignity has not only rejected Church teaching but intends to develop its own ethical position. This was proclaimed by Mary Hunt, the keynote speaker at the 1985 National Convention. Dignity members are called "to lead healthy and holy lives as sexually active gays and lesbians. That struggle sends shivers down the spineless episcopacy. It threatens to replace rigid hierarchical authority with communal sharing of responsibility —responsibility to love our brothers and sisters."[52]

Since Dignity does not disapprove of homosexual activity, it will see the crisis created by AIDS as demanding the practice of "safe" sex. Thus, J. Champagne writes that Dignity/New York members should seek detailed information concerning healthy sex practices published by Gay Men's Health Crisis (GMHC). Guidelines are concerned with the avoidance of any exchange of body fluids and with ways of obtaining erotic and carnal pleasure with little risk. The point made is that not even the fear of

[50] In the Gay Synagogue in Greenwich Village a symposium was held on Executive Order 50 on the last Friday of July 1984. Father Carter spoke as a representative of Dignity/New York.

[51] *Calendar*, June 1985, p. 4.

[52] *Calendar*, Oct. 1985, p. 1. Reported by Ken Goldstein. The same issue exhorts members to "play safe. Follow safe sex guidelines."

this dread disease has caused many Dignity members to reflect on the immorality of all homosexual activity. It is a hedonistic approach that the writer attempts to canonize when he concludes, "But for those who choose to continue to lead a sexually active life, safe sex is a low-risk alternative to unrestricted behavior. And it might even be considered a Christ-like activity, an opportunity to nurture and guard the life of another, and to care for the Christ in oneself."[53]

In 1982 Father Rueda referred to the practice of *commitment* expressed in religious ritual, for homosexual couples. He gives the Dignity/New York statement, together with samples of "liturgies", commenting that these are becoming institutionalized in America.[54] Apparently, Dignity/New York has had a hard time making decisions on the implementation of its statement, as John Rash writes in *Calendar*. He recounts that he receives about twelve calls per month for such ceremonies and that 90% are from women. He believes that policies should be worked out to satisfy the need of so many women and men. Considering the large number of men in Dignity/New York, I think the adjective "many" refers to women.[55] This tells us a great deal about the difference between male and female homosexuals. Female homosexuals tend far more than males toward some form of stable relationship. In any case, it also reveals that Dignity members, seeking to legitimize their relationship, want the blessings of religion, however rebellious they may be toward the Church.

I believe I have provided sufficient evidence—as does Rueda in his *Homosexual Network* (1982)—to state that Dignity has established itself within the Church with support of clergy, religious, and laity, but against the teaching of the Church. It uses every means in its power to undermine that teaching on homosexual activity.[56] It does not hesitate to distort the message of Courage, which in its words, "preaches essentially 'celibacy' or 'damnation' to those gay men and lesbians who are privately interviewed and found guilty enough about their sexuality to be admitted within its closed-door meetings".[57] I shall add, however, the testimonial evidence of Brother Joe who belonged to Dignity for a number of years.

While in college Joe learned about Dignity through a priest who was

[53] *Calendar*, Feb. 1986, pp. 1–2. Each *Calendar* contains a fine-print note that "the views expressed in *Calendar* are not necessarily those of Dignity/New York, Inc." Yet we may have reasonable certitude that such views are typical of Dignity/New York when so many of their articles are written by its leaders.

[54] *The Homosexual Network*, appendix V, pp. 571–578.

[55] "Commitment Ceremonies", Feb. 1986, pp. 1–2.

[56] *The Task Force on Sexual Ethics* has issued a questionnaire to Dignity members to get their opinions on genitality and spirituality and related matters, with the idea that sexual morality will be determined by the vote of the community.

[57] John Rash, *Calendar*, May 1986, p. 3.

asked to say Mass at the newly formed chapter in Boston. Dignity seemed to Joe like an answer to a prayer. Dignity would provide an alternative to the one-night stands and promiscuity to which he was at times tempted. Within the religious and social activities of Dignity, Joe looked for a more stable and Christ-centered commitment. He established a Dignity chapter at the college where he was a student. He came to believe that his homo-sexuality was a gift from God. Moving to San Francisco, he immersed himself in the work of the Dignity chapter there. At a shared prayer meeting he met Tom, and within six months they had moved in together. Dignity had given him just what he wanted. Tom had helped him to establish a committed and consistent prayer life. Together they would show others that a committed Christian relationship was possible.

Instead, after a year and a half of this, Joe began to have doubts. Why did he feel so empty after Tom and he had been together physically? "I had a distant sense that somehow God was expecting something more of my life." In his prayer he began to sense that Christ was calling him to give up everything. He resisted the call and became difficult to live with. Finally, at the suggestion of Tom he went home to pray about his future. During the few months before he left, however, he became disillusioned with Dignity:

> What I saw was that, instead of finding Dignity a challenge to the gay subculture, more and more people were coming to it, wanting to rubberstamp their lifestyle, whatever it was. I had hoped it would challenge the promis-cuous mentality that prevailed, particularly among gay men. Instead I found that many of the priests who came to minister to us were becoming romantically involved with members; many had left their vocations. In addition, there were many ex-religious (priests, brothers, nuns) who were members. Some of them advocated having more than one lover. . . . This was deeply disturbing to me. It was this mentality, along with my questioning of my sexual relationship with Tom, which led me to seriously question whether God indeed approved of such relationships.[58]

After a conversion experience at home he gave up both Tom and Dignity. He realized in the process of conversion that Dignity had brought him to "a self-acceptance based on a false identity". Taking this step was not easy. He lost all his former friends, although now he has the support of H.A. and a Baltimore spiritual support group known as Regeneration. Through prayer he discovered his true identity as a child and man of God. He has worked that reality into his life through a new relationship with his earthly father. No longer does he limit his self-acceptance and identity to his sexuality.

[58] "Dignity Regenerated", Regeneration News, P.O. Box 10574, Baltimore, MD 21285, pp. 5–7.

9. NEW WAYS MINISTRY

Already in 1982 Father Enrique Rueda had documented the close inter-relationships among Catholic pro-homosexual organizations, as well as their cooperation with secular homosexual organizations. This is why he calls his book *The Homosexual Network*. Among the closest of networks is that between Dignity and New Ways Ministry (NWM). This latter was founded in 1977 at Mt. Rainier, Maryland, by Father Robert Nugent, a Salvatorian priest, and Sister Jeannine Gramick, S.S.N.D. The organization specializes "in publishing pro-homosexual literature with a Catholic flavor, lobbying for pro-homosexual legislation, holding educational and religious meetings for homosexuals and their sympathizers, and generally promoting the movement's ideology. One of the group's most important activities is serving as a center for a very extensive network of homosexual and pro-homosexual activists within the Church. . . ."[59]

NWM describes itself as "an organization founded in 1977 to serve as a bridge between gay and nongay groups, . . . which has provided educational programs, resources, and consultation services for a wide variety of dioceses, seminaries, colleges, religious orders, universities, peace and justice groups, and has published articles from Holland and England."[60]

In his analysis of NWM, Rueda notes that neither its leaders nor its board members, staff members, and interns are on record as accepting the official teaching of the Church that homosexual actions are always objectively evil. In fact, Rueda could not find any statements from speakers at its workshops condemning or attacking any homosexual practices. This has also been my experience. As with Dignity, the nature of NWM is apparent to anyone reading its materials or observing its networking with Dignity. Its quarterly newsletter, *Bondings*, gives the reader insight into the purpose of NWM. For example, in *Bondings*, Father Nugent shows how NWM regards the magisterial teaching on homosexual activity by distinguishing three theological positions on homosexuality.

The first position is the official teaching that homosexual activity is intrinsically evil. The second is a mediating position that views homo-sexual actions, not as objectively wrong, but as a deviation from the norm. While not measuring up to the norm, these acts can be tolerated for the overall good of the parties concerned. The third is the relational position, which finds the value of sexual acts, not in genital activity per se, but in the quality of the relationships thereby established. Logically, this

[59] Rueda, *The Homosexual Network*, p. 354.
[60] Press release, NWM, April 9, 1981; quoted by Rueda, *op. cit.*, p. 354.

view leads to the acceptance of homosexual relationships as ethical if their quality is good.[61]

As Rueda points out, presenting three alternative positions is

> a clever way of opening the door to the acceptance of the morality of homosexual actions, since according to traditional Catholic moral teaching on probabilism, when there is disagreement among experts concerning the morality of a certain action, people are free to choose any "probable" opinion. The fact that the principle of probabilism does not apply in this case, because the second and third opinions are not technically probable, is never mentioned. In fact, no opinion contrary to what the pope and the bishops teach explicitly can be presented as "probable".[62]

By attempting to use probabilism, Nugent effectively nullifies the clear teaching of the Church by reducing it to an opinion, however venerable, that one is free to follow or to disregard. It places opinions opposed to official teaching on the same level as the official teaching. In effect, it allows homosexuals who engage in homosexual activity to remain in good conscience, provided it is a steady, loving relationship. NWM again attempts to use the principle of probabilism in its critique of Archbishop John Quinn's pastoral, which clearly condemns homosexual activity. New Ways was disappointed that the pastoral gave celibacy as the *only* option for homosexual persons when there are "others who are aware of a solidly probable opinion among American Catholic moralists that 'homosexual expression in the context of a faithful, stable relationship tending toward permanency is not beyond their moral reach.' "[63] The use of the term "solidly probable" for opinions opposed to the Church's position is false and misleading.

The response of NWM to Archbishop Quinn's pastoral indicates that New Ways holds that homosexual acts can be morally correct if they are loving and stable, and that NWM must continue to "educate" the Church so that she will come to see that a homosexual lifestyle can be morally acceptable.[64]

Rueda details other incidents showing that NWM was not really in agreement with official Church teaching, including a letter that Archbishop Hickey of Washington, D.C., wrote to all Catholic bishops in the U.S.A. as well as to religious personnel in the Washington area. In this letter he indicated that in his judgment NWM was in direct conflict with Church teaching: "I must inform you that I found their [NWM's] position

[61] *Bondings*, Winter 1980–1981, p. 12.

[62] *The Homosexual Network*, p. 333.

[63] *Bay Area Reporter*, "Catholic Gay Group Calls Quinn's pastoral on homosexuality 'Inadequate' " (San Francisco, June 19, 1980; quoted in *The Homosexual Network*, pp. 333–334).

[64] *The Homosexual Network*, p. 357.

ambiguous and unclear with regard to the morality of homosexual activity. While presenting the teaching of the Church as contained in the *Declaration on Sexual Ethics* of the Sacred Congregation for the Doctrine of the Faith (1975), they present as viable other options which hold that it is morally permissible for homosexuals to live together in a sexually active, stable relationship."[65]

That fall (1981), NWM held its symposium in Washington, D.C., with 180 attending, including a number of major superiors of women's and men's religious orders, diocesan representatives, and vocation directors. In the following years Archbishop Hickey took steps to have both Father Nugent and Sister Jeannine Gramick removed from their leadership roles in NWM. As the result of this intervention, the Sacred Congregation for Religious and Secular Institutes ordered both Father Nugent and Sister Jeannine to relinquish their positions as coordinators of NWM and to leave the Archdiocese of Washington. The Sacred Congregation worked through the major superiors of each in the summer of 1984. Archbishop Hickey felt it was his responsibility to take such action. Had he allowed NWM to continue as it was, his silence could have been interpreted as passive encouragement.[66] Still, NWM continues under lay leadership.

Indeed during the fall of 1985 and the winter and spring of 1986, NWM organized three symposia in Lanham, Maryland, San Francisco, and St. Louis. A large number of religious and priests attended these symposia. In the Lanham symposium (Nov. 8–10) more than three dozen Catholic organizations and religious orders planned a drive to raise publicly the issue of homosexual priests and nuns despite strong objections from Archbishop Hickey, who had asked that the conference not be held. Spokesmen for the conference said that the issue of the increasing numbers of acknowledged homosexuals entering communities of priests, nuns, and brothers must be addressed.[67]

While NWM in its symposium at Lanham claims that it agrees with official Catholic teaching, it is difficult to understand its opposition to Archbishop Hickey. Meanwhile, Father Nugent and Sister Jeannine continue to hold seminars for the Catholic Coalition for Gay Civil Rights, often in Protestant facilities.[68]

From a perusal of *Bondings* from 1984 to 1986 it is clear that NWM

---

[65] "To the Priests, Deacons, and to the Communities of Religious Women and Men in the Archdiocese of Washington", Oct. 27, 1981. Quoted by Rueda in *The Homosexual Network*, p. 359.

[66] *Homosexual Network*, p. 362. The letter from the Sacred Congregation was dated July 14, 1984.

[67] *Bondings*, Spring-Summer, 1986.

[68] Religious News Service, Nov. 12, 1985, by William Bole. Reprinted in *Bondings*, Spring-Summer 1986.

supports the teaching that steady-lover relationships are a morally acceptable option for Roman Catholics. Although members support celibacy
for priests and religious, they advocate that lay Catholics be allowed to
have steady-lover relationships. The writers who appear in *Bondings* are
familiar for their opposition to Catholic teaching on homosexuality:
Daniel Maguire, Kevin Gordon, and Rosemary Ruether. One will find
representative pieces reflecting the views of NWM in *Challenge to Love*,
edited by Father Nugent.[69]

In addition to Dignity and NWM there is another publication, *Communication*, that circulates among homosexual priests and nuns of the
Catholic Church. It is secretive by its very nature, and thus not open to the
same scrutiny given to Dignity and NWM. In *The Homosexual Network*,
pp. 549–570, Father Rueda gives a sampling of *Communication* newsletters
that develop themes similar to those of Dignity and NWM. Many of the
letters give homosexual priests and religious an opportunity to express
their inner feelings without fear of repercussions from superiors. In
a sense such letters may have a therapeutic value, but they also reflect
much confusion about the meaning of the vow of celibacy. One brother
mentions that in attending *Communication* events he is "severely out-
numbered by those religious who have chosen a different path in regard to
celibacy. In other words the support and interaction I need is lacking."[70]

---

[69] Robert Nugent, *Challenge to Love* (New York: Crossroad, 1983).
[70] Rueda, *The Homosexual Network*, p. 569.

CHAPTER EIGHT

SPECIAL CONCERNS

In my pastoral experience I have encountered three problems not open to ready solutions: (1) the married homosexual person; (2) the apparent homosexual adolescent; and (3) Acquired Immune Deficiency Syndrome (AIDS). This is not to say there are no other complex problems among homosexual persons—for example, pedophilia and sado-masochism—but only that I have not had to deal as frequently with these particular ones. Although my perspective is primarily moral and pastoral rather than psychologically speculative, it will be necessary to relate both psychological theory and canonical considerations concerning the validity of marriage to the pastoral approach. Like many other pastoral theologians, I am searching for better ways of bringing these special persons to some degree of *spiritual* cure. I use the word *spiritual* advisedly. I know that so far there is no physical remedy for AIDS, but in our pastoral care, with the help of God we can be instruments of the healing power of the grace of Christ. Again, my experience with these special concerns, although considerable, is necessarily limited; nonetheless, I hope that others who share these concerns will enlarge our perspectives and deepen our insights. I proceed first to the question of homosexuality and marriage.

1. THE MARRIED HOMOSEXUAL

It is not a rare occurrence for priests and religious counselors to meet married persons engaged in homosexual activity or gravely beset with homosexual fantasy. From listening to the homosexual man or woman (more often it is a man) for the first time it is difficult, if not impossible, to discern where the person is on the seven-point Kinsey scale. It is advisable that for diagnostic tests one refer such a person to a clinical psychologist who is not an advocate of homosexuality so that the priest or counselor can make prudent recommendations based upon the judgment of an experienced clinician. One should not jump to the conclusion that because there have been homosexual acts the person is homosexual. The pastoral situations are usually very complex. Usually the spouse does not know; frequently the person has children. More often than not, the "homosexual" person wants to go on with his marriage, insisting that the priest or counselor keep his secret. Sometimes the problem is rendered even more complex, because the person is drinking heavily and the spouse believes the problem is alcoholism. Rather than suggest guidelines that will seem simplistic, I shall describe some pastoral situations and my response to them.

Case 1. Stanley was in his late twenties when he came to me for spiritual direction. He was married and had three preschool boys. He engaged in periodic homosexual promiscuity, with intervals of abstinence. He frequently came home from bars intoxicated. He made regular visits to a psychiatrist. Besides doing his government job in the day, he attended evening school for a graduate degree. He had given permission to his psychiatrist and me to discuss his situation. The psychiatrist was concerned about whether Stanley could succeed in his marriage and considered telling his wife. Then Stanley began to have longer periods of abstinence. His wife became pregnant, and the pressure to keep the marriage going increased in Stanley. He relapsed into promiscuity, which was always joined with heavy drinking. He suffered blackmail, and partially admitted to his wife his homosexual activity, but he blamed it on alcohol. She wanted to keep the marriage going. For a while things went well, but then for the first time he formed an attachment to another man and moved out of the house to live with him. Legal separation and divorce followed, and she obtained an annulment of the marriage. He visited the three boys regularly.

Although Stanley was periodically promiscuous and drinking heavily, he tried to keep his marriage going. But as soon as he formed a relationship with another man, he gave up on his marriage and moved out. He was also unwilling to admit using his drinking as an excuse for promiscuous activity. He stopped counseling with both the psychiatrist and me. Eventually he went back to live with his mother. The most important characteristic of Stanley was that he was compulsive. It was the judgment of the psychiatrist that Stanley was predominantly homosexual, but that was not as important as his refusal to take the necessary steps to handle sexual promiscuity and possible alcoholism. Had he become involved in both A.A. and a homosexual support group, he might have remained in his marriage. Even after his wife was told that Stanley was homosexual, she wanted to do all she could do for the sake of their three boys, with whom he was on good terms. This raises the pastoral question of whether a priest, believing that the man who has come for counsel is homosexual, should demand that the person seek an annulment of the marriage. I shall treat this pastoral-canonical question later.

Case 2: Jerry, fifty-one, married twenty-five years, with three children, has been involved in promiscuous homosexual activity over the past several years. It takes place on the way to or from work in a metropolitan area, usually in restrooms. His activity is sporadic—continent for several weeks, then three or four times in a week. He comes more for sacramental absolution than for counseling. Although fully contrite at the time, he soon relapses. I have explained that he needs a support group such as S.A. (Sexaholics Anonymous). So far he has not gone to their meetings. For twenty-three of the twenty-five years of his marriage he was able to have good heterosexual relations with his wife, suppressing homosexual desires. During the last several years, however, he has neglected marital relations. His wife, he says, is very patient with him, blaming it on his going through "a change of life". She has no knowledge of his problem. When questioned whether he felt that he was homosexual before marriage, he said he had had homosexual activity before marriage but had resolved to give it up, and he had done so for over twenty years.

Jerry's situation poses several questions. Without doubt he has homosexual tendencies, but is he predominantly homosexual? He is compulsive, so he needs to get into some form of group spiritual therapy to get control over his compulsive activity. Should the spiritual advisor or counselor insist on such group counseling? I think Jerry should be told he has an obligation to join such a group. Without revealing the nature of the compulsion, he should explain to his wife that he needs group therapy.

Case 3: Rita, thirty-nine, mother of four children, married twelve years, had homosexual tendencies as a teenager. She entered a convent and a few years later found herself involved emotionally and physically with another sister. She decided to leave the convent. Several years later she married a man ten years older than she who had had serious emotional problems. She wanted to have a family. Although she enjoyed sexual relations with her husband, she was not emotionally involved with him; instead, she found herself emotionally and physically attracted by another married woman with whom she has had an affair sporadically over several years. Feeling deeply guilty after each episode, she sought sacramental absolution. In group therapy sessions she wondered out loud whether she was heterosexual or homosexual. It was pointed out to her that she had a pattern of emotional involvement with women but not with any man, not even her husband. She agreed with this analysis. Since her husband gave her no help with the four small children, since she had little time to come to group support meetings, and since she feared any revelation to her husband about the nature of her difficulty, she found her marriage increasingly more difficult. She continued to have marital relations but had to keep fighting off homosexual fantasies of the other married woman.

Rita's situation raises additional questions about the pastoral treatment of female homosexual persons. Rita believes she was homosexual long before marriage, but she wants to maintain the marriage and family. Suppose the spiritual adviser, aware of the trend in diocesan marriage tribunals to grant annulments if there is sufficient evidence that the homosexual orientation was present before marriage, decides to tell Rita that she should seek an annulment. Would this be a prudent thing to do? I think not. I believe that the principle of good faith applies. Rita is a religious person who is following a spiritual program to overcome homosexual tendencies, which, in my judgment, are a form of compulsion. The good of the children, which requires a stable family environment, and the good of her husband motivate her to maintain her marriage.

If, moreover, psychological theorists and psychiatrists continue to disagree on the nature and etiology of homosexuality, how is the ordinary pastoral counselor or priest going to discern the traits of the "true" homosexual during the course of a few interviews? Would he not be in danger of basing his judgment concerning the existence of homosexuality on rather flimsy evidence? Even if the evidence is more substantial, as in this case, it does not amount to moral certitude. Unless, then, the evidence in favor of homosexuality is overwhelming, the counselor should presume in favor of maintaining the marital relationship and should present to the counselee a program of spiritual direction.

Case 4: Bill, thirty-four, married eight years, with a five-year-old boy and a two-year-old girl, informed his wife, Isabel, he had always been homosexual, and that he could not go on with the marriage. He asked her to agree to a separation and divorce. Isabel was upset by this information, and both sought counsel. He continued to insist, however, that he wanted to move out and find companionship in the metropolitan "gay" community. Eventually, she obtained both a civil divorce and a canonical annulment. While he provided some financial support for the children and visited them regularly, he did not really spend enough time with the children, and this concerned Isabel, particularly because the son needs his father.

Bill's wife, Isabel, did not have great difficulty in obtaining an annulment of her marriage. Years ago, the fact that a marriage was physically consummated and that children had been born led to a presumption in favor of the validity of a marriage involving homosexuality, but during the last twenty-five years many articles in canon law journals have proposed new arguments for the invalidity of marriages involving one person who is predominantly homosexual. This scholarship, in turn, has significantly influenced diocesan marriage tribunals so that cases involving homosexual orientation and activity are usually resolved by a decree of annulment that allows the heterosexual person to remarry, if such is what is desired.[1] I shall sum up these arguments at the end of this section; at this point I am concerned with the situation of Bill's wife.

What happens to the wife of a homosexual after she gets an annulment? Usually she is in her thirties or forties and often has three or four children. She will worry about the absence of a father for her son(s) and daughter(s), but more so for her son(s), because she knows his need for parental guidance during the teenage period. (I have recommended to Bill's wife the option of enrolling her son in Boys' Clubs so he can have the male companionship he needs.) The wife feels cheated, and she may seek out another marital partner too quickly, sometimes marrying a divorced person without waiting to see whether he has had an invalid previous marriage. (Isabel did that, and she is not alone in it.) In any case, the pastoral guide should not think his task is over as soon as the wife gets her decree of annulment. She will need help in rearing her children as a single parent. She will also need understanding, since she may nurse much anger and resentment about what happened to her.

Case 5: Alex, fifty-two, has five children. He attends spiritual support groups for homosexual persons, because four years ago he had what he calls a religious conversion. Previously, he had frequent promiscuous encounters, but by the grace of God and the help of the support group he has overcome his desire for impersonal sex and continues to relate well with his wife and children. His wife is not aware of his past, which means that sometimes he cannot come to the support group because of a family engagement. He has become an inspiration to young unmarried members

---

[1] Paul K. Thomas, "Marriage Annulments for Gay Men and Lesbian Women: New Canonical and Psychological Insights", *The Jurist* 43, no. 2 (1983):318–342. At the end of his article Thomas presents an annotated bibliography of articles in canonical and medicoscientific journals vis à vis the nullity of marriages in which one person is predominantly homosexual in orientation. While the canonical references are very useful, the medicoscientific references reflect the bias of Father Thomas in favor of the questionable judgment by the American Psychiatric Association in 1973 that "homosexuality per se implies no impairment in judgment, stability, reliability, or general social or vocational capabilities." In the interest of objectivity, Thomas might have set down some of the authors of distinction who disagree with the decision of the American Psychiatric Association, authors who hold that homosexuality involves "affective disturbance" and addictive characteristics. Thomas refers to such authors as "old medical literature" (read "outmoded"), but this is not true. See Charles Socarides, *Homosexuality* (New York: Aronson, 1978). Socarides, "The Sexual Deviations and the Diagnostic Manual", *Amer. J. of Psychotherapy* 32 (1978):414–425. See also Ruth T. Barnhouse, *Homosexuality: A Symbolic Confusion* (New York: Seabury Press, 1977), wherein she points out that the decision of the A.P.A. "was far from unanimous and was predominantly arrived at on socio-political rather than scientific grounds" (pp. 45–46); see also Gerald van den Aardweg, *Homosexuality*, Introduction, pp. xi–xv.

of the group. From a psychological point of view I can find no explanation for the way Alex has turned his life around. One will find instances of such conversions among the Protestant ministries to homosexuals, such as Metanoia Ministries, Love in Action, and Outpost. In my view it raises the question of whether the so-called constitutional homosexual can change his sexual orientation to the degree that he is capable of valid marriage.

Case 6: Virginia, forty-seven, is married and has one son, nineteen, a sophomore in college. Virginia joined a Catholic support group but soon made it clear that she did not accept Catholic teaching on the morality of homosexual activity. She knew she was homosexual before she married, but she thought she could overcome it. After a few years, however, she found no attraction in the marital relationship and later refused all sexual relations. In the support group she found an unmarried woman with whom she formed a very close relationship. When both left the group they wrote a letter saying that in conscience they could no longer come to Courage when they were unwilling to live by its principles. They were convinced that faithful love relationships are good.

Case 7: Lynn, thirty-nine, twice divorced, has a nine-year-old daughter, who she says was the only reason for her second marriage. Lynn was engaged to be married for several years when she fell in love with a woman. She broke her engagement and moved in with her lover; meanwhile, her fiancé committed suicide. After about a year she left her lover and entered into promiscuous relationships with men. Both her marriages were short-lived, and when she became pregnant in the second she began to think about divorce, which came a year or so after the birth of her daughter. Learning of Courage as a spiritual support group for homosexual persons, she became one of the few women in a Courage unit. Now a practicing Catholic and devoted mother, she still carries a heavy weight of guilt over the suicide of her former fiancé. She wants to live a celibate life and at present is not interested in dating men, although she relates well to the other members of her support group, all male. She believes she is homosexual in orientation, but she is not interested in probing her own sexuality. Determined to be a good mother, she supervises her child's education closely. She has a full-time job and has completed her college education in the evenings. She admits she feels very lonely in her struggles.

From listening to Lynn over many private sessions I would not be able to say whether she is heterosexual or homosexual. Some would say she is bisexual, and she appears to be, having had genital relations with members of both sexes. Realizing that Kinsey makes room for bisexuality (point 3 on the Kinsey scale), I believe that a person is either homosexual or heterosexual and that the best criterion we have to help persons decide whether they are *now* one or the other is the degree of their emotional involvement toward a member of their own sex as compared with the degree of emotional involvement with a person of the other sex. I have already alluded to this criterion in the case of Rita above.

Yet in using this criterion I do not in any way imply that one cannot change one's sexual orientation. The fact that individuals have moved from so-called constitutional (true, confirmed) homosexuality to hetero-sexuality over a period of time—say, five years—means that this transition, even this transformation, is truly possible, albeit difficult.[2] Working out a faith perspective rooted in Christ as Redeemer of the whole person, Colin Cook and others have been able to make this arduous journey.[3]

Other similar situations of married homosexual persons could be considered, but I believe this sampling of cases reveals the complexity of the problems and the need to proceed cautiously in setting up a pastoral program for any married homosexual person. Lynn, for example, needs time to work through the bitter memories of the past before she will be ready to consider whether she wants to move toward heterosexual orien-tation—which, after much struggle, she possibly may not attain. She eventually needs to be told that, but not at present, in my judgment. Again, all these cases raise the question of canonical annulment of marriages in which one of the parties seems to be a confirmed homosexual. Since I do not intend this work to be a canonical treatment of the subject, I shall review as briefly as possible some pertinent canonical and psychological studies on the subject.

Canonical and psychological considerations

Lawrence Wrenn defines the diriment impediment of impotence as the antecedent and perpetual incapacity of a man or a woman to have physical intercourse. In saying that it is antecedent Wrenn means that it exists before the marriage contract, at least virtually and causally. It is necessary and sufficient that the proximate disposition to impotence and the proxi-mate cause of its onset be present at the time of marriage. This, he adds, could be verified in the case of a homosexual.[4]

[2] Gerald van den Aardweg, *On the Origins and Treatment of Homosexuality* (New York: Praeger, 1986), pp. 252–258.

[3] Colin Cook, *Homosexuality: An Open Door?* (Boise, Idaho: Pacific Press, 1985).

[4] *Annulments*, 4th edition (Washington, D.C.: Canon Law Society of America, 1983), pp. 8–9. Wrenn comments on the canon concerning impotence, 1084:1. In 1969 Clara Maria

John Cavanagh, M.D., integrates a great number of canonical and psychological insights in his 1977 study *Counseling the Homosexual*. From his long years of psychiatric care of homosexual persons he concluded that the vast majority were impotent in the canonical sense and that this condition opposes the very essence of marriage. He gives the following reasons for the invalidity of the homosexual–heterosexual marriage.

1. The homosexual cannot give the consent necessary to bring into existence the reality of marriage.

2. The homosexual is incapable of the genuine conjugal love required for a proper marriage.

3. The homosexual is psychologically impotent.[5]

With regard to the first reason, the consent of marriage is a loving covenant leading to a full sharing of life together. But heterosexuality is an indispensable condition for this to take place. Each partner should expect the other to be capable not only of performing but also of desiring the marriage act in its full meaning. The capacity to give full personal consent to the marriage act in its total meaning is an essential condition for establishing marriage, and the homosexual person is not capable of giving such a consent.[6]

With regard to the second reason, Cavanagh shows that marriage demands a spiritual and disinterested love of the spouses for each other. It should be truly complementary, as described in Genesis 2:18–24: "For this reason a man shall leave father and mother and cleave to his wife, and they shall be two in one flesh." But Cavanagh holds that the homosexual person is not capable of such conjugal love, but only a sexual love. This needs to be explained. The union of man and wife is a union of whole persons, far more than merely a physical act:

> It is a mutual compenetration of two human beings who are united body and soul with each other. The sexual act is incomplete unless this physical compenetration is effected with its psychical counterpart. Thus, it is not permissible for the partners in a marital act to separate the psychical component of the act from the physical, nor the physical from the psychical. Such separation would be the rule rather than the exception in the case of the homosexual.[7]

Henning had argued that in women, homosexuality did not lend itself to the legal provisions of a marital impediment, because the orientation develops differently in females than in males. In women it may develop long after the day of marriage. I think that subsequent canonical and psychological research has answered her objection, though it still should be admitted that our knowledge of female homosexuality is incomplete. See footnote 16 on Henning.

[5] *Counseling the Homosexual* (Huntington, Ind.: Our Sunday Visitor, 1977), p. 147.

[6] *Ibid.*, p. 149.

[7] *Ibid.*, p. 150.

In the absence of true heterosexual love, says Cavanagh, there is a continuous threat to the permanence of the marital relationship. To prove his point he refers to a series of authorities in psychology.[8]

With regard to the third reason, Cavanagh holds that the homosexual is psychologically impotent in heterosexual relations, because both the stimulus and the desire for such relations are absent. The homosexual lacks capacity for that unselfish love necessary for marriage. He admits that the Rota holds that one cannot say without qualification that homosexuality always produces impotence and that therefore each case must be judged on its own merits.[9] Even without this third argument, however, it seems that the first two constitute sufficient proof for the invalidity of the heterosexual–homosexual marriage. It remains to review several canonical authorities on the invalidity of such a marriage.

Charles Ritty, Pierre Menard, and John Rogg Schmidt have each stressed the personal incapacity of the homosexual person to make a contract he cannot fulfill. Menard stated that marriage is essentially a heterosexual interpersonal relationship that the confirmed homosexual is radically incapable of fulfilling. Schmidt sees the invalidation of such a marriage as arising from the incapacity of the homosexual person to fulfill the essential requirements of a heterosexual relationship. John R. Keating believed that

> if constitutional homosexuality invalidated marriage, the grounds for nullity would derive not from a defect in the act of marital consent, but from the existent condition itself, rendering the persons objectively incapable of binding themselves *sub gravi* to an essential obligation of conjugal life. For instance, he indicated that with regard to indissolubility, if the homosexual individual is constitutionally incapable of a lasting union with a member of the opposite sex, then that person cannot conceivably bind himself or herself *sub gravi* to a permanent relationship.[10]

Prevention of homosexual marriages

If it is true that the condition of homosexuality incapacitates the person for marriage, then it would seem necessary to counsel an engaged couple one

---

[8] *Ibid.*, p. 151. See also Cavanagh's references in footnote 26 on pp. 300–302 of his book.

[9] *Ibid.*

[10] The above quote is taken from Paul Thomas' article, "Marriage Annulments for Gay Men and Lesbian Women", *The Jurist* 43, no. 2 (1983):341, footnote 58. The references for the above summary of canonical authorities is also taken from Thomas' article: Pierre Menard, "The Invalidating Force of Homosexuality", *Studia Canonica* 3 (1969):5–21; Charles Ritty, "Possible Invalidity of Marriage by Reason of Sexual Anomalies", *The Jurist*, 23 (1963):394–422; John B. Schmidt, "Homosexuality and Validity of Marriage", three articles in *The Catholic Lawyer*: 19 (1973):84–101, 169–199; 21 (1975):85–121. The first two articles also appeared in *The Jurist* 32 (1972):381–399, 494–530.

of whom gives signs of confirmed homosexuality that they should not enter into sacramental marriage.[11] The pastoral difficulty for the priest or counselor lies in evaluating the *degree* of homosexual orientation present in either partner. One must adapt his pastoral approach to the specific persons with whom one is dealing after obtaining a complete personal history of the apparently homosexual person. In practice, unfortunately, for a variety of reasons evidence of homosexual orientation does not usually surface during the engagement period. The person may not be aware of his homosexual tendencies; he may be aware of them but believe he is in love with this woman and that such love will help him keep his homosexual tendencies under control; he may have experienced attraction to the opposite sex previously and have had sexual relationships with them and, despite the memory of homosexual encounters, believe that on balance he can manage to maintain a heterosexual commitment; he may think that his homosexual activity was just a passing phase of his young life. In all these reasoning processes the person is engaged in denial and not very likely to seek counsel from a clinical psychologist or psychiatrist. Besides, he is often in his late twenties and wants to settle down and raise a family with a lovely young woman. He may even tell her of his previous escapades, but he assures her that they are a matter of the past. Usually she will respond that with her help he will not slip into such promiscuity again. She does not want to believe that this nice man could be homosexual, and even if he has been involved in such actions in the past, he is different now. Unconsciously, she believes that her love will take care of such difficulties. Besides, she really wants to be married and to have a family. As a result, the priest preparing the couple for marriage remains innocent of this knowledge until one or the other comes back some years later seeking divorce and annulment. In short, there are understandable reasons why persons who are homosexual either do not reveal this before marriage or else disclose it to the other person in such a way as to minimize its importance.

It should also be noted that some homosexuals marry because of the pressures of family and business relationships or even as a protection for continuing clandestine homosexual practices, as has happened with certain movie idols. Suppose, however, the heterosexual person or the priest or the minister receives a warning from acquaintances of the homosexual person that amounts to a solid suspicion of the presence of *pronounced* homosexual traits. Perhaps these revelations come through the future bride, who is all too ready to dismiss them. However they come, they should be investigated by the priest or minister.

[11] Van den Aardweg holds that we have no conclusive answer to the question of how many homosexual men marry. He assumes that at least one-tenth of homosexual men are married and that for lesbians this percentage could be higher. *Ibid.*, 144.

Again, suppose the person opens his conscience to a priest or minister and reveals a past of sexual activity with both men and women, as well as a pattern of compulsive masturbation. He has reformed and intends marriage in the next six months. In such a situation the spiritual counselor should recommend that the young man practice complete chastity for an extended time and join a support group, such as S.A., and get regular spiritual direction so the counselor can ascertain whether he is capable of truly relating in a heterosexual manner to a woman and of practicing marital fidelity. The extended time should be at least a year. He should let his fiancée know at least his propensities, but not his sins, as the reason for extending the engagement. She has the freedom to break it under such circumstances. During this trial period the young man should discuss with a counselor the degree of physical attraction he has for his fiancee, and the success he has had with controlling fantasy, masturbation, and promiscuous acts. Unless he has a strong physical attraction for his fiancée, and control over all sexual tendencies, he should not marry. Pastoral experiences reveal that where these conditions are not fulfilled, marriages do not last more than a few years. Often they begin well, but within a few years homosexual fantasy and activity often recur.

What is more significant than sexual behavior is the fantasy of the person. A man who has engaged in homosexual behavior as a substitute for the other sex will not have homosexual fantasy. Nevertheless, there is a lack of self-control present, which is a danger sign for marriage. The higher the degree of self-control exercised before marriage in suppressing deviate tendencies, the greater the chance the person has of making a happy marriage: "To the extent that a person of either sex has engaged in sex variant activity he or she is less likely to make a satisfactory heterosexual adjustment. The chances of making such an adjustment are less to the extent that substitutive sexual behavior has been prolonged."[12]

Again, unless the apparent bisexual *definitively* gives up his homosexual friends and milieu, the priest should advise him not to marry. It is tragic illusion to imagine that marriage will transform him into a heterosexual person.

It also should be reiterated that the same principles apply to the apparent female bisexual.

The female bisexual and the female homosexual person

At this point in our discussion of marriage it is useful to recall a few observable differences between male and female homosexuals or bisexuals. The female differs from the male in such matters as the greater depth of her

[12] George W. Henry, *Sex Variants* (New York: Harper, 1948), one-vol. edition, p. 1048.

attachments, her avoidance of erotic transvestism, her ability to keep her anomaly secret, and the allegedly deeper sensitivity of her conscience to the guilt of homosexual desires and acts. This seeming deeper sensitivity of conscience may still be present in many female homosexuals or bisexuals, but it is seldom brought to Catholic priests in the forum of conscience, because these women, by and large, are angry at the Church for other reasons, mainly because the Church has not allowed the ordination of women to the priesthood. The "right" of women to ordination and the "right" of homosexual women to a stable, loving genital union have been made a common cause opposed only by the "enemy" Church. Father Rueda documents the close cooperation between the Women's Ordination Conference (WOC), a radical Catholic feminist organization, and the Catholic homosexual movement. "Increasing involvement in WOC correlates strongly with increasing involvement in the Catholic homosexual movement."[13]

While generalizations are risky when it comes to the relative sensitivity of male and female homosexuals, I have observed in pastoral practice that the female is more docile than the male, less likely to defend her way of life by sophisticated arguments of a pseudo-intellectual stripe, and more ready to admit the obviously emotional character of her homosexual attachments, to which she may continue to cling, not as a rebellion against the moral teaching of the Church, but really out of fear of the vacuum she imagines will follow renunciation of the beloved. In general, I find more weakness and less pride in the female homosexual person, but it should be kept in mind that those homosexual women who are angry because of the Church's position on the ordination of women are not likely to speak with a priest about their personal situation.

Several questions emerge as one studies this problem. The first is whether a homosexual woman or a female bisexual has a better chance of having a happy marriage than a male homosexual. I had held the opinion that true female homosexuals should not marry,[14] but Dr. Cavanagh believes that under special circumstances it could be allowed. While agreeing with me that a homosexual woman who was active and wished to get married only for the sake of appearance should be strongly discouraged from doing so, Dr. Cavanagh conjectures that a highly motivated homosexual woman could be a good mother to her children and show

---

[13] *The Homosexual Network*, pp. 330–332.

[14] John F. Harvey, O.S.F.S., "Homosexuality and Marriage", *Homiletic and Pastoral Review*, Dec. 1961, pp. 227–234. On the basis of pastoral experience and of research into other authors, I remain of the opinion that wherever I find strong homosexual inclinations marriage is inadvisable, and I discourage it. Yet I want to find more satisfactory solutions than we have.

proper interest and affection for her husband. He adds that if the husband had a low sex drive, it would be less difficult for her to submit to intercourse.[15] This may be true in some instances, but I agree with Clara Henning that it is very difficult to determine *canonically* whether a marriage in which it is claimed that the wife is homosexual is open to an annulment. Our present canonical jurisprudence has not addressed adequately the nature of female homosexuality. Henning reminds the canonists that they have treated homosexuality too indiscriminately as a uniform problem.[16]

There seems less difficulty in such a marriage than in one where the woman is heterosexual and the man homosexual. After a time the man's homosexual feelings may reemerge in such a way that he neglects having intercourse with his wife. Nevertheless, I still hold to the opinion that *before* marriage the female homosexual should be discouraged from marriage. *After* marriage I try to help the person to fulfill her duties as wife and mother. Often she does not want a divorce; she wants to keep her family; she has intercourse whenever her husband requests it.

Van den Aardweg takes a position different from both Cavanagh's and mine. He says that few counselors nowadays will advise that marriage will solve the homosexual problem, but

> it is also a fact that our time tends to underestimate the possible positive influence of married life in some cases of homosexuality. Whether this influence is a healthy one depends upon several factors, the most important of which are the person's conscious intentions and will, the severity of his overall neurosis, and the nature of the relationship with his partner. . . . The situation of many married homosexuals is identical with that of other married neurotics. It is sensible to warn a homosexual, as well as his future marriage partner, of the difficulties they will almost certainly face if they decide to marry, but it must not be an iron rule to discourage such intended marriages.[17]

Van den Aardweg believes it irresponsible that divorce take place if the homosexually oriented partner ran into trouble because of his sexual longings. The couple can work out their problems through counseling; the homosexual person must take all the steps mentioned in anti-complaining therapy.[18] While I have difficulty in accepting the attempt to gain a divorce as irresponsible, I am open to further consideration of this view in those situations where the homosexual person has been faithful to his spouse. We need more empirical evidence that such a marriage

---

[15] *Counseling the Homosexual*, p. 152.

[16] "Lesbianism and the Canon Law of Marriage", *Homiletic and Pastoral Review* 69 (1969):691–698.

[17] *Origins and Treatment of Homosexuality*, p. 147.

[18] *Ibid.*, pp. 147–150; 205–258 (anti-complaining therapy).

can be repaired, and we are more likely to find it in the work of H.A., Colin Cook, and the umbrella of Protestant ministries called Exodus International.

I believe it is pastorally consistent to discourage marriages *before* the reception of the sacrament where there are clear signs of homosexuality in either partner, but to do everything psychologically and spiritually possible to heal a marriage where one of the partners is homosexual. At the same time we cannot deny the right of the non-homosexual partner to seek divorce and annulment where the homosexual partner leaves or has been flagrantly unfaithful.

Another unresolved question in this issue is that of bisexuality. From his research, van den Aardweg calls the bisexual the least neurotic of the homosexuals, but he does not say that the bisexual-heterosexual marriage will be easier to maintain. Indeed, he points out that there is "no peaceful coexistence" between homosexual and heterosexual feelings, and he gives examples to substantiate his position.[19] Given the perennial controversy concerning the very nature of bisexuality, it is difficult to say that the bisexual person can change his orientation more easily than one who is clearly homosexual.

From this study of homosexuality and marriage I draw several guidelines. First, we need to be cautious in premarital investigations whenever there seems to be any evidence that one of the persons is homosexual or bisexual. Secondly, when someone who is married reveals to us in the forum of conscience that he is homosexual or bisexual, we must get the full picture in order to help. If such persons desire to remain in the marriage, they must be willing to follow a rigorous spiritual program such as H.A. or Courage. If they believe they are not able to continue the marriage, it is advisable to consult with a clinical psychologist or psychiatrist who will not interfere with the conscience of a Catholic. Then it may be necessary to consult with a canonist in the event that divorce is recommended. The person concerned will be asked to write his autobiography for the tribunal. Thirdly, we need to keep abreast, not only of psychological studies, but also of the results of spiritual support groups among both Protestants and Catholics. Realistically speaking, when change from homosexual or bisexual orientation does take place, it takes as long as five years, as a young minister pointed out to me recently. In this context the word *change* should give way to the word *healing*. Healing means control over compulsive tendencies before it means change in sexual orientation. A person who has gained real control over sexual desires is already healed.

---

[19] *Ibid.*, pp. 145–147. In comparison with confirmed homosexuals, the bisexual is less feminine, less marked by fears, less passive. "The situation seems mirrored for the lesbian woman with bisexual inclinations" (p. 147).

2. THE APPARENT ADOLESCENT HOMOSEXUAL

Over twenty years ago, before homosexual organizations had flooded the media with the message that "gay is good", I received a letter from a twenty-year-old that expressed very well the uncertainty and ambivalence I have noted in other youth. He wrote:

> I have delayed taking action along the proper lines for so long, I sincerely hope there is a vestige of my true self left to salvage and to improve. . . . Yes, I am a homosexual. . . . I thought I could be a bisexual, or maybe that this was just a stage I was passing through. . . . At this point I feel quite powerless to do very much for myself. I also know that I both enjoy the life and am repulsed by it at the same time. I cannot face this thing by myself any longer. . . . If only I could have an escape. I want you to know that I need your help. . . .[20]

These revealing excerpts pose problems for the person counseling this apparent adolescent homosexual person. After I had interviewed this young man I told him I did not think he was homosexual, but I asked him to visit a clinical psychologist who could make a professional evaluation and could give appropriate counsel. The pastoral point I stress is that whenever anyone under twenty-five claims to be homosexual, his assertion should not be accepted uncritically, particularly since our young people are exposed to massive gay propaganda through media, literature, and hundreds of gay clubs throughout the country. Without denying that some homosexuals sense their sexual orientation very early, it is also true that other persons enter adolescence with their sexual orientation unresolved. It is immoral, then, to subject such teenagers and young adults to the kind of propaganda that holds that a stable homosexual relationship, in which two persons of the same sex live together in a "holy union" is as good as a heterosexual marriage. That the teenage and young adult person may be seduced unnecessarily into a homosexual way of living is affirmed by Ruth Tiffany Barnhouse in *Homosexuality: A Symbolic Confusion* (New York: Seabury, 1977).

Barnhouse's definition of homosexuality stresses this point:

> I use the word *homosexuality* to refer to an *adult* adaptation characterized by *preferential* sex behavior between members of the same sex. The emphasis on *adult* is very important. Much of today's rhetoric does not allow for the fact that adolescence is often accompanied by a period of transitional anxiety or confusion about sexual identity. . . . To lump discussion of homosexual phenomena in teenagers together with those occurring in adults is such an

[20] John F. Harvey, O.S.F.S., "Counseling the Apparent Adolescent Homosexual", *Bulletin of the Guild of Catholic Psychiatrists*, Oct. 1963, pp. 204–214 at 204.

inappropriate confusion of categories as to render meaningful discourse virtually impossible.[21]

Barnhouse does not accept the view that the origins of homosexuality are sealed in the first six years of life, however important these years may be. She believes that experiences during the so-called latency period (between the age of six and the onset of puberty) are also significant. During this period one develops satisfactory peer relationships and experiences of aggressiveness and competitiveness, success or failure.[22] More to our present thesis, she adds that "it is the internal and external experiences of adolescence which are probably decisive in most cases."[23] At the same time she admits that it would take an exceptionally fortunate set of circumstances in this period to prevent some adolescents from moving toward homosexuality, given the environmental circumstances that predispose boys and girls to a homosexual lifestyle. Sometimes the young person may find a new environment far away from the pernicious circumstances in which he had been living.

In the early teenage period youngsters tend to associate principally, if not exclusively, with same-sex peers. This seems more true of boys than of girls. Some "homosexual" acting out in group masturbation is not uncommon. These homosexual acts, however, do not prove that these boys are homosexual. In every instance we should distinguish homosexual acts from homosexual identification, but particularly in the case of teenagers. Teenage boys sometimes fear they are "queer" because they do not measure up to a macho culture. They become involved in homosexual prostitution to prove they can be the aggressor.[24] Many return to a heterosexual way of life as adults, although sometimes "homosexual acts engaged in during this adolescent stage may trigger unresolved difficulties from earlier stages and may precipitate a more serious or lasting homosexual commitment."[25]   Barnhouse goes on to show how our extremely competitive and power-oriented culture affects the adolescent. Pushed by his parents to the "pursuit of excellence" he may become involved for a time in homosexual adaptational behavior.[26] "It becomes easy to see that if a youngster is in any way torn by these problems, it may make a

[21] Ruth T. Barnhouse, *Homosexuality: A Symbolic Confusion* (New York: Seabury Press, 1979), p. 22.

[22] *Ibid.*, p. 58. Van den Aardweg, *On the Origins and Treatment of Homosexuality*, p. 83, also views the years between 8–16 as very important in the development of homosexual orientation.

[23] *Ibid.*, p. 59.

[24] Arno Karlen, *Sexuality and Homosexuality*, pp. 521–523.

[25] Barnhouse, *op. cit.*, p. 60.

[26] *Ibid.*, pp. 56–57; also Lionel Ovesey, *Homosexuality and Pseudohomosexuality* (New York: Science House, 1959), pp. 9–31.

difference if he is surrounded by a climate of opinion which rejects homosexuality as an acceptable life-style rather than by one which tells him that homsexuality is not only acceptable, but probably normal."[27]

In the years since Barnhouse expressed this opinion, the propaganda in favor of "gay is good" has spread far and wide through gay organizations on college campuses, including Catholic Dignity chapters for college students. Dignity/New York reports, for example, the Dignity Region II Scholarship Award of $500.00 to a young man who wrote an essay entitled "The Development of the Gay and Lesbian Student Movement" (September 1985, *Calendar*, Dignity/New York's newsletter). The essay is militant, noting that "the dominant attitude against which the students fought was, quite simply, that homosexuality was wrong." The author claims that gay and lesbian students are not passive, but "continue to participate actively in the larger gay and lesbian movement". It does not take much imagination to picture the difficulties of the apparent adolescent homosexual on campuses where he encounters intelligent and aggressive leaders like the essayist.

We need to keep two facts in balance: (1) In some instances the individual adolescent boy or girl goes through a temporary period of homosexual infatuation and activity but grows out of it; and (2) in other situations the pattern of homosexual activity becomes fixed. Many men, Barnhouse reports, come for treatment "who regret having made the choice at an age when they were too immature to understand its full implications".[28] It is my opinion that even in the situations where the person feels it is too late to change, he should be encouraged to make the effort, using recent insights on the psychological level from Moberly and van den Aardweg and on the theological and spiritual levels from the experience of Colin Cook and others. Even if one does not change one's sexual orientation, one will experience healing of the heart and will be helped to live a celibate life out of love for the Lord. Courage has members like that. In helping the apparent young homosexual, then, we have no sure way of knowing whether a given boy or girl now involved in homosexual activities will continue this pattern for the rest of his or her life, but we should presume that with sound psychological and spiritual guidance we can help such youth to break out of a homosexual way of living.

The first need of so many confused adolescents who think they are homosexual is *education* in the basic meanings of human sexuality. Considering the fact that a young person has been exposed to false views of sexuality in general, and homosexuality in particular, this becomes a difficult task for

[27] Barnhouse, *op. cit.*, p. 60.
[28] *Ibid.*

the spiritual counselor. The idea that the purpose of genital activity is to express love and secondarily to have fun (and in some individuals the other way round) is so pervasive in our culture that it is little wonder that young people who sense homosexual longings come to believe that homosexuals have as much right to their form of genital pleasure as heterosexuals have to theirs. Meanwhile the procreative aspects of human sexual expression are ignored, because sexual intercourse has become a commodity. People begin to feel that it really does not make any difference which sex one has genital acts with so long as these acts are affectionate or pleasurable. Thus you will find many heterosexual persons in sympathy with the homosexual's lifestyle; after all, they reason, how else can a homosexual express his love? Seemingly, it does not occur to either the supportive heterosexuals or the homosexuals that love can be manifested in many other ways besides genital acts. The first step, then, in the reeducation of the confused adolescent is to present the full meaning of sexuality in a Christian context.[29]

The second step is to demonstrate the falsehood of identifying homosexual persons as part of a minority similar to ethnic or racial groups. Gay organizations portray homosexual persons as an oppressed minority like the blacks or the Hispanics, and therefore they must fight for their civil rights as other minorities have done. I examined this fallacy in Chapter Five. There I pointed out that minorities that are such by the color of their skin or their nationality are significantly different from minorities who are *known* to be such through their *free* actions. Again, other segments of the population have civil rights as well as the homosexual civil rights activists, and in certain instances the rights of others in the community take priority over civil rights activists. For example, a civil community could deny to a declared homosexual the right to teach its children, because they do not consider him an appropriate role model. This is not homophobia, which in no way do I justify.

On the volitional and emotional levels the apparent adolescent homosexual needs understanding and firm guidance. The counselor must be aware of a strong element of *ambivalence* in these persons. They profess too loudly that there is nothing wrong in homosexual activity. A young woman in a lesbian relationship may be uncertain about her behavior but verbally defend it in terms of the enjoyment derived from the physical

---

[29] Dr. Jean Benjamin of Sydney, Australia, told me in the summer of 1979 that the teenager is unduly impressed by the public acceptance of the homosexual lifestyle. This causes the uncertain to think that the law allows it now, so it can't be too bad. This leads them to join the ranks of homosexuals. Dr. Benjamin was opposed to the decriminalization laws in New South Wales, Australia.

intimacy in the relationship; besides, it is so superior to her previous relationships with "insensitive" males. (Strangely, male homosexuals think their love superior to love of women.) In pastoral experience with adolescent and young adult apparent lesbians I have noticed initial resistance. More often than not, having had heterosexual genital experience, she has found it wanting, whereas she is deeply in love with the woman with whom she is now involved. Frequently, these women do not come back. Those who do keep in contact with a spiritual counselor gradually come to realize the *narcissistic* nature of their relationship. This is typical of the male adolescent as well. It is necessary, then, to examine more closely the elements of these relationships. In doing so it should be kept in mind that narcissism and infatuation are not the exclusive possessions of adolescent apparent homosexuals.

Narcissism and infatuation

When one develops fixation or a "crush" upon another person of the same sex, one experiences emotional reactions very similar to those of teenage boy-girl love. While a situation of this kind may begin with a spiritual but exclusive bond, it very often degenerates into mutual masturbation. Just as often, or oftener, it begins on a frankly sexual level among boys or among girls. Such contacts are usually shallow, transient, and not emotionally charged. One may ask why youngsters will form such exclusive and self-defeating friendships. Usually, filled with a feeling of their own *inadequacy*, they seek to project themselves into the persons they admire and love. The desire to be what one cannot be leads one to form a friendship with the kind of person he would desire to be but feels he cannot be. A homely woman, for example, or one who *thinks* she is, will seek friendship with an attractive woman. Should the two women express love passionately, the unattractive person will derive vicarious satisfaction from arousing the passions of her beautiful partner. In thus experiencing the emotions of her beloved, the unattractive person comes as close as possible to being the beautiful beloved. In fantasy, very intimate physical contact with the other means *becoming* that other beautiful person.

Such a narcissistic longing involves polarity, the attraction of opposites for each other. Different forms of polarity are found among male homosexuals. Not merely beauty, but physical strength and what the male considers esoteric intelligence are sometimes found to be magnetic points between male homosexuals. The history of pederasty among the ancient Greeks placed the accent on the attraction of older men for adolescent physical beauty, usually for genital pleasure. In turn, the Spartan youth were conceived of as receiving in a sort of magic way some of the physical strength and bravery of their adult lovers.[30] Among others, however, physical beauty does not seem to count as much as more spiritual traits, such as similarities of interests, mutual perception of mutual loneliness, idolization of another's intelligence, and the notion that both youths are far above the mediocre herd in their intellectual and artistic gifts.[31]

Leanne Payne, however, provides us with deeper insight concerning narcissism when she writes: "The flipside of the wrong kind of self-love will always be some form of self-hatred. Inordinate self-love, which is, psychologically speaking, an immaturity in the personality, is the reverse side of a deep insecurity."[32] Payne treats this insecurity in her patients with a program that integrates the psychological with the spiritual. The third chapter of *The Broken Image*, "Matthew's Story", illustrates her method of getting at narcissism. After learning of his strong homosexual desires for another young man, she asked him a series of questions: What specifically do you admire in this person? He responded that it was looks, intelligence, and the fact that he was successful. These were *"outstanding traits in himself*, but traits that because he could not as yet accept himself, he was denying."[33] When asked what he did in his fantasies he replied that he dreamed of physical union with his beloved. Payne countered then with an inquiry about cannibals: *Why* do they eat people? Astonished, Matthew said that he had no idea, but Payne quoted a missionary who had told her: "Cannibals eat only those they admire, and they eat them *to get their traits*. What was happening to Matthew was very clear: he was looking at the other young man and loving a lost part of himself, a part that he could not recognize and accept."[34]

Before making some pastoral suggestions to help the adolescent apparent homosexual I want to advert to several other explanations of their exclusive friendships. Ovesey makes a distinction between pseudo-homosexuals and true homosexuals. Ovesey stresses the motivational context in which the fear of being homosexual became manifest in heterosexual males. He seeks to discover the unconscious motivations that impel a heterosexual

[30] John A. Symonds, *A Problem in Greek Ethics* (London, 1901, privately printed). See also Robin Scroggs, *The New Testament and Homosexuality* (Philadelphia: Fortress Press, 1983), pp. 29–43, pederastic practices; Arno Karlen *Sexuality and Homosexuality*, pp. 29–39. "The word pederasty means, literally, love of boys, and mostly Greek homosexuality was between men and adolescents, not adult males" (p. 25).

[31] Meyer Levin, *Compulsion* (New York: Simon and Schuster, 1956). The novel, based on the Leopold-Loeb case, reveals the contempt with which two narcissistic youths regarded the rest of society, against which they attempted to perpetrate the perfect crime.

[32] *The Broken Image* (Westchester, Ill.: Crossway Books, 1982), p. 94.

[33] *Ibid.*, p. 46.

[34] *Ibid.*, pp. 46–47.

male in his *fantasies* to seek contact with another man's genitals. In every instance he found where there was no evidence of homosexual arousal, the fantasies were motivated either by *dependency* needs or by *power* needs. The patient misperceived them as homosexual because of the *content* of the fantasies. Thus in his clinical practice Ovesey has discovered that the homosexual act is not governed by the wish for sexual gratification alone but also by two nonsexual motivations—dependency and power.[35] "These two motives played the same symbolic roles for the homosexual that they played in the nonerotic, pseudohomosexual fantasies of the heterosexual male."[36]

In further research Ovesey discovered the feminine counterpart of the pseudohomosexual conflict in men. Subjecting the wish to be a man to an adaptational analysis, he shows that it is a symbolic expression of dependency and power needs. He proposes, moreover, three fundamental assumptions as a basis for therapy: (1) Homosexuality is not a natural biological phenomenon; (2) homosexuality is an overdetermined *treatable* illness; (3) through treatment the normal heterosexual direction of the sexual drive can be reestablished.[37] The value of Ovesey's research and clinical experience is that it can help not only confused adolescents but also confused adults concerning their homosexual fantasies and feelings, offering hope that even the "true" homosexual can change sexual orientation. It is part of a respected professional body of thought that refuses to believe that homosexuality is both immutable and the basis for an acceptable alternative lifestyle.

Another aspect of these intensive and exclusive friendships of apparent homosexuals is a false understanding of human love. The youth believes that he can love with the soul alone another young man who loves him in the same way. These individuals see their love as superior to the love of a man for a woman; they fancy themselves as Davids and Jonathans, presupposing that there is something angelic about love between man and man, while love for a woman is simply a means of gratification for the carnal passions of men. Supposedly, each loves the other with the soul only. Aptly, the French term this form of friendship *angelism*.[38] How such an attitude develops is a matter of speculation. Failure to teach in the home

[35] *Homosexuality and Pseudohomosexuality*, pp. 10–11.

[36] *Ibid.*, p. 18.

[37] *Ibid.*, p. 119. For a full understanding of the author's theory I recommend his book. Terms like *adaptational analysis*, *power*, and *dependency needs* require further refinements beyond the scope of my work. It should be noted that Ovesey in 1969 had already concluded that homosexual orientation was a treatable disorder.

[38] Charles La Rère, "Passage of the Angel through Sodom", *New Problems in Medical Ethics*, vol. 1 (Cork: Mercier, 1952), pp. 110–119.

and the school that chastity is a virtue involving the body, and not a concern of angels, may be a contributing factor. This attitude is a total denial of the flesh-and-blood nature of human love and chastity. The love called angelism discovers a reflection of self in another being, and rejoices in the recognition of one's own reflection. The smug feeling of superiority that usually accompanies it is really a form of compensation.

Yet I have also seen persons drawn into homosexual practices through fear of physical contact with the other sex. One may regard all hetero-sexual behavior as degrading or as barely licit even in marriage. Since nothing was said in school or home about homosexuality, one may come to regard sexual explorations with members of one's own sex as of no great importance, surely not hurting anyone the way one could injure the reputation of a girl were she to become pregnant (or in the case of a girl, to get a boy in trouble by her becoming pregnant). Obviously, this same-sex fondling is found among adolescent girls as well as boys. But it is not necessarily homosexual, as we have already seen.

Crushes

Among adolescents one notes a phenomenon that is usually painful and comically idealistic, but not homosexual. An older teenage girl, for example, strives deliberately to win the affections of one of the younger students, and when she perceives the latter completely dependent upon her friendship, she toys with the other's feelings by a sort of emotional freeze play. Confused, the younger girl goes about as if some great tragedy had smashed her dreams. All this the older girl enjoys, interpreting as a sign of her triumph that in any altercation the younger girl feels obliged to make the first overtures of reconciliation; thereupon, she condescends to treat her young friend with a warmth born of illusory grandeur. After a time she will drop this youngster and go to another who will suffer the same fate. This game bolsters her ego, which may not be homosexual but is certainly narcissistic. Such heartless tactics are not exclusively nor principally feminine, however. Nor is it always the older person who initiates a crush relationship. Often the younger person initiates and controls the progress of the pseudo-romance, which, like true romance, demands that someone take the lead.

While it is important that the priest or counselor recognize the difference between a crush and the beginnings of a real homosexual relationship, in practice it is not always easy to discern the difference. Even if the exclusive friendship between two boys or two girls has been expressed by physical acts of love, it does not mean that either or both of the individuals involved are homosexual. That can be discerned only by a more complete investigation of the person's history, and usually it is better to send the youngster to a professional therapist if one is still in doubt. Still, the counsel one would give adolescents on the subject of crushes applies equally to heterosexual or homosexual persons, male and female. It is also pertinent to adults who in this regard are just as immature as adolescents.

In pastoral practice, I try to help the young person understand why he has formed a crush on another person. He needs to see that it comes from a sense of inadequacy and loneliness. He can learn that true love is found not merely in intensity of emotion but in going out to a real world in the service of God and neighbor. The example of the young Augustine can also be cited. He had an emotional friendship with another young man, and when the young man died, Augustine went into a deep depression. Looking back on it twenty-five years later, Augustine concludes how foolish it is for any human to love another human as if he were divine and to expect another to love him as if he were divine.[39]

Show the youngster that this excess is found in every exclusive friendship. The remedy, then, is implicit in the excess. Humans should learn to love other humans in a human way: not expecting too much from any other human, accepting limitations in both self and neighbor, and not seeking from a friend a kind of love the friend cannot give—indeed, a love that God alone can give; moreover, he should not give another the kind of love due to God alone. Since we are *God's* creatures, we are not meant to love with intense, concentrated exclusiveness another member of our own sex, and whenever we violate the law of moderation in love, we suffer in our own persons all the turbulence of disordered emotions.[40] This may sound heavy, but young people are interested in the many meanings of love.

The priest or counselor must be aware that the adolescent person who is convinced he is homosexual harbors much bitterness toward himself and God. He has the feelings of inferiority that van den Aardweg has described, but he will probably not admit their existence. But when the subject of God and religion is broached, he will usually respond that the Church does not understand his condition and that it condemns him whenever it speaks about homosexuality. In speaking with several college homosexual women I ran into hostility toward the Church: "The Church doesn't care, and I don't need her." Usually they are involved in some group that

---

[39] *Confessions of St. Augustine*, bk. 4, ch. 7, Frank Sheed transl., p. 51.

[40] *Ibid.*, bk. 4, ch. 9. Augustine teaches that the sinner brings on his own punishment in the sin itself—the sin becoming, as it were, the instrument of God's justice. A special kind of sin brings a special kind of punishment.

supports the homosexual lifestyle. They do not want to hear any talk of changing their sexual orientation. They claim they are happy just the way they are.

If one probes beneath the surface of the apparently contented homosexual, one will find a great bitterness toward God and at least one parent: "Why did God allow me to be this way? I really didn't want to be this way." If, fortunately, the person gives vent to these feelings, one should listen, not interrupting and not moralizing. By your empathy he realizes that you accept him as a person. Later he will be strong enough spiritually to discuss the role of divine Providence in his life. What he needs now is a sense of hope, a sense that someone cares about him. At this point he may be a fatalist, regarding an active homosexual lifestyle as inevitable, especially if he is the long-standing victim of seduction by older persons. He is like one enslaved by drug or alcoholic addiction. In this situation the counselor can become the power "greater than oneself" to help the person break out of the prison of self-alienation.

Like the adult, the adolescent also needs a spiritual support group. I would invite him to a Courage meeting where he will have the support of adults who have been able to regain *some degree of control* over their lives. If there is no Courage unit in the area, I would suggest that he join an H.A. chapter, where he will receive both support and spiritual direction to live a chaste life. Indeed, H.A.'s encouragement of individuals who are striving to change their sexual attraction will benefit the young person because it demands a moratorium on sexual activity and a concentration on the profound spiritual meaning of being a person redeemed by Christ. Yet he must be impressed with the truth that any road to recovery is long and difficult. Living the five principles of Courage or the Fourteen Steps of H.A. or following the anti-complaining therapy of van den Aardweg or the gender-specific approach of Moberly is hard work.

At the same time we all know that adolescents involved in other forms of addiction (drugs, alcohol, fantasy, and masturbation) are reshaping their lives in rehabilitation centers with strong follow-up meetings after "graduation". Why should not the adolescent or young-adult homosexual person be willing to struggle as hard to regain control of his life, although not necessarily changing sexual orientation? Finally, I used the phrase "some degree of control" to indicate that members of Courage or H.A. may have relapses but that these should not discourage the adolescent joining the group. On the contrary, he will be encouraged when he sees that those who have fallen have got up again by the grace of God. Furthermore, he may be able to accept his own weakness better when he realizes that others are in the same boat as he is. In the fellowship of the weak, strength is born.

Some practical directives for adolescent homosexual persons

1. Avoid styles of dress that signal that he is looking for someone for sexual reasons.

2. Avoid situations wherein immunity from adult observation is combined with a high degree of physical exposure (such as private swimming pools, summer camp cabins, dressing rooms for athletes).

3. Avoid membership in body-culture or weight-lifting clubs and subscriptions to physical culture magazines.

4. Drink moderately, if at all.

Only number 4 applies to adolescent girls. Usually the path of seduction for the teenage or young-adult woman is not through direct genital satisfaction prior to an intense emotional bond with an older person or a peer. Usually, the girl forms an emotional bond with another woman before she becomes involved in genital activity. There are, however, individual variations from this pattern. What is frequently noted among female homosexual persons is the fact of early seduction by older males, often members of their immediate family; subsequent promiscuity may be a cloak for homosexuality. Naturally, the sense of hopelessness pervading these young women makes it unlikely that they will seek help from a spiritual counselor.

The practical directives given above are really concerned with the *external* occasion of serious sin; they will be of greater value if the individual is aware of another factor that might be termed the *internal* occasion of sin. Pastoral experience reveals that before an individual visits the gay-porno theatre, the restrooms, the baths, or the bars he has allowed either a down-mood of self-pity or an up-mood of triumph to take over his imagination. Anger, bitterness, loneliness, and an attitude of defiance are components of these moods. From listening to the young person the counselor should be able to show the *connection* between mood and entering the external occasion of sin. Whenever I have pointed this out to a person after a fall, I have observed that he or she recognized this connection. The obvious inference is the need to control dangerous moods; it will be useful to make some further practical suggestions to all homosexual persons for overcoming negative moods and breaking emotional attachments.[41]

1. Recognize that this has happened before. On previous occasions you

[41] Patrick Carnes, *The Sexual Addiction*, pp. 134–139, analyzes the belief system of Theresa (*Looking for Mr. Goodbar*); he shows the interconnection among her romantic beliefs, her moods, and her behavior.

have fallen in love with the same kind of person. Perhaps a clinical psychologist can help you understand the reasons for this compulsion.

2. Seek spiritual direction from a guide who will help you see the elements of *irrationality* and *idolization* involved in seeking from another creature what one is not able to give. In this regard read the chapter on the "absolutizing instinct" in *Images of Hope* by William F. Lynch (New York: 1966).

3. Admit the limitations of the other person. Your romantic notion of his or her perfection must yield to reality.

4. Ask God to help you break this tendency, and meanwhile see your weakness as a cross to be borne, one that will lead you to a deeper prayer life. In place of resentment and self-pity, pour out your feelings to the Lord—not just your thoughts, but your heart.

5. Do not place yourself unnecessarily in the presence of the person from whom you wish to be free. In this way you will prove to yourself the sincerity of your desire to break away from emotional dependency.

6. Prepare yourself for a period of grief and depression after the break by going to a close friend or adviser and expressing these feelings. Do not be afraid to express these feelings to a trusted third party, but not to the person of concern. Experienced counselors believe that *the person must prepare for the long haul, disciplining emotions lest one slip again into a neurotic pattern of dependence.*

7. Cultivate throughout this struggle an interior life of dependency upon the Lord by spending at least thirty minutes daily in prayer.

The counselor should urge the counselee to begin to show affection to others to fill up the void, explaining that we are all meant to be inter-dependent; this is the reason behind group support. We are meant, first of all, to be dependent upon God, upon Whom we cannot be too dependent. We can be too dependent upon other humans—or too independent of them. Interdependence is sharing love. Explain that in forming friendships one should avoid the excesses of the past, not trying to be the center of attention in the relationship, not giving in to the desire to *be* loved, understood, and pitied—all infantile demands. One must be honest enough to admit that there are dangers even in a seemingly noble friendship, because of human weakness. There is no need to make a *cult* of friendship, for this is egocentric. "If you behave normally toward others, you shall find good friendships now and then, but don't *deliberately seek them*, either, for the sake of a 'cure'. It is infinitely better to try really to love other people, men and women alike and to search yourself and see how little you in fact do love and give" (Correspondence, van den Aardweg, Oct. 1, 1986).

3. ISSUES OF AIDS
(ACQUIRED IMMUNE DEFICIENCY SYNDROME)

The AIDS epidemic is not going away; in fact, in 1986 more persons were diagnosed as having the disease than in all previous years (1978–1985) combined.[42] News reports on November 24, 1986, stated that in Africa the virus had infected millions and was out of control. Gene Antonio holds that between two and three million Americans are considered to be permanently affected with the AIDS virus.[43] He refers to the statement of Dr. James Curran of the Centers for Disease Control (CDC) that "in many areas, the number of persons infected with the AIDS virus is at least one hundred times greater than reported cases of AIDS."[44] As the name implies, the Acquired Immune Deficiency Syndrome is best known for producing an inability of the body's immune system to ward off infections. The person acquires the full-blown disease or its precursor condition ARC (AIDS Related Complex) by becoming infected with the AIDS virus. Children born to infected mothers have acquired the disorder both in the womb and during and after birth.

The term *AIDS* was first used by the CDC in 1982 to describe what seemed to be a new disease. The term is misleading because it does not describe situations where the AIDS virus attacks *many cells of the body apart from those in the immune system*. Again, the term *acquired* does not explain how a child can be born with AIDS, or how there is a spectrum of diseases caused by the virus, a spectrum much wider than that encompassed by the CDC definition of AIDS. "Errors of fact are then propagated by the innocent. There are, for example, many mistakes in the article by Jonathan Lieberson in the January *N. Y. Review of Books*. These canards are extremely dangerous because the disease itself is lethal and because we know neither how serious the problem is now nor how serious it will become . . . for without proper information we will not have rational action."[45] I would add that our moral analysis depends upon such facts. For this reason I sum up three basic known stages of the virus.

The first stage is an asymptomatic carrier stage. Although infected with

[42] J. W. Curran, "The Epidemiology and Prevention of the Acquired Immunodeficiency Syndrome", *The Annals of Internal Medicine* 103 (1985):657–662. Referenced in Gene Antonio, *The AIDS Cover-Up?* (San Francisco: Ignatius Press, 1986), Introduction, p. xi.

[43] *The American Spectator*, March 1986, p. 13: AIDS is caused by infection with a virus that was isolated in France from a patient with chronically swollen glands and was called LAV. In America the virus has been called HTLV-III and ARV. In this book it is called "the AIDS virus".

[44] Gene Antonio, *op. cit.*, p. xi.

[45] James Grutsch, Jr., and A. D. J. Robertson, "The Coming of AIDS", *The American Spectator* 19, no. 3 (March 1986):12–15. See also Antonio, *op. cit.*, pp. 15–30.

the virus, the person shows no detectable signs. He can disseminate the virus to others just as well as those in the full-blown stage three of the virus can. Once this infection has taken place it is there for the lifetime of the person. Dr. Haseltine reiterates: "Once infected, a person remains infected for the rest of his life. Once infected a person is infectious. It is not safe to assume otherwise."[46] This means that once a person becomes infected with the AIDS virus, he or she can never engage in intimate sexual activity without endangering the life of another person. Regulations drafted by CDC state that such persons would have to be told "that they cannot engage in sexual intercourse, kiss someone, or seek medical or dental care without exposing their partner or health care provider to this possibly deadly virus."[47]

It should be noted that authorities in this research are insisting that in every act of sexual intercourse the asymptomatic carrier places the other person at risk. The infection is *lifelong*, and the gestation period of the AIDS virus can be protracted.

There is at least one moral conclusion from such data. If one knows that one is a carrier, one has a serious obligation in conscience to inform anyone with whom one intends to have a sexual contact in which there would be a transmission of fluids. Thus a person who knows that he or she is infected would be obliged to inform the spouse. If the spouse is still willing to take the chances involved in marital coitus, one must also consider the danger of conceiving a child with AIDS. In this situation one should use Natural Family Planning methods to avoid pregnancy. Incidentally, contrary to the advice of Dr. C. Everett Koop, U.S. Surgeon General,[48] the efficacy of condoms in preventing AIDS is unproven.[49]

The second stage of the AIDS virus infection manifests itself in a variety of symptoms, such as sudden unexplained weight loss, persistent diarrhea, swelling of the lymph nodes in the armpits and groin, and chronic fatigue. This has been called the AIDS-related complex (ARC) or the pre-AIDS syndrome. Since persons developing ARC are critically infected with the AIDS virus, the use of the prefix "pre" is inappropriate. The virus itself

[46] D. Gelman et al., "AIDS", *Newsweek*, Aug. 12, 1985, p. 22; quoted by Antonio, *op. cit.*, p. 11.

[47] Joel L. Nitzkin, M.D., and Mark J. Merkens, M.D. (Rochester, N.Y.: Monroe Co. Department of Health), letter to the editor, *JAMA*, 253 (1985):398, citing draft federal regulations in the MMWR, 1985; 34:1–5. Quoted by Antonio, *op. cit.*, p. 11.

[48] U.S. Department of Health and Human Services, *Surgeon General's Report on Acquired Immune Deficiency Syndrome*, p. 17: ". . . you must protect your partner by always using a rubber [condom]. . . ."

[49] J. Curran, "The Epidemiology and Prevention of the Acquired Immunodeficiency Syndrome, *Ann. of Int. Med.* 103 (1985):660.

can directly attack the brain and central nervous system and bring about severe psychiatric and neurological disturbances.[50] *Lancet* (August 17, 1985) reports the case of a twenty-two-year-old man with ARC symptoms who developed paranoid psychosis. Significantly, he had no opportunistic infection or Kaposi's sarcoma; thus he would be excluded from a diagnosis of AIDS according to the Centers for Disease Control (CDC).[51] Since only persons with full-blown AIDS are reported by the CDC, and since it is estimated that the number of those with ARC is much greater than those with AIDS,[52] the public has no idea how many are infected with the AIDS virus. Persons in this second stage are also capable of transmitting the AIDS virus to others.

The third stage, full-blown AIDS,[53] involves the breakdown of the immune system; it leaves the body vulnerable to a series of opportunistic infections, including the development of various cancers and the occurrence of deadly infections from normally nonlethal organisms. In the media the two most frequently mentioned are Pneumocystis carinii pneumonia (PCP) and Kaposi's sarcoma, but there are others as well. So far those in this stage are terminal.

Several other bleak facts about the AIDS virus are: (1) *It is a slow-acting lentivirus*, which means that it will very probably prove deadly to all persons infected by inducing degenerative brain disease in those who do not succumb to opportunistic infection; (2) since the adverse effects of AIDS may take many years to become visible, the infection can spread more rapidly; and (3) the AIDS virus mutates very rapidly, making the development of a vaccine more difficult.[54]

Researchers concerned with the manner in which the AIDS epidemic has spread reveal a combination of factors that have contributed to making practicing homosexual males prime targets for rapidly acquiring and

[50] Deborah M. Barnes, "AIDS-Related Brain Damage Unexplained", *Science*, May 30, 1986, pp. 1091–93: "A very large percentage of AIDS patients have neurological problems. The exact incidence is not known, but as many as 60% will eventually develop dementia."

[51] Antonio, *op. cit.*, pp. 13–14. See also C. S. Thomas et al., "HTLV-III and Psychiatric Disturbance", *Lancet*, Aug. 17, 1985, pp. 395–396.

[52] J. I. Slaff and J. K. Brubaker, *The AIDS Epidemic: How You Can Protect Yourself and Your Family—Why You Must* (New York: Warner Books, 1985), pp. 159–160.

[53] "It is worth repeating that the name 'AIDS' is not synonymous with the AIDS virus, though the vast majority of the people infected with the virus have not yet developed AIDS—which is the name given to a number of diseases known to be caused by the AIDS virus. The rapid spread of AIDS among 'high risk' groups in the United States has obscured our perception of the equally or more serious spread among other groups in other countries and the beginning of the spread to what are considered 'low risk' groups here" (Grustch and Robertson, *op. cit.*, p. 13). Antonio shares this view.

[54] Antonio, *op. cit.*, pp. 30–31.

widely disseminating AIDS *and other virulent* diseases. Physiologically damaging sexual practices facilitate the transmission of infectious agents. Among male homosexuals sodomy is substituted for normal vaginal intercourse. But when sodomy is performed, the forced inward expansion of the anal canal results in a tearing of the lining as well as producing bleeding anal fissures. Colitis, a severe inflammation of the mucous membrane of the colon, often occurs as sodomy is repeatedly indulged in. Interestingly, a study made before the discovery of the AIDS virus (HTLV–III/LAV) found that blood from rectal mucosal lesions, which are known to be common in homosexual males engaging in rectal intercourse, "could contain the infectious agent responsible for this epidemic."[55] This important study, correlating homosexual behavior and diseases with the prevalence of AIDS, was published by the American College of Physicians in 1983. Yet there has been only occasional mention in the media of the relationship between homosexual acts or diseases and the probability of the transmission of AIDS.

Prior stimulation and *suppression of the immune system* as the result of sodomy, together with repeated venereal disease, seems to increase susceptibility to devastation by the AIDS virus. By way of contrast, during normal heterosexual intercourse the dynamic qualities of sperm enable penetration and fertilization of the female ovum with resultant pregnancy. But the walls of the vagina are elastic and several layers thick, with glands that provide natural lubrication during sexual relations. This blocks large quantities of sperm from entering the bloodstream. A 1984 study in the *Journal of the American Medical Association*, after noting the association of sperm-induced immune dysregulation with the practice of anal intercourse, underscores "the critical structural differences between the rectum and the vagina . . . the lining of the rectum is made of a single layer of columnar epithelium. . . . [It], unlike the vaginal epithelium, is not only incapable of protecting against any abrasive effect, but also promotes the absorption of an array of sperm antigens, *thus enhancing their exposure to the immune apparatus in the lymphatic and blood circulation.*"[56]

In so-called education to prevent the spread of AIDS it is often said that "monogamous" sodomy is an acceptable alternative to promiscuous sodomy. Antonio reports a study, however, involving monogamously paired homosexual males, in which three-fourths of the passive partners

[55] H. W. Jaffe et al., "National Case-Control Study of Kaposi's Sarcoma and Pneumocystis Carinii Pneumonia in Homosexual Men: pt. 2, Laboratory Results", *Ann. of Int. Med.* 99 (1983):145–151; quoted in Antonio, *op. cit.*, pp. 34–35, at 35.

[56] G. M. Mavligit et al., "Chronic Immune Stimulation by Sperm Alloantigens; Support for the Hypothesis That Spermatozoa Induce Immune Dysregulation in Homosexual Males", *JAMA* 251 (1984):237–241. Quoted in Antonio, *op. cit.*, pp. 37–38.

manifested sperm-induced immune dysregulation—a dysregulation quite apart from infection by the AIDS virus, yet preparing the way for it.[57] Citing an additional study concerning the vulnerability of the rectal mucosa, Antonio observes that "from a purely biological perspective, sodomy, even apart from the transmission of AIDS, *is an intrinsically unsanitary and pathological act*."[58] From a theological point of view I would add that it is a violation of the human body and of the plan of the Creator for the procreation of the human race, as well as a parody of true marital love. I think the use of the word *pathological* is justified when one considers that the practice of sodomy does direct harm to anal tissues and has been a transmitting agent in the spread of AIDS.

AIDS spreading to the general population

Antonio holds that another factor in the spread of AIDS is the aggressive growth of the homosexual liberation movement (joined with legislative sanction of homosexual behavior), since it fosters "extremely high levels of anonymous, multiple-partner sexual encounters."[59] John Sonnabend argues that any hypothesis regarding the genesis of AIDS must explain the recent emergence of the syndrome. He suggests that an unprecedented level of promiscuity has developed in urban areas during the past decade, attacking first the homosexual population and likely to invade the general public. When one considers the relatonships between bisexual men and prostitutes, it is not difficult to understand the spread of AIDS to the wives or sexual partners of bisexual men, or indeed of heterosexual men who visit prostitutes. In his report on AIDS, C. Everett Koop warns against sex with prostitutes. Infected male and female prostitutes are frequently also intravenous drug abusers; therefore they may infect clients by sexual intercourse and also infect other intravenous drug abusers by sharing their intravenous drug equipment. Female prostitutes can infect their unborn babies.[60]

According to Dr. William Haseltine of Harvard Medical School, more than ten million persons are presently infected with the AIDS virus in Africa. The modes of transmission are not known at this date, but it must *not* be assumed that AIDS in Africa is spread *only* through heterosexual contact. AIDS is also spread by multi-use, nonsterile needles and by "the

[57] Antonio, *op. cit.*, p. 39. Antonio references the work of Mavligit et al., p. 241 (note 56).

[58] *Ibid.*, p. 39. See also my Chapter Five with arguments against homosexual activity. Antonio on p. 39 refers to Goedert et al. in *ibid.*, p. 214, note 3.

[59] *Ibid.*, p. 64.

[60] *Time*, Nov. 3, 1986, "A Most Explicit Report", pp. 76–77. See also *Surgeon General's Report* on AIDS, p. 18.

close, nonsexual contact between cuts, sores, and abrasions and the blood or serum of other people which commonly occur, particularly in children in the crowded and unsanitary conditions in which most people on earth live."[61]

Various researchers in several countries suggest that in Africa the Anopheles mosquito is an important transmitter of AIDS. But whatever the primary routes of AIDS in Africa may have been, there is now a lethal pandemic spreading throughout the crowded cities and villages of developing nations on a scale unparalleled in human history.[62] What has taken place in Central Africa can happen in the Western world and in the United States. Concerning our own country the following facts are pertinent:

1. Drug-addicted male homosexuals who shared contaminated hypodermic needles with heterosexual addicts introduced AIDS into this segment of the population (33% of IV drug abusers with AIDS were homosexual or bisexual men—159 out of 485).

2. Intravenous drug abusers, primarily heroin addicts, have been the next largest group developing the AIDS virus (17% of the cases with AIDS).

3. The AIDS blood-screening test is not as reliable as it has been hailed to be; it still permits a significant number of persons who are asymptomatically carrying the virus to slip through. The blood is safer than it was before, but how safe we do not know.

4. It is alarming that some active male homosexuals who have not been tested still donate blood; proper measures should be taken to discourage this practice.

5. In the United States *until now* heterosexual sexual transmission has comprised only a fraction of diagnosed AIDS cases. Only 1% of all AIDS cases have been linked directly to heterosexual relations. There are reasons for this: "Normal heterosexual coitus is not an intrinsically damaging act as is sodomy. . . . The anatomical differences between the vagina and the rectum appear to be largely responsible for the fact that AIDS may be acquired more readily by anal-receptive sodomy."[63] Again, there are lower levels of sexual intercourse among heterosexuals than among homosexuals. The extremely high frequency of homosexual encounters facilitates massive invasion of the AIDS virus.

6. But the proportion of reported AIDS cases occurring through heterosexual relations will increase.[64] Reported cases include both male-

[61] Slaff and Brubaker, *The AIDS Epidemic* (New York: Warner Books, 1985), p. 236.

[62] Antonio, *op. cit.*, pp. 71–74.

[63] *Ibid.*, p. 81.

[64] Katie Leishman, "Heterosexuals and AIDS—The Second Stage of the Epidemic", *Atlantic Monthly*, Feb. 1987, pp. 39–58.

to–female transmission, and vice versa. The present increase in AIDS cases among heterosexuals in this country may follow the pattern of increase among homosexuals of several years ago. A contributing factor is the fact that more than a million and a half homosexual and bisexual men are presently infected with the AIDS virus. Bell and Weinberg, moreover, report that 65% of practicing homosexuals have engaged in heterosexual intercourse, and 20% are or have been married.[65] As Dr. Koop and others have pointed out, there is the potential for the spread of AIDS through female prostitutes. Dr. William Haseltine of Harvard's Dana-Farber Cancer Institute reports: "There is accumulating evidence that infection is transmitted from prostitutes to their customers. A recent study conducted by the United States Army revealed that five per cent of United States soldiers reporting to venereal disease clinics in Berlin are now infected with the AIDS virus."[66]

Proposed responses to the spreading AIDS epidemic

With very little hope for a cure or vaccine, the Institute of Medicine, an affiliate of the Natural Academy of Sciences, called for expenditures of one billion dollars a year by 1990 for research and another one billion dollars for AIDS education. The report urges that the president take a strong leadership role in the fight against AIDS to prevent its further spread and that a national commission on AIDS be established to monitor the program and report periodically to the public. The report goes on to say that the level of funding is but a small fraction of the billions of dollars for care that the epidemic is sure to cost, particularly if it is not curbed rapidly. Samuel Thier, president of the Institute of Medicine, stated: "We expect approximately 179,000 deaths from AIDS in the United States by the end of 1991." Pointing out that AIDS is now spreading among heterosexuals, he warned that "there is potential for much wider spread of AIDS within this group, and as a result we can expect to see increased transmission of AIDS from mothers to newborns."[67]

On the basis of medical studies, Antonio draws a far more grim picture of the future than does the Institute of Medicine study.

In the next several years, close to one million persons, mostly between the ages of twenty and forty-nine, will have their physical and mental health inexorably and progressively devastated by AIDS virus infection. Hundreds

[65] *Homosexualities: A Study of Diversity among Men and Women* (New York: Simon and Schuster, 1978), pp. 162, 286. Antonio, *op. cit.*, p. 91.

[66] W. A. Haseltine (response to a letter to the editor), *N. Eng. J. of Med.* 314 (1985):55–56.

[67] Alison Bethel, "2 Billion AIDS plan urged by '90", *Philadelphia Inquirer*, Oct. 30, 1986, pp. 1 and 19 A.

of thousands—perhaps more—will die of full-blown AIDS. Hundreds of thousands—perhaps more—will suffer from the severe immunological and neurological disorders induced by the HTLV-III virus.[68]

In any case I think we can agree that our country has to face a very grave crisis for the foreseeable future. What is not clear is the best way to stop the spread of AIDS. The Institute of Medicine says that we need money for research to discover a vaccine to cure those already afflicted with the virus and to educate the public in methods of prevention. Since Dr. Koop has given us some advice in his 36-page booklet on AIDS, we might regard this as our first lesson on the subject. He says that we need sex education in schools, including information on homosexual and heterosexual relationships. In this sex education curriculum there should be a heavy emphasis on the prevention of AIDS and other sexually transmitted diseases.

But who is going to give this information on homosexual relationships? What will be the moral premises of such directives? Those of the Judeo-Christian tradition? or those of secular humanism and gay liberation holding that homosexual acts, including sodomy, are good? If one regards sodomy between faithful lovers as good, then why not recommend the use of condoms to be "safe"? On the CBS Dan Rather show on AIDS (8 P.M., Oct. 22, 1986) nurses were shown recommending condoms.

Again, it is agreed that the avoidance of the AIDS virus is a matter of life and death, yet Dr. Koop says nothing about the unreliability of condoms, either in the context of youth education or in the situation of a "partner" who suspects that his "partner" has been exposed by previous homosexual or heterosexual behavior or use of intravenous drugs. It is clear that the directives assume that the vast majority of students in school, or adults in various kinds of sexual relationships, do not desire to practice sexual abstinence even if it is a matter of life or death. It is assumed, moreover, in a pluralistic society that all expressions of sexuality are good as long as no one is hurt and that sodomistic intercourse between two homosexuals is, as a way of life, equal in value to marriage and family. The assumptions may be those of the vast majority, but the suggestion of self-control and sexual abstinence should also be proposed as a practical way of avoiding the AIDS virus. Such a proposal, however, would be regarded as oppressive, an imposition of a code of morality on the public. Thus, since no serious challenge has been issued to practice the virtue of self-control, millions have already been put in jeopardy of getting AIDS. Unfortunately, our leaders have assumed that the practice of sexual abstinence is *in practice*

---

[68] Antonio, *op. cit.*, pp. 131–139 at 132. For medical references see footnotes to Antonio, *op. cit.*, pp. 231–232.

impossible and that it is more prudent to take a chance on a condom to save one's life.

Granted, the directives of the Surgeon General include practical advice concerning tears in the vagina or rectum for those who are determined to indulge. It is also true that the risk of infection becomes greater the more partners one has. The warnings about the use of drugs are also on target. The advice about giving blood is reassuring.

These guidelines of the Surgeon General, however, are misleading by omission. They fail to point out that the virus began to spread in large homosexual communities such as San Francisco and New York City through promiscuity, particularly through sodomy and that these communities have the prime responsibility to use effective means to prevent the further spread of AIDS. They were slow to recommend the closing of bathhouses and other establishments where sodomitic homosexual intercourse continues unbridled.

Antonio holds that the AIDS epidemic is being treated in a markedly different manner from other plagues of the past.[69] Less virulent venereal diseases have been met with greater efforts at control and prevention than has AIDS. Dr. Restak writes that "efforts are being made by medically unsophisticated politicians and attorneys to dictate policy in regard to an illness that has the potential for wreaking a devastation such as has not been encountered for hundreds of years."[70] One may ask why such a highly politicized wall of opposition has been raised against presenting the facts concerning the nature of AIDS to the public. Why does the Surgeon General issue palliative pansexual directives to stop the spread of this killer-virus? I think Antonio answers this question well with medical opinion to document his position: "This lethal barrier stems from the inability of major health and political officials and others to reconcile their philosophical presuppositions regarding the nature of human sexuality with the empirical contradiction of the epidemiology of AIDS and other virulent diseases."[71]

In trying to understand why there is such a coverup on the AIDS crisis one should not overlook judicial decisions; for example, in its 1981 decision holding the state's antisodomy law to be unconstitutional, the Supreme Court of New York concluded that there was no rational basis for the law. No showing had been made in the briefs "that physical injury

[69] Antonio, *op. cit.*, 141–167.

[70] Richard Restak, "Worry about Survival of Society First; Then AIDS Victims' Rights", *Washington Post*, Sept. 8, 1985.

[71] *Op. cit.*, p. 144. Read the section "AIDS Control and the Medical Establishment", pp. 144–151.

is a common or even occasional consequence of the prohibited conduct."[72] Yet one year prior to the ruling, the *New England Journal of Medicine* had editorialized that

> oral and anal intercourse present physicians with surgical as well as medical problems, ranging from anal fissures and impaction of foreign bodies in the rectum to major diagnostic dilemmas. Infection in traumatized rectal mucosa and in amebic or herpetic ulcers above the level of the anal ring may produce formations that mimic rectal carcinoma.[73]

Antonio also gives examples of media censorship of the AIDS epidemic, together with a summary of the legislative goals of the homosexual movement. One of the stated major goals of this movement is to have homosexuality taught in the public schools as a healthy alternative sexual lifestyle. This movement is naturally afraid that the truth about AIDS will damage the image of homosexuality it wishes to present.[74]

Antonio believes that federal action is imperative to stop the spread of AIDS. He handles the sophism that one cannot legislate morality well, drawing support from Dr. Restak, who writes:

> Only sentimentalists refuse to make any distinction between the victims of a scourge and those not presently infected. . . . The threat of AIDS demands from us all a discrimination based on our instinct for survival against a peril, that if not somehow controlled, can destroy this society. This is a discrimination that caution is in order when knowledge is incomplete so that the public interest is protected. . . . This is not a civil rights issue; this is a medical issue. To take a position that the AIDS virus must be eradicated is not to make judgments on morals or lifestyle. It is to say that the AIDS virus has no "civil rights".[75]

Finally, Antonio proposes legislative steps, which include a federal order closing down all known homosexual bathhouses; federal bans on all high-risk group members from donating blood or plasma, contributing semen to sperm banks, or donating organs; federal registration of all persons diagnosed with full-blown AIDS or pre-AIDS, as well as those testing positive with the AIDS blood screening test; a crackdown on computerized solicitation for high-risk sexual activities; a kind of sex education in the public schools that will prevent the spread of AIDS

---

[72] Onofre, 434 N.Y.S. 2d at 951, cited in Charles Rice, *Legalizing Homosexual Conduct: The Role of the Supreme Court in the Gay Rights Movement* (Cumberland, Va.: Center for Judicial Studies, 1984), pp. 19–20. Antonio, *op. cit.*, pp. 151–152.

[73] K. Dritz, *op. cit.*, p. 464. Antonio, *op. cit.*, p. 152.

[74] Antonio, *op. cit.*, pp. 151–167.

[75] Restak, *op. cit.*, quoted by Antonio, *op. cit.*, pp. 172–173.

(obviously this would be a contradiction of the pansexuality currently taught in many public schools).

I believe his proposals should be given due consideration, although I have reservations about some of them, particularly the federal registration of those testing positive in the AIDS blood screening test. It is beyond the scope of this work properly to evaluate these proposals. Yet, believing that most of them make good sense, I hope that those who have considered the urgency of the situation will write to congressmen, senators, the Attorney General, the Surgeon General, and the Secretary of Education. Perhaps a small group of persons will assume the responsibility to write the necessary legislation to present to the American public through democratic processes. It is an arduous task to transform Christian convictions into law in order to stop the spread of AIDS, but we cannot afford *not* to attempt to do it.[76]

The pastoral care of those with AIDS

Besides doing everything possible to stop the spread of AIDS, we must minister to those already afflicted with AIDS as is occurring already in some dioceses. In New York City, Cardinal O'Connor announced a comprehensive plan for the care and study of AIDS patients (Aug. 20, 1985). St. Clare's and St. Vincent's hospitals have units devoted to the care of AIDS patients. Mother Teresa has opened a hospice for AIDS patients at an abandoned rectory in Greenwich Village. In San Francisco, a former convent has been converted into a hospice for those dying of AIDS.

In 1986 Mother Teresa opened another hospice in Washington, D.C. Meanwhile in Los Angeles, Archbishop Roger Mahoney has pledged to do what he can to provide care for those suffering from AIDS. One layman, Jim Johnson, has established three small home hospices in Los Angeles, mainly at his own expense, giving up a profitable business and spending personal income to keep the hospices going. He is also a founder of Courage in Los Angeles, seeking volunteer help from the small Courage units in the city. In Boston, Cardinal Law has asked his priests and laity to plan ways of helping those afflicted with AIDS, carefully avoiding harsh judgments. Other dioceses (Chicago, New Orleans, Minneapolis, and Sacramento)[77] have set up hospices; but while isolated examples of the

---

[76] Antonio, *op. cit.*, pp. 164–184.

[77] Bishop Francis Quinn of Sacramento writes: "If the yardstick of our faith is unconditional love, particularly love of those whom society regards as outcasts, then our response to people suffering from AIDS will be a measure of our faith." "Ministry to AIDS Victims", *Origins*, 16, no. 12 (Sept. 4, 1986).

Catholic response to the AIDS crisis are noteworthy, the Church must make a more concerted effort on the national level to serve those suffering from AIDS.[78]

Attitudes toward persons with AIDS

Personally, I have ministered over a two-year period to two Courage members who died of AIDS and to the families of others with AIDS. The question I have encountered frequently is: What should be the proper Christian attitude toward this tragic illness? I have heard people say that AIDS is a punishment from God afflicted upon homosexuals violating the law of God; it is Sodom and Gomorrah repeated. I cannot accept this explanation. Why are not heterosexual persons who are involved in fornication, adultery, incest, and rape similarly punished by a fatal illness? The judgment of responsibility and guilt is properly that of Christ. We need to keep in mind that many women and children are the innocent victims of the disease. Even homosexual persons who knew they were engaging in high-risk activity may not be as guilty as one would think, because these same persons tend to act compulsively while under the illusion of freedom. I do not say that such persons are absolved from all responsibility, but I do say we should give them the benefit of the doubt and treat them with love. From my pastoral experience I believe that the vast majority of persons suffering from AIDS had no clear idea what they were getting into. Judgment is the Lord's.

Another attitude I heard on Dan Rather's CBS Special on AIDS (Oct. 22, 1986) was that of a man commenting on the situation of a woman dying of AIDS contracted from her bisexual husband. The husband said he felt no guilt, that it was just a biological accident. This is really a denial of responsibility; *humans* do the kinds of acts that transmit the AIDS virus. This same attitude is found in members of the Gay Liberation Movement, revealing itself in their resistance to the closing of homosexual bathhouses in New York and San Francisco when they knew the AIDS virus was spreading in those cities. The words of the "Letter to the Bishops of the Catholic Church on the Pastoral Care of Homosexuals" from the Sacred Congregation for the Doctrine of the Faith (Oct. 1, 1986) are pertinent: "Even when the practice of homosexuality may seriously threaten the

[78] Michael G. Meyer, "The Catholic Church and AIDS", *America*, June 28, 1986, pp. 512–514, adds that "if the church is to play an effective part, it must examine the cause of its reticence, accept the grace of conversion and plan a rational course" (p. 512). In this same issue one finds Archbishop Quinn's Pastoral Response, a thoughtful piece by James Stulz: "Toward a Spirituality for Victims of AIDS", and an article by James Whitehurst entitled "AIDS the New Leprosy: If Only Father Damien Were Here!"

lives and well-being of a large number of people, its advocates remain undeterred and refuse to consider the magnitude of the risks involved."[79]

Another attitude toward AIDS is found in two members of Dignity in the Washington and Baltimore areas who made it clear they did not regard their homosexual activity as sinful. AIDS was a cross they had to carry. As has been pointed out, this view that homosexual activity in a stable relationship is morally good is widespread among Dignity members.

Eileen Flynn in her book *AIDS, A Catholic Call for Compassion* does not assert that such relationships are good or bad, but instead presents both the opinions of dissenting theologians and the official teaching of the Church. The fact that she does not explicitly state that homosexual activity is always wrong weakens the value of her work, which otherwise helps the public to understand the terrible suffering of AIDS patients.[80]

I agree, however, with her conclusion that "the lot of the AIDS patient will improve only when the attitudes of well people reflect genuine concern and compassion. Religious and government leaders should use the power of the pulpit and the podium to shape a new attitude which will lead to a comprehensive plan of action."[81] There are difficulties, however, in the fact that government leaders take the view that homosexuality is a morally acceptable alternative lifestyle, and some religious leaders hold the same view. From a practical point of view, the safest way for the homosexual person to avoid AIDS is to be sexually abstinent, but he is not about to be such as long as he believes that he has a right to homosexual activity and can manage to avoid AIDS by "safe" sex.

In helping the person suffering from AIDS, nothing is accomplished by denying the *objective* immorality of homosexual activity. On the *subjective* level the person may be without serious guilt because of ignorance or the power of compulsion. In ministering to such a person we stress the mercy of God to all of us sinners; if the sick person wants to confess his sins, and he feels that he has sinned in his homosexual activity, let him say it. To be sure, he may have only diminished responsibility, and the minister should

---

[79] PCHP, 9.

[80] *AIDS, A Catholic Call to Compassion* (Kansas City, Mo.: Sheed and Ward, 1985), pp. 62–80. On p. 69 Eileen Flynn refers to the Church's teaching on sexuality as "idealistic"; it would be more accurate to say that such teaching is a difficult ideal binding in conscience and possible by the grace of God. Flynn, moreover, accurately describes the position of some contemporary moral theologians who hold that "based on psychological data . . . committed, monogamous homosexual unions may be a morally acceptable solution for those homosexuals who are unable to embrace a life of celibacy" (p. 75). The weakness of this dissenting position is that it ignores the psychological data in favor of celibate living, and it does not take into account the power of divine grace to help a homosexual person to live without genital sex in accord with the Church's understanding of the moral law.

[81] Flynn, *AIDS: A Catholic Call to Compassion*, p. 94.

say so. Christ truly loves sinners, as He showed in His love for Mary Magdalen. He loves homosexual sinners too. In my actual ministering to such persons I found that what occupied their thoughts most of the time was the acceptance of pain through the Cross of Christ and the meaning of heaven.

POSTSCRIPTUM

As I finish this chapter, the AIDS crisis continues to grow, and both the U.S. government and private agencies of all kinds are searching for effective ways of halting the spread of this dread disease. In every diocese bishops are seeking ways of ministering to those so afflicted. Meanwhile both media and homosexual propagandists perpetuate the myth that condoms are a form of "safe sex", whereas common sense dictates that only sexual abstinence qualifies as safe. Even the Surgeon General, C. Everett Koop, advocates condoms for those who will not accept his recommendation of sexual abstinence. In this spiritual vacuum we need to speak about prevention of AIDS through sexual abstinence or monogamy in marriage, recognizing that this can be accomplished only by the grace of God, for which everyone must pray. As one liberal columnist has said, "It is either faithful monogamy in marriage or celibacy."

CHAPTER NINE

PSYCHOLOGICAL AND PASTORAL REFLECTIONS ON PEDOPHILIA

Unfortunately, during the past two years sexual abuse of young boys by priests or brothers in various parts of the country has been highlighted in the media. While only a very small number of priests have been convicted of such behavior, the Church and society are concerned to protect the young as well as bring adequate professional care and pastoral guidance to anyone, including priests and religious who have become sexually involved with prepubertal or adolescent males. Until very recently there has been widespread ignorance, even among psychiatrists and clinical psychologists, concerning pedophilia, and that is why I shall give a brief overview of the problem. In writing this chapter I have had the assistance of Dr. John F. Kinnane, and we shall begin with the definition of pedophilia.

Pedophilia is one species of the paraphilias described in *The Diagnostic and Statistical Manual of Mental Disorders*, Third Edition (*DSM III*) as a subclass of "unusual or bizarre imagery or acts [that] are necessary for sexual excitement." Such imagery and acts tend to be "insistently and involuntarily repetitive."[1] *DSM III* then describes pedophilia:

> The essential feature is the act or fantasy of engaging in sexual activity with prepubertal children as a repeatedly preferred or exclusive method of achieving sexual excitement. The difference in age between the adult with this disorder and the prepubertal child is arbitrarily set at ten years or more. For late adolescents with this disorder, no precise age difference is specified.[2]

Adults with this disorder are twice as likely to be oriented toward children of the other sex as toward children of the same sex. Here, however, I concentrate on homosexual pedophilia. Homosexually oriented males tend to prefer slightly older children than those heterosexually oriented, who prefer eight- to ten-year-old girls. The percentage of those

[1] *DSM III* p. 266. See also John Money, *Lovemaps* (New York: Irvington Publishers, Inc., 1986). This is an updated compendium of the pedophilias, with strong emphasis on their biological roots. Together with Dr. Fred Berlin, Dr. Money has conducted extensive research into the paraphilias, and pedophilia in particular. Money says that the word *paraphilia* is derived from two Greek roots. *Philia* means love, and *para* means the love that goes beyond what is ordinarily expected or is apart from it. "Thus, in medical usage, it also means abnormal" (p. 1).

[2] *DSM III*, p. 271.

couples who know each other only casually is higher among the hetero-sexually oriented. Again, most individuals oriented homosexually have not been married.[3]

1. THE THOUGHT OF BERLIN AND MONEY ON THE NATURE OF PEDOPHILIA

Dr. Fred Berlin of the Sexual Disorders Clinic at the Johns Hopkins School of Medicine presents as comprehensive a view of the pedophile person as is presently attainable. He stresses that men do not choose to be pedophiles, that they are *predisposed* to certain kinds of partners (young boy or girl) or to certain kinds of behavior (oral, anal intercourse, or merely touching genitalia) by a series of factors, not all of which are completely understood. Like the other paraphilias, pedophilia is charac-terized by very strong and persistent urges to perform the sexual act with prepubertal children. "As with other appetites, the pedophilic appetite craves satiation, with recurrence of hunger an expected event."[4] While Berlin distinguishes between those pedophiles who are not concerned with this tendency (ego-syntonic) and those who desire to be rid of the tendency (ego-dystonic), our concern is only with the ego-dystonic pedophile.

Berlin provides direct testimony that shows how tortured and conflicted a man may be by the sexual lusts he feels toward young boys:

> What starts a person like myself doing what I am doing?. . . Why can't I be normal like everybody else? You know, did God put this as a punishment or something toward me?. . . Why can't I just go out and have a good time with girls? I feel empty when a female is present. An older "gay" person would turn me off. I have thought about suicide. I think after this long period of time I have actually seen where I have an illness. It is getting uncontrollable to the point where I can't put up with it anymore. It is a sickness. . . . But as far as society is concerned you are a criminal and should be punished. . . .[5]

How do pedophilic sexual desires come about? Berlin gives us one explanation. Most of us yearn for a loving, adult sexual relationship, while children elicit from us emotional responses that do not include feelings of lust or erotic love. We usually do not fall in love with children

---

[3] *Ibid.*

[4] Fred Berlin and Edgar Krout, "Pedophilia: Diagnostic Concepts, Treatment, and Ethical Considerations", *Amer. J. of Forensic Psychiatry*, 7 (1986):13–30 at 13.

[5] *Ibid.*, p. 14. See also F. S. Berlin and C. F. Meinecke, "Treatment of Sex Offenders with Antiandrogenic Medication: Conceptualization, Review of Treatment Modalities, and Preliminary Findings", *Amer. J. of Psychiatry*, 138 (1981):601–607; F. S. Berlin and G. S. Coyle, "Sexual Deviation Syndromes", *Johns Hopkins Med. J.* 149 (1981):119–125.

in a romantic or sexual way, but the pedophile does. It is, then, an issue of sexual and affectional orientation. In Berlin's view, life, experience, and constitution play a role in the acquisition of such an orientation. He points to research showing that many men who experience pedophilic erotic urges as adults were sexually involved with adults when they were children. In treating the pedophile, one is often treating the former "victim". We do not know, however, whether his pedophilia is directly the result of childhood seduction or of the nature of his biological constitution, or both. We do know that other men who were involved in sexual relationships as children do not become pedophiles.

John Money holds that excessive prohibition of early sexual expression may also put one at risk of developing pedophilic sexual desires.[6] He attributes this to what is known as the *opponent-process* principle. If a boy is discovered by his parents in a sexual act, either as seduced or seducer, and is punished and mortified, he will tend in later life, usually as a middle-aged adult, to perform a similar sexual act with a child. Aversion becomes addiction. Usually there is a long period of repression before the act is repeated, only in adult life and *compulsively*. This addiction is resistant to change, which, Money believes, is due to the fact that "a paraphilic attraction is the equivalent of the normophilic attraction of falling in love."[7]

Drawing on findings gained in their Sexual Disorders Clinic, both Berlin and Money point out that biology also plays an important role in the development of sexual orientation and sexual paraphilias. According to their theory, sexual desire itself is apparently unlearned and is rooted in biology. As in the case of language and dialect, once acquired, sexual desires are not readily modified. It is reasonable, then, to ask whether certain biological abnormalities could be related to pedophilia. In an effort to throw some light on this question, Berlin evaluated forty-one men, all of whom had met the *DSM III* diagnostic criteria for some form of paraphilia. The majority of the men were pedophiles or exhibitionists. Berlin concluded that there may indeed be an association between the presence of certain kinds of biological abnormalities and the presence of certain kinds of unconventional behavior, such as pedophilia.[8] At the Clinic it is unusual to see a man who experiences recurrent pedophilic

---

[6] *Love and Love Sickness* (Baltimore: Johns Hopkins Press, 1980).

[7] *Lovemaps*, p. 38. Money credits Richard L. Solomon with the formulation of the opponent-process theory of learning, according to which one becomes positively addicted to what initially was negatively aversive: "Even the victims of cruel child abuse become addicted to abuse" (p. 39).

[8] F. S. Berlin, "A Biomedical Perspective and a Status Report on Biomedical Treatment", in *The Sexual Aggressor: Current Perspectives on Treatment*, ed. J. C. Greer and I. R. Stuart (New York: Reinhold, 1983), pp. 83, 123.

cravings in the absence of a significant biological abnormality, a history of sexual involvements with an adult during childhood, or both.[9]

Berlin notes the different approach of *DSM III* from *DSM II*. In the latter, pedophilia was categorized as an antisocial personality disorder, but *DSM III* acknowledges that this is not necessarily so. Diagnosing a person as pedophilic gives us information concerning the nature of his sexual desires and orientation, but it does not tell us anything about his temperament or about traits of character, such as caring versus uncaring, and so on. Such a diagnosis does not necessarily mean that a person is lacking in conscience or flawed in character.

Thus, in evaluating a person who has become involved with a child, one has to determine whether this behavior is the effect of psychosis, psychological immaturity, lack of conscience, a pedophilic sexual orientation, other influences, or a combination of several of these. The point to be made is that one must concentrate independently on the nature of an individual's sexual drives and interests as distinguished from what the person is like in terms of character, intellect, and other mental capacities.[10]

This brings us to the question of the responsibility of the pedophile to change his behavior.

Berlin adverts here to the common view that the pedophile could stop acting out if only he made up his mind to do so: "People can invariably control their behavior through the exercise of 'willpower' alone. After all, some people give up smoking or drinking after many years." Berlin shows that many people are not able by will power *alone* to control their cravings when such drives are influenced by biological regulatory systems. He gives the example of a person on kidney dialysis made thirsty by the procedure who often has great difficulty maintaining necessary fluid restrictions, even though not doing so can be life-threatening. Researchers have shown that the limits set by the physician for such a patient may not suffice, because they differ from the patient's own physiology. Analogically, the pedophilic person suffers in many cases from another kind of physiological drive and is sometimes compelled to act out his craving. Will power alone will not suffice in these compulsive situations.

Again, Berlin refers to a confusion in the public's understanding of other compulsions. It is objected that a pedophile will not approach a child when a policeman is present and that a chain smoker will not smoke in his doctor's office. What is not observed is that these individuals were able to exercise self-control because of something *beyond* will power, the stabilizing influence of another person.[11] This is part of the meaning conveyed in

[9] Berlin and Krout, *art. cit.*, *Amer. J. of Forensic Psychiatry*, 7 (1986):15.

[10] *Ibid.*, pp. 16–17.

[11] *Ibid.*, p. 17.

Step Two of A.A.—turning to a power greater than oneself, to the spiritual support of the group.

Thus, Berlin concludes that we need to be very prudent in assessing the responsibility of the pedophile. On the one hand, he is not the passive product of life experiences and constitution; on the other hand, he does have great difficulty gaining greater control over his compulsive activity. Without excusing irresponsible behavior as "psychopathology", we must avoid double-standard judgments, that is to say, judgments in which we condemn the pedophilic person out of hand after the fashion of the culture. If a person says he is trying to stop smoking or to stop compulsive handwashing, he is often believed and given help. But if a person says he needs help in order to avoid having sex with children, and that he cannot control himsef by will power alone, he is often rejected.[12] Since Berlin believes that pedophiles do need help to regain control over their sexual fantasies and acts, he and John Money propose a program of treatment. But before considering their program, I should like to introduce the thought of Gerald van den Aardweg on the nature of pedophilia.

2. VAN DEN AARDWEG ON THE NATURE OF PEDOPHILIA

Van den Aardweg believes that the most adequate definition of homosexual pedophilia was given by André Gide, himself a pedophile: "Sexual interest in boys who do not yet manifest the marks of adult manhood." In this definition the criterion is subjective, lying in the view of the afflicted person himself. How does he see his object? A young man of seventeen or eighteen without markedly manly characteristics may be appealing to a pedophile, although he is usually attracted by boys around twelve years of age. While granting that the majority of homosexuals are not aroused by young boys, the distinction between homosexuality and homosexual pedophilia is not quite absolute. In some cases the interest oscillates between young adolescents and adults, in others between boys and adolescents; in exceptional cases a man may be interested in boys at one time and adults at another.[13]

From research and clinical practice, van den Aardweg explores the possibility that pedophilia may be related to different parental relationships in childhood. He was impressed by the recollections of pedophilic patients concerning overcritical mothers who did not give them sufficient freedom to play, to explore, or to bring their friends home. There were also instances of pampering—overpermissive mothers who tied their sons to

---

[12] *Ibid.*

[13] *On the Origins and Treatment of Homosexuality*, p. 157.

their apron strings. Both types of mothers *restrict* the contacts of their sons with other children. The father was more detached, as is often the case with homosexuals.

This factor of *inhibition* with regard to normal boyish enterprises assumes various forms: keeping the boy away from others by inducing anxiety toward the outside world, tying him too close to mother, forbidding boyish activities. Such measures induce the feeling of loneliness in the boy and impede him from forming friendships. This is the most conspicuous psychological factor in pedophiles: "They nearly all relate having been lonely outsiders in the boyhood community. Often they did not have even one friendship, or merely a temporary one (which made them feel all the more desperate after its termination)."[14]

In the preadolescent period, then, the future pedophile admires other boys, judging them more "boyish", rougher and tougher. But he admires these qualities from a hurting feeling of loneliness and inferiority. He thinks "If only I could be like them!" Admiration mixed with self-dramatization! Later, the adult pedophile will harbor this self-pity and will hanker for prepubertal boys.

The specific elements in the adult pedophile's self-view are reflected in the traits in which he exults in boys. If he is enchanted by mischievous boys, he has felt himself too much of the "well-mannered, well-educated boy" in childhood; if he is attracted by the tricks of boys, it will be because in childhood he has been restrained by all sorts of rules. This is interest, not only in the appearance, but also in the behavior of boys. The wishes of the pedophile are primarily "a yearning for togetherness with the idolized and inaccessibly superior other boys, an outcrying for belonging".[15] He painfully misses the friendship of other boys, although externally he may play the father role toward boys or the teacher or the youth leader. But he will never know this unless he looks into himself. According to the "inner boy" theory of van den Aardweg, one sees that a second personality survives even with the same contact and sex wishes as in childhood: "Not the grown-up, but a 'boy' within craves for the appreciation of other children. . . . What Gide said about himself (in his *Journal*, 1906) that he 'never was a man, and would remain but a child grownup' was an adequate description of the psyche of all people with this neurosis."[16]

Loneliness is so much a part of the pedophile that he automatically puts himself in advance in the position of the outsider, not socializing but retreating from other people. This behavior, in turn, justifies new complaints of loneliness and a repetition of feelings of rejection, which lead to craving for company. All this triggers the pedophile's erotic obsession.

[14] *Ibid.*, p. 158.
[15] *Ibid.*
[16] *Ibid.*, p. 159.

The pedophile differs from the ordinary homosexual in that the former admires *boyishness* in the object of his affections, while the latter admires *manliness*. As soon as a boy begins showing signs of physical masculinity in adolescence, the pedophile loses interest in him, while the ordinary homosexual becomes interested in the boy only when he sheds a boyish appearance. Interestingly, some homosexuals concentrate their interests in adolescent males, and they are known as *ephebophiliacs*. The ephebophiliac has a kind of sexual neurosis different from that of the pedophile.[17]

Van den Aardweg notes that, contrary to public opinion, which associates pedophilia with serious acts of aggression against children, only a small minority of men with homosexual pedophilic inclinations commit crimes such as rape or murder. In some cases, however, aggressive and sadistic tendencies coexist with the erotic drive. In these cases the very feeling of rejection could engender hatred, a desperate kind of anger, and a lust for revenge. In van den Aardweg's theory, the real cause of murder by a pedophilic after having sex contact with a child may be that he is enraged that his victim does not like him.[18]

3. TREATMENT OF PEDOPHILIA BY THE SEXUAL DISORDERS CLINIC

Dr. Berlin introduces his presentation on the treatment of the homosexual with several preliminary observations: (1) The attempt to provide treatment for the pedophile is not to condone his behavior; on the contrary, professional assistance is crucial, because it is imperative that he totally stop his prior sexual behaviors immediately and indefinitely. This is both necessary and formidable. It may lead the pedophile to rationalize his past conduct and the need for treatment. This must be counteracted. (2) We need to use our imaginations to understand how difficult is the task which faces the pedophile seeking to change. It would be difficult for any of us to stop feeling the sexual attractions we have felt throughout our lives. Imagine the average man trying to find little boys sexually appealing, while at the same time losing all erotic interest in adult females. Yet this is precisely what the fixated homosexual pedophile has to accomplish—in reverse.[19]

---

[17] *Ibid.*, p. 160. See also John Money, *Lovemaps*, p. 73: "The paraphilic age range of the pedophile's partner of either sex is rather rigidly set as juvenile. Homosexual pedophilia has little overlap with homosexual ephebophilia, and both of these have little overlap with homosexual attraction for adults. The same applies heterosexually."

[18] *On the Origins and Treatment of Homosexuality*, pp. 160–163.

[19] In this section I have used two articles by Dr. Berlin: "Treatment of Pedophilia", *The Medical-Moral Newsletter* 21, no. 6 (June 1984):21–24, and "Pedophilia", *Medical Aspects of Human Sexuality* 19, no. 8 (Aug. 1985): 79, 82, 85, 88. The word *fixated* applied to the

Four major treatments have been proposed for pedophilia: psychotherapy, behavior therapy, surgery, and medication. With regard to *psychotherapy*, it is doubtful that persons can come fully to understand the basis of their own sexual interests through the process of introspection alone. Just as the average man cannot figure out why he prefers women to men, so the pedophile cannot understand the basis of his sexual inclination. Even if he did understand, it is doubtful that he could continue to resist these strong sexual drives. There is little convincing evidence to show that traditional psychotherapies have had much success in helping the pedophile.

The approach of *behavior therapy* is concerned, not with the historical roots of the pedophile, but with helping him to overcome his behavior. This method seeks to extinguish erotic feelings associated with children while teaching the individual to become sexually aroused by age-appropriate partners who were formerly non-arousing. While there is some evidence that in the laboratory situations some pedophiliac men no longer show signs of sexual arousal when looking at pictures of unclothed children, and that they begin to respond to stimuli of age-appropriate partners, there is insufficient evidence that such changes *regularly* carry over into nonlaboratory or real-life situations.

Two types of *surgery* have been proposed for pedophilia: (1) stereotactic neurosurgery and (2) removal of the testes. Since neurosurgery for this purpose is still in a preliminary stage, Berlin omits discussion of it; instead he turns to the surgical procedure for removal of the testes (castration). Castration has been suggested as a treatment for pedophilia, because the testes are the major producers of testosterone, a hormone that can fuel sexual appetite. In animal research, lowering testosterone by removing the testes eventually leads to a marked reduction in almost all forms of sexually motivated behavior. Berlin believes that the same is true of humans, as several European studies have indicated, particularly one in Denmark, where Sturup reported on a thirty-year investigation of 900 castrated "sex offenders", including 4,000 follow-up examinations. "He documented a recidivism of less than 3%."[20] That there is a correlation between low testosterone levels and low sexual libido is also indicated by evidence from a variety of medical sources.[21]

---

homosexual pedophile means that only prepubertal boys arouse him. The treatment suggested is primarily for him.

[20] "Treatment of Pedophilia", *The Medical Moral Newsletter*, June 1984, p. 24. The reference to the Denmark investigation is G. K. Sturup, "Castration: The Total Treatment", in H. Resnick and M. Wolfgang, eds., *Sexual Behaviors: Social, Clinical and Legal Aspects* (Boston: Little, Brown and Co., 1972), pp. 361–382.

[21] "Pedophilia", *Medical Aspects of Human Sexuality*, Aug. 1985, p. 85.

Today, however, Berlin indicates, it is no longer necessary to perform surgical castration in order to reduce testosterone levels; *medication* can be used. This can be done *pharmacologically* without the physical or psychological trauma of surgery.[22] In the United States the drug most often used is medroxyprogesterone acetate (Depo-Provera). This drug is injected intramuscularly once a week, and it gradually moves into the bloodstream over the course of several days. The major side effects have been weight gain and, in some cases, hypertension. But it consistently reduces serum testosterone levels significantly. Lowering testosterone lowers libido, which, in turn, seems to help many men control their sexual behavior. If unwanted sexual desire can be removed from an otherwise trustworthy relationship between an adult and a child, then it seems that such a relationship should be allowed to continue in a healthy way.

It is important to note, however, that most pedophiles receiving Depo-Provera also attend *group counseling* sessions similar to those of A.A. Berlin stresses the importance of such sessions, where the men acknowledge that they have been tempted to do something they know they must not do. They then discuss among themselves strategies intended to help them resist such temptations (whom to call, what situations to avoid, early warning signs, and so on). Here Berlin is really referring to the spiritual support that pedophiles and exhibitionists can give one another at such gatherings.[23]

Berlin reports that in the year 1983–84, seventy men were treated with Depo-Provera at Johns Hopkins for some form of paraphilia, mainly exhibitionism and pedophilia. Counseling was also part of the treatment. Fewer than 5% relapsed. Approximately eighty others who—in Berlin's judgment—did not require Depo-Provera received counseling only, and compliance was 90%. In short, Depo-Provera is one important element in the process of recovery of the pedophile. In no way should it be viewed as a punishment. More study of its effects and side effects is in order.

Now I turn to some reflection on the ethical aspects in the treatment of the pedophile. First, I shall review Dr. Berlin's ethical views, and then I shall add my own.

---

[22] *Ibid.*

[23] A new group called Sexaholics Anonymous (S.A.) has begun, adapting the Twelve Steps of A.A. and using the insights of Patrick Carnes in *The Sexual Addiction*. At these meetings there is a mixture of single and married persons of both sexes, as well as members of the clergy, both Catholic and non-Catholic. Contrary to the impression created by the media, pedophilia is not a problem unique to Roman Catholic clergy because of the vow of celibacy and chastity. Sexual disorders are no respecters of persons.

4. ETHICAL CONSIDERATIONS IN THE TREATMENT
OF THE PEDOPHILE

Berlin believes that Depo-Provera should be given to pedophiles on legal probation if it is necessary, and that judgment should be made by a psychiatrist familiar with the problem. The pedophile who needs the drug should be given it even if he is in prison. Incarcerated men report that Depo-Provera (D-P) freed them from obsessional sexual preoccupations. Persons should be given the opportunity to see whether this drug confers upon them an increased capacity for self-control, particularly when individual psychotherapy and group counseling have failed to help the person to avoid pedophilic acts.

The next objection Berlin considers is the argument that psychotropic drugs, such as D-P, are "mind controlling". In response, he cites the legitimate medical indications for the use of psychotropic drugs: decrease of suffering, restoration of normal functions, and increase of the personal capacity successfully to exercise self-control. Since in many men the capacity for self-control is increased by D-P, it follows that this is a legitimate use. The Sexual Disorders Clinic of Johns Hopkins, of which Berlin and Money are directors, makes the following statement:

> Studies begun at Johns Hopkins in 1966 have shown that sex offenders or paraphiliacs, for example, pedophiliacs, treated with the antiandrogenic hormone, Depo-Provera, plus counseling, have gained in self-regulation of sexual behavior. Depo-Provera suppresses or lessens the frequency of erection or ejaculation and also lessens the feeling of libido and the mental imagery of sexual arousal.[24]

Berlin next considers the phenomenon of the pedophile falling in love with a child and desiring sex. It is easy for the pedophile to become convinced that the relationship is good and healthy and not harmful, particularly when the child does not seem to mind or even enjoys the sexual act. Such self-deception must be confronted by the counselor. The person must learn to stop rationalizing and to develop strategies for overcoming sexual and affectional temptations. I would add that the best place to bring this about is through group spiritual support systems such as Sexaholics Anonymous (S.A.).

Berlin asks that society begin to treat the pedophile with justice and compassion, recognizing his rights as a person and making allowances for

[24] "Antiandrogenic and Counseling Treatment of Sex Offenders", The Johns Hopkins University School of Medicine, Baltimore, Maryland. This statement also says that, as a result of the discovery and medical use of antiandrogen, castration is disfavored in "contemporary American legal-medical management of sex offenders".

his past conduct in the sense that he did not choose to have such an orientation. In no way is one justifying his activity; indeed, society and he have a joint responsibility to bring it to an end to protect the innocent child. At the same time he must be shown the same respect we accord the recovering alcoholic or drug addict. Ultimately, innocent children will benefit by such compassion shown to the pedophile.

Berlin believes that in counseling the child it may help to let the child know that the pedophilic person genuinely cared about him, even if that care was expressed in the wrong way. I believe this is good advice, but, unfortunately, whenever such behavior has become public knowledge and criminal suits have been brought against the offender (and perhaps his employer), it has become almost impossible to reach the child who would certainly benefit from such counsel.

Berlin makes one final point. Granted the responsibility of the pedophile to make use of adequate means to bring his propensity under control, society has the correlative duty to provide those means in the forms of medication and individual and group counseling. In the counseling situation, moreover, the pedophile must be able to trust his counselor or counselors completely: "Only under such circumstances can one expect the individual to talk candidly about the innermost aspects of his own sexuality."[25]

Evaluation of Berlin's ethical reflections

In general, I agree with Berlin's ethical reflections, and I shall add a few of my own. With regard to the use of Depo-Provera (D-P), the principle of the twofold effect can be applied to the situation of the pedophile who desires to regain control over his sexual conduct. His intention is good. The act in itself is good: the use of medication for the sake of personal well-being. The good effect—gradual but increasing control over undesirable fantasy and act—is directly proportionate to the *known* bad effects: weight gain and hypertension. Finally, the good effect of increasing capacity for self-control does not come about through the evil effects of weight loss and hypertension, which are really by-products of the medication. The use of D-P under these circumstances, therefore, is morally good and indeed mandatory for the pedophile whenever it is professionally indicated as a necessary means of avoiding pedophilic acts. (In some instances it is not indicated as necessary, and then its use is not mandatory.)

[25] Berlin and Krout, *art. cit.*, *Amer. J. of Forensic Psychiatry*, 7 (1986):30.

I do have reservations, however, about the view of the Sexual Disorders Clinic that the only alternative proposed to the pedophile, recovering from his compulsive tendency, is "to have a sex life with a socially suitable consenting partner instead".[26] It is understandable that the Sexual Disorders Clinic may have no place for celibacy in its philosophy, but there are homosexual pedophiles, both lay and clerical, who feel bound in conscience to live a life of sexual abstinence. I should like to suggest some guidelines for such pedophiles, since I have had the experience of working with them and with celibate ephebophiles (who had sought adolescent males).

I do not doubt that celibates may have an obligation to use D–P to avoid relapses, but they also have a duty to use both individual counseling and spiritual group support systems. They need to integrate the human wisdom of therapy with the principles of the Gospel, understood in a life of prayer. The Christian homosexual pedophile needs a spiritual plan of life even more than the ordinary homosexual does, because his spiritual survival depends upon it. It is not enough, then, to propose medication, counseling, and support systems to the celibate homosexual pedophile. The spiritual dimension is not just another dimension, but the all-important motivator to use all possible natural means to regain control over one's sexuality so that it may be used properly in the service of the Lord. If such a celibate is sincere, he will find a spiritual director in addition to his professional counselor and group support system.

For several years I have been engaged in what is best described as *crisis intervention*, working with clinical psychologist John F. Kinnane, of Catholic University, Dr. Richard Fitzgibbons of Philadelphia, and with treatment centers in the rehabilitation of clerics and religious who had become emotionally and sexually involved with boys or adolescent males. It is a program involving regular clinical counseling, participation in group retreats, attendance at A.A. or S.A. meetings, and vigilant pastoral supervision of the counselee. With the explicit permission of those with whom Dr. Kinnane and I have worked, we have been able to share our perception of them and to help fourteen clerics get some measure of control over their lives. Our shared clinical and counseling impression is that these persons have not grown up psychologically, morally, or spiritually. Psychologically, they are like little boys; morally, they lack sensitivity concerning the damage they may have done to these young people; and spiritually, they have lost contact with their God in the depths of their souls.

We are therefore dealing with more than a physical and psychological disorder; it is a profoundly spiritual crisis, and all that has been already said

---

[26] "Antiandrogenic and Counseling Treatment of Sex Offenders", p. 2.

in describing a spiritual program such as A.A. for homosexual persons applies preeminently to the pedophile. He has to live the Twelve Steps. In my role as spiritual director I see my counselees at regular intervals. There is hope, then, for the homosexual pedophile who is willing to cooperate with professionals and spiritual directors. But he must realize that every step he takes back to spiritual sanity is possible only by the grace of God.

One practical insight I have garnered from working with celibate pedophiles and with those attracted by adolescent males is their need to begin to cultivate friendships with *adults*. This they had not done in the past. Both the counselor and the spiritual director should inquire into the progress of the individual in this regard. Consciously or unconsciously, he will gravitate toward children or adolescents, and he must resist this tendency by regularly meeting with adults, perhaps with other clerics or religious, in social events or at meetings of S.A. or A.A.

CHAPTER TEN

SUMMARY AND CONCLUSIONS

As I was in the process of preparing this manuscript, the statement of the Congregation for the Doctrine of the Faith on homosexuality was issued (Oct. 1, 1986), and I incorporated it into the first chapter because it raised a series of issues I intended to discuss in the following chapters. It also explained in what sense homosexual orientation is an "objective disorder", and it developed the argument from Holy Scripture beyond the 1975 CDF document. In Chapter Two, necessary distinctions are made between homosexual inclination and activity, and between noncompulsive and compulsive acts. Since the notion of compulsion is at once so important and yet so complex, I entered into the nuances of this phenomenon.

Again, if one hopes to understand homosexual persons, one needs to study recent thinking concerning the origins and treatment of homo-sexuality, and in Chapter Three one will find two diverse explanations of the homosexual condition. I leave it to the reader to decide which of the two approaches he wishes to take; or he may choose neither of them. In my judgment, Moberly has given valuable insight into the origins of the homosexual orientation, but she needs more empirical verification of her principles of gender-specific therapy. On the other hand, van den Aardweg provides much evidence in favor of his theory of *feeling* inferior as *masculine* or *feminine*, but in my judgment he does not explore sufficiently possible causal relationships between failure to identify with the same-sex parent and difficulties with the opposite parent and inability to relate to peers in the preschool period. Yet my pastoral practice bears out his detailed and true-to-life descriptions of the feelings and moods of homosexual persons. Both authors have contributed greatly to my under-standing of the homosexual person, and I hope they will also deepen the perceptions of the reader. I introduce the faith premises of Colin Cook at the end of the psychological section to underline the necessity of integrating psychological insight into pastoral practice.

In Chapter Four, Father Jeffrey Keefe, O.F.M. Conv., sharpens the focus on certain complexities in the emotional development of the homo-sexual person. He brings to his study over twenty years of clinical and pastoral experience coupled with research.

I devote Chapter Five to major theological views that are contrary to the official teaching of the Church, because the Church needs to explain *how* these views do not provide adequate explanation for homosexual activity as an action morally good under certain sets of circumstances or *why* the Church should *not* say such actions are always morally wrong. The public has the impression that the position of the Church is an *ipse dixit* with no substantiation in reason. For this reason in Chapter Six I develop the argument from Holy Scripture at some length, and I follow that up with arguments from the very nature of homosexual activity. I add psychological arguments that I have found persuasive with homosexual persons.

But since one must also consider the freedom and responsibility of the person performing homosexual acts, I show that the traditional teaching of the Church makes room for all the ways in which human freedom and responsibility can be significantly reduced or even removed. At the same time, one retains the responsibility to take those measures necessary to regain one's freedom and responsibility. With "fear and trembling", then, I turn to the controversy concerning the rights of the homosexual person.

Gay-rights advocates constantly speak of the freedom of the homosexual person—but seldom, and then vaguely, of what he is free to do. These claims include the "right" to sodomitic intercourse and the "right" to live together with all the legal protections given to marriage. The Archdiocese of New York does not stand alone in opposing these claims. Both Jewish and Protestant organizations also believe that the rights of homosexual persons are limited by the rights of other individuals and by the rights of groups, such as parents' organizations with regard to the education of their children. At the same time the Church opposes any unjust treatment of homosexual persons, insisting on their equal dignity before God and firmly correcting anyone who in any way ridicules homosexual persons. It is also the duty of the Church in every diocese to provide adequate pastoral programs to help homosexual men and women live the Gospel to the full.

In Chapter Seven I draw the distinction between one-to-one counseling and group counseling, explaining the nature of a group spiritual support system. The tremendous influence of the Twelve Steps of A.A. on both Protestant and Catholic spiritual support groups is spelled out by drawing comparisons of A.A. both with H.A. (interdenominational) and with Courage (Roman Catholic). But since group spiritual direction is inadequate without concurrent individual direction, I describe the specific elements of a spiritual plan of life for homosexual Catholics. I also note the differences between H.A. and Courage in terms of goals and purposes. Courage is designed to help the homosexual person to live a celibate life for the Lord, but it does not discourage one from seeking to change his sexual orientation; Homosexuals Anonymous and related Protestant organizations, under the umbrella of Exodus International, endeavor to help the person move from the condition of homosexuality to that of heterosexuality. Finally, as part of this chapter, I describe the activities of Dignity and New Ways Ministry as *not* in agreement with official Church teaching. I found it necessary to document my position by using the writings of these two organizations.

While I have treated many aspects of homosexuality, in Chapter Eight I select three I have encountered in ministry to homosexual persons. (1) The problems of married homosexuals, the question whether a homosexual person should not marry, and the difficulties of ascertaining whether a marriage involving a female homosexual person is valid are discussed. (2) Then there is the puzzle of the apparent adolescent homosexual and what can be done to help him recognize his sexual orientation. It should be kept in mind that similar uncertainty is found in adolescent girls. (3) The moral and pastoral issues emerging from the growing AIDS crisis are treated in full detail. Our churches need volunteers to minister to the victims of AIDS and to their families.

In Chapter Nine I present some brief psychological descriptions of *pedophilia* and of the treatment given to pedophiles in the Sexual Disorders Clinic of Johns Hopkins School of Medicine. Before we minister to pedophiles pastorally, we need to understand their condition psychologically. We need to know the way in which this compulsive urge operates and how it is distinct from the tendency to seek sexual gratification from adolescents—also a form of sexual neurosis. Above all, we need to exercise compassion in helping these men to overcome their neurosis.

From the study of researchers in the field and from pastoral experience I have drawn two general conclusions. The first is concerned with whether a homosexual person can change his sexual orientation. On this possibility it is difficult for both the public and the homosexual person to keep an open mind. Among professional therapists, moreover, the weight of opinion continues to hold that the chances of changing sexual orientation are rather slim, although a small number of researchers and therapists, including both Moberly and van den Aardweg, continue to hold that change in orientation is in practice possible. I agree with this minority, recalling the insightful comment of Arno Karlen in his scholarly review of this question:

> There is no doubt that psychotherapy—like surgery, corporate law, and original mathematics—is as much an art as it is a science. In the thirties, when schizophrenics were considered almost impossible to treat, Harry Stack Sullivan became famous for his special, personal gift for gaining rapport with patients no one else could reach. Dr. Bruno Bettelheim has made a similar breakthrough with autistic children who not long ago were considered untreatable. Some doctors who report high change rates in homosexuals may simply have a gift for dealing with them. . . . I feel sure this is true of a

number of clinicians I have interviewed. Fortunately, psychotherapy, surgery, and mathematics are also sciences, and the personal gifts of one creative man can be, within limits, routinized into standard procedures by men who read his ideas and case histories. Thus conditions once considered untreatable become treatable by more and more practitioners.[1]

Since this statement was made in 1971 we have learned much more about the treatment of homosexual persons through the experiences of both group therapy and group spiritual direction, as well as through new insights from researchers such as Moberly and van den Aardweg. Unresolved in any consideration of the contributing factors in the genesis of homosexuality is the question of which is the *predominating* factor in any given case. I have little doubt that identification with same-sex parent is extremely important, and that its lack *may* contribute to homosexuality; but I also believe that relating to the other parent and feeling that one *belongs* to a peer group of one's own sex are important in the development of homosexuality. *Feeling* inferior precisely as a *boy* or *girl* is part of the history of many homosexual persons.

One must not overlook other theories stressing hormonal influences on the brain of the prenatal infant as contributing factors. But no one has explained how these diverse factors converge in a given individual to produce homosexual orientation; hence it seems prudent not to put great faith in any one theory, but to use elements of each in helping the homosexual person to overcome personal deficits and even to change his sexual orientation.

It would be a mistake, however, to remain on the level of psychological insight, valuable as this is, in the pursuit of an adequate program for homosexual persons. A truly spiritual program should integrate the psychological truths provided by different theorists. Homosexuals Anonymous (H.A.) and Courage are examples of such attempts at integration. Both utilize the spiritually integrating principles of A.A. Again, just as the practice of the Twelve Steps of A.A. demands in the beginning ninety meetings in ninety days, and afterward regular attendance at weekly meetings as a minimal requirement, so the practice of the Fourteen Steps of H.A. or their equivalent in Courage requires regular weekly attendance in addition to daily meditation on the virtues necessary for chastity. There is no shortcut to chastity or to the development of a heterosexual orientation. We do not acquire the virtues of a Christian way of life overnight but only by renewed cooperation with God's grace in daily struggle.

The second conclusion is: It is *in practice* possible for a homosexual man

---

[1] *Sexuality and Homosexuality*, p. 585. Chapter 30, "Cure or Illusion", should be read in its entirety: pp. 572–606.

or woman to lead a celibate life through a program of group spiritual support, which helps one develop an interior life of prayer and form close and intimate friendships with persons of the same or other sex.

As I was completing this chapter, I received a letter typical of many others received over the last six months. A forty-four-year-old member of Courage wrote to encourage me "in the vital project in which you are engaged, writing a book to help gays find the inner peace and self-respect that the spirituality of abstinence affords". This man works on two hotlines "for the suicidal and despairing" in a metropolitan area, and he has talked with a number of homosexual men and women. Describing his experience as "eye-opening", he adds: "I've found that a very large number of gays are struggling to understand and know what the right thing to do is; they have high ideals and want to lead an ethical life." Many homosexual persons call the hot line when a relationship has just broken up, since they find it "painfully difficult to deal with their feelings of rejection, anger, loneliness, and alienation".

From listening on the hotline, particularly to young men, my correspondent concludes:

> My own belief is that it probably takes some time before a thinking gay realizes that chance encounters and casual relationships do not bring the emotional fulfillment that is desired. What Courage offers, I'm convinced of it, is the answer. The inner peace, the deep self-acceptance and the self-restraint that the choice of chastity imposes are far more enduring and self-affirming than the momentary gratifications of self-indulgence. Speaking for myself, I'm really extremely happy—and relieved—to have the opportunity to work at spiritual self-growth in the context of a group of gay men who lead consecrated lives in the service of the Lord and their fellow men. It's a lot harder to live a celibate life without emotional support. Courage offers that support.

It is my desire that this book will plant a seed of hope in the hearts of many homosexual persons who do not know about group spiritual support.

LETTER TO THE BISHOPS OF THE CATHOLIC CHURCH ON THE PASTORAL CARE OF HOMOSEXUAL PERSONS

1. The issue of homosexuality and the moral evaluation of homosexual acts have increasingly become a matter of public debate, even in Catholic circles. Since this debate often advances arguments and makes assertions inconsistent with the teaching of the Catholic Church, it is quite rightly a cause for concern to all engaged in the pastoral ministry, and this Congregation has judged it to be of sufficiently grave and widespread importance to address to the Bishops of the Catholic Church this Letter on the Pastoral Care of Homosexual Persons.

2. Naturally, an exhaustive treatment of this complex issue cannot be attempted here, but we will focus our reflection within the distinctive context of the Catholic moral perspective. It is a perspective which finds support in the more secure findings of the natural sciences, which have their own legitimate and proper methodology and field of inquiry.

However, the Catholic moral viewpoint is founded on human reason illumined by faith and is consciously motivated by the desire to do the will of God our Father. The Church is thus in a position to learn from scientific discovery but also to transcend the horizons of science and to be confident that her more global vision does greater justice to the rich reality of the human person in his spiritual and physical dimensions, created by God and heir, by grace, to eternal life.

It is within this context, then, that it can be clearly seen that the phenomenon of homosexuality, complex as it is, and with its many consequences for society and ecclesial life, is a proper focus for the Church's pastoral care. It thus requires of her ministers attentive study, active concern and honest, theologically well-balanced counsel.

3. Explicit treatment of the problem was given in this Congregation's "Declaration on Certain Questions Concerning Sexual Ethics" of December 19, 1975. That document stressed the duty of trying to understand the homosexual condition and noted that culpability for homosexual acts should only be judged with prudence. At the same time the Congregation took note of the distinction commonly drawn between the homosexual condition or tendency and individual homosexual actions. These were described as deprived of their essential and indispensable finality, as being "intrinsically disordered", and able in no case to be approved of (cf. no. 8, § 4).

235

In the discussion which followed the publication of the Declaration, however, an overly benign interpretation was given to the homosexual condition itself, some going so far as to call it neutral, or even good. Although the particular inclination of the homosexual person is not a sin, it is a more or less strong tendency ordered toward an intrinsic moral evil; and thus the inclination itself must be seen as an objective disorder.

Therefore special concern and pastoral attention should be directed toward those who have this condition, lest they be led to believe that the living out of this orientation in homosexual activity is a morally acceptable option. It is not.

4. An essential dimension of authentic pastoral care is the identification of causes of confusion regarding the Church's teaching. One is a new exegesis of Sacred Scripture which claims variously that Scripture has nothing to say on the subject of homosexuality, or that it somehow tacitly approves of it, or that all of its moral injunctions are so culture-bound that they are no longer applicable to contemporary life. These views are gravely erroneous and call for particular attention here.

5. It is quite true that the biblical literature owes to the different epochs in which it was written a good deal of its varied patterns of thought and expression (Dei Verbum, no. 12). The Church today addresses the Gospel to a world which differs in many ways from ancient days. But the world in which the New Testament was written was already quite diverse from the situation in which the Sacred Scriptures of the Hebrew people had been written or compiled, for example.

What should be noticed is that, in the presence of such remarkable diversity, there is nevertheless a clear consistency with the Scriptures themselves on the moral issue of homosexual behavior. The Church's doctrine regarding this issue is thus based, not on isolated phrases for facile theological argument, but on the solid foundation of a constant biblical testimony. The community of faith today, in unbroken continuity with the Jewish and Christian communities within which the ancient Scriptures were written, continues to be nourished by those same Scriptures and by the Spirit of Truth whose Word they are. It is likewise essential to recognize that the Scriptures are not properly understood when they are interpreted in a way which contradicts the Church's living Tradition. To be correct, the interpretation of Scripture must be in substantial accord with that Tradition.

The Vatican Council II in Dei Verbum, no. 10, put it this way: "It is clear, therefore, that in the supremely wise arrangement of God, Sacred Tradition, Sacred Scripture, and the Magisterium of the Church are so connected and associated that one of them cannot stand without the others. Working together, each in its own way under the action of the one Holy Spirit, they all contribute effectively to the salvation of souls." In that spirit we wish to outline briefly the biblical teaching here.

6. Providing a basic plan for understanding this entire discussion of homosexuality is the theology of creation we find in Genesis. God, by His infinite wisdom and love, brings into existence all of reality as a reflection of His goodness. He fashions mankind, male and female, in His own image and likeness. Human beings, therefore, are nothing less than the work of God Himself; and in the complementarity of the sexes, they are called to reflect the inner unity of the Creator. They do this in a striking way in their cooperation with Him in the transmission of life by a mutual donation of the self to the other.

In Genesis 3, we find that this truth about persons being an image of God has been obscured by original sin. There inevitably follows a loss of awareness of the covenental character of the union these persons had with God and with each other. The human body retains its "spousal significance" but this is now clouded by sin. Thus, in Genesis 19:1–11, the deterioration due to sin continues in the story of the men of Sodom. There can be no doubt of the moral judgment made there against homosexual relations. In Leviticus 18:22 and 20:13, in the course of describing the conditions necessary for belonging to the Chosen People, the author excludes from the People of God those who behave in a homosexual fashion.

Against the background of this exposition of theocratic law, an eschatological perspective is developed by St. Paul when, in 1 Corinthians 6:9, he proposes the same doctrine and lists those who behave in a homosexual fashion among those who shall not enter the Kingdom of God.

In Romans 1:18–32, still building on the moral traditions of his forebears, but in the new context of the confrontation between Christianity and the pagan society of his day, Paul uses homosexual behavior as an example of the blindness which has overcome humankind. Instead of the original harmony between Creator and creatures, the acute distortion of idolatry has led to all kinds of moral excess. Paul is at a loss to find a clearer example of disharmony than homosexual relations. Finally, 1 Timothy 1, in full continuity with the biblical position, singles out those who spread wrong doctrine and in v. 10 explicitly names as sinners those who engage in homosexual acts.

7. The Church, obedient to the Lord who founded her and gave to her the sacramental life, celebrates the divine plan of the loving and life-giving

union of men and women in the sacrament of marriage. It is only in the marital relationship that the use of the sexual faculty can be morally good. A person engaging in homosexual behavior therefore acts immorally.

To choose someone of the same sex for one's sexual activity is to annul the rich symbolism and meaning, not to mention the goals, of the Creator's sexual design. Homosexual activity is not a complementary union, able to transmit life; and so it thwarts the call to a life of that form of self-giving which the Gospel says is the essence of Christian living. This does not mean that homosexual persons are not often generous and giving of themselves; but when they engage in homosexual activity they confirm within themselves a disordered sexual inclination which is essentially self-indulgent.

As in every moral disorder, homosexual activity prevents one's own fulfillment and happiness by acting contrary to the creative wisdom of God. The Church, in rejecting erroneous opinions regarding homosexuality, does not limit but rather defends personal freedom and dignity realistically and authentically understood.

8. Thus, the Church's teaching today is in organic continuity with the Scriptural perspective and with her own constant Tradition. Though today's world is in many ways quite new, the Christian community senses the profound and lasting bonds which join us to those generations who have gone before us, "marked with the sign of faith".

Nevertheless, increasing numbers of people today, even within the Church, are bringing enormous pressure to bear on the Church to accept the homosexual condition as though it were not disordered and to condone homosexual activity. Those within the Church who argue in this fashion often have close ties with those with similar views outside it. These latter groups are guided by a vision opposed to the truth about the human person, which is fully disclosed in the mystery of Christ. They reflect, even if not entirely consciously, a materialistic ideology which denies the transcendent nature of the human person as well as the supernatural vocation of every individual.

The Church's ministers must ensure that homosexual persons in their care will not be misled by this point of view, so profoundly opposed to the teaching of the Church. But the risk is great and there are many who seek to create confusion regarding the Church's position, and then to use that confusion to their own advantage.

9. The movement within the Church, which takes the form of pressure groups of various names and sizes, attempts to give the impression that it represents all homosexual persons who are Catholics. As a matter of fact,

its membership is by and large restricted to those who either ignore the teaching of the Church or seek somehow to undermine it. It brings together under the aegis of Catholicism homosexual persons who have no intention of abandoning their homosexual behavior. One tactic used is to protest that any and all criticism of or reservations about homosexual people, their activity and lifestyle, are simply diverse forms of unjust discrimination.

There is an effort in some countries to manipulate the Church by gaining the often well-intentioned support of her pastors with a view to changing civil statutes and laws. This is done in order to conform to these pressure groups' concept that homosexuality is at least completely harmless, if not an entirely good thing. Even when the practice of homosexuality may seriously threaten the lives and well-being of a large number of people, its advocates remain undeterred and refuse to consider the magnitude of the risks involved.

The Church can never be so callous. It is true that her clear position cannot be revised by pressure from civil legislation or the trend of the moment. But she is really concerned about the many who are not represented by the pro-homosexual movement and about those who may have been tempted to believe its deceitful propaganda. She is also aware that the view that homosexual activity is equivalent to, or as acceptable as, the sexual expression of conjugal love, has a direct impact on society's understanding of the nature and rights of the family and puts them in jeopardy.

10. It is deplorable that homosexual persons have been and are the object of violent malice in speech or in action. Such treatment deserves condemnation from the Church's pastors wherever it occurs. It reveals a kind of disregard for others which endangers the most fundamental principles of a healthy society. The intrinsic dignity of each person must always be respected in word, in action and in law.

But the proper reaction to crimes committed against homosexual persons should not be to claim that the homosexual condition is not disordered. When such a claim is made and when homosexual activity is consequently condoned, or when civil legislation is introduced to protect behavior to which no one has any conceivable right, neither the Church nor society at large should be surprised when other distorted notions and practices gain ground, and irrational and violent reactions increase.

11. It has been argued that the homosexual orientation in certain cases is not the result of deliberate choice; and so the homosexual person would then have no choice but to behave in a homosexual fashion. Lacking

freedom, such a person, even if engaged in homosexual activity, would not be culpable.

Here, the Church's wise moral tradition is necessary since it warns against generalizations in judging individual cases. In fact, circumstances may exist, or may have existed in the past, which would reduce or remove the culpability of the individual in a given instance; or other circumstances may increase it. What is at all costs to be avoided is the unfounded and demeaning assumption that the sexual behavior of homosexual persons is always and totally compulsive and therefore inculpable. What is essential is that the fundamental liberty which characterizes the human person and gives him his dignity be recognized as belonging to the homosexual person as well. As in every conversion from evil, the abandonment of homosexual activity will require a profound collaboration of the individual with God's liberating grace.

12. What, then, are homosexual persons to do who seek to follow the Lord? Fundamentally, they are called to enact the will of God in their life by joining whatever sufferings and difficulties they experience in virtue of their condition to the sacrifice of the Lord's cross. That cross, for the believer, is a fruitful sacrifice since from that death come life and redemption. While any call to carry the cross or to understand a Christian's suffering in this way will predictably be met with bitter ridicule by some, it should be remembered that this is the way to eternal life for *all* who follow Christ.

It is, in effect, none other than the teaching of Paul the Apostle to the Galatians when he says that the Spirit produces in the lives of the faithful "love, joy, peace, patience, kindness, goodness, trustfulness, gentleness and self-control" (5:22) and further (v. 24), "You cannot belong to Christ unless you crucify all self-indulgent passions and desires."

It is easily misunderstood, however, if it is merely seen as a pointless effort at self-denial. The cross *is* a denial of self, but in service to the will of God Himself who makes life come from death and empowers those who trust in Him to practice virtue in place of vice.

To celebrate the Pascal Mystery, it is necessary to let that Mystery become imprinted in the fabric of daily life. To refuse to sacrifice one's own will in obedience to the will of the Lord is effectively to prevent salvation. Just as the cross was central to the expression of God's redemptive love for us in Jesus, so the conformity of the self-denial of homosexual men and women with the sacrifice of the Lord will constitute for them a source of self-giving which will save them from a way of life which constantly threatens to destroy them.

Christians who are homosexual are called, as all of us are, to a chaste life. As they dedicate their lives to understanding the nature of God's personal call to them, they will be able to celebrate the Sacrament of Penance more faithfully and receive the Lord's grace so freely offered there in order to convert their lives more fully to His Way.

13. We recognize, of course, that in great measure the clear and successful communication of the Church's teaching to all the faithful, and to society at large, depends on the correct instruction and fidelity of her pastoral ministers. The bishops have the particularly grave responsibility to see to it that their assistants in the ministry, above all the priests, are rightly informed and personally disposed to bring the teaching of the Church in its integrity to everyone.

The characteristic concern and good will exhibited by many clergy and religious in their pastoral care for homosexual persons is admirable, and, we hope, will not diminish. Such devoted ministers should have the confidence that they are faithfully following the will of the Lord by encouraging the homosexual person to lead a chaste life and by affirming that person's God-given dignity and worth.

14. With this in mind, this Congregation wishes to ask the bishops to be especially cautious of any programs which may seek to pressure the Church to change her teaching, even while claiming not to do so. A careful examination of their public statements and the activities they promote reveals a studied ambiguity by which they attempt to mislead the pastors and the faithful. For example, they may present the teaching of the Magisterium, but only as if it were an optional source for the formation of one's conscience. Its specific authority is not recognized. Some of these groups will use the word "Catholic" to describe either the organization or its intended members, yet they do not defend and promote the teaching of the Magisterium; indeed, they even openly attack it. While their members may claim a desire to conform their lives to the teaching of Jesus, in fact they abandon the teaching of His Church. This contradictory action should not have the support of the bishops in any way.

15. We encourage the bishops, then, to provide pastoral care in full accord with the teaching of the Church for homosexual persons of their dioceses. No authentic pastoral program will include organizations in which homosexual persons associate with each other without clearly stating that homosexual activity is immoral. A truly pastoral approach will appreciate the need for homosexual persons to avoid the near occasions of sin.

We would heartily encourage programs in which these dangers are avoided. But we wish to make it clear that departure from the Church's teaching, or silence about it, in an effort to provide pastoral care is neither caring nor pastoral. Only what is true can ultimately be pastoral. The neglect of the Church's position prevents homosexual men and women from receiving the care they need and deserve.

An authentic pastoral program will assist homosexual persons at all levels of the spiritual life: through the sacraments and in particular through the frequent and sincere use of the sacrament of Reconciliation, through prayer, witness, counsel and individual care. In such a way, the entire Christian community can come to recognize its own call to assist its brothers and sisters, without deluding them or isolating them.

16. From this multi-faceted approach there are numerous advantages to be gained, not the least of which is the realization that a homosexual person, as every human being, deeply needs to be nourished at many different levels simultaneously.

The human person, made in the image and likeness of God, can hardly be adequately described by a reductionist reference to his or her sexual orientation. Every one living on the face of the earth has personal problems and difficulties, but challenges to growth, strengths, talents and gifts as well. Today, the Church provides a badly needed context for the care of the human person when she refuses to consider the person as a "heterosexual" or a "homosexual" and insists that every person has a fundamental identity: the creature of God, and by grace, His child and heir to eternal life.

17. In bringing this entire matter to the bishops' attention, this Congregation wishes to support their efforts to assure that the teaching of the Lord and His Church on this important question be communicated fully to all the faithful.

In light of the points made above, they should decide for their own dioceses the extent to which an intervention on their part is indicated. In addition, should they consider it helpful, further coordinated action at the level of their National Bishops' Conference may be envisioned.

In a particular way, we would ask the bishops to support, with the means at their disposal, the development of appropriate forms of pastoral care for homosexual persons. These would include the assistance of the psychological, sociological and medical sciences, in full accord with the teaching of the Church.

They are encouraged to call on the assistance of all Catholic theologians who, by teaching what the Church teaches, and by deepening their reflections on the true meaning of human sexuality and Christian marriage with the virtues it engenders, will make an important contribution in this particular area of pastoral care.

The bishops are asked to exercise special care in the election of pastoral ministers so that by their own high degree of spiritual and personal maturity and by their fidelity to the Magisterium, they may be of real service to homosexual persons, promoting their health and well-being in the fullest sense. Such ministers will reject theological opinions which dissent from the teaching of the Church and which, therefore, cannot be used as guidelines for pastoral care.

We encourage the bishops to promote appropriate catechetical programs based on the truth about human sexuality in its relationship to the family as taught by the Church. Such programs should provide a good context within which to deal with the question of homosexuality.

This catechesis would also assist those families of homosexual persons to deal with this problem which affects them so deeply.

All support should be withdrawn from any organizations which seek to undermine the teaching of the Church, which are ambiguous about it, or which neglect it entirely. Such support, or even the semblance of such support, can be gravely misinterpreted. Special attention should be given to the practice of scheduling religious services and the use of Church buildings by these groups, including the facilities of Catholic schools and colleges. To some, such permission to use Church property may seem only just and charitable; but in reality it is contradictory to the purpose for which these institutions were founded, it is misleading and often scandalous.

In assessing proposed legislation, the bishops should keep as their uppermost concern the responsibility to defend and promote family life.

18. The Lord Jesus promised, "You shall know the truth and the truth shall set you free" (Jn 8:32). Scripture bids us speak the truth in love (cf. Eph 4:15). The God who is at once truth and love calls the Church to minister to every man, woman and child with the pastoral solicitude of our compassionate Lord. It is in this spirit that we have addressed this Letter to the Bishops of the Church, with the hope that it will be of some help as they care for those whose suffering can only be intensified by error and lightened by truth.

During an audience granted to the undersigned Prefect, His Holiness, Pope John Paul II, approved this Letter, adopted in an ordinary session of the Congregation for the doctrine of the Faith, and ordered it to be published.

Given at Rome, October 1, 1986.

Joseph Cardinal Ratzinger, *Prefect*

Alberto Bovone
Titular Archbishop of Caesarea in Numidia
Secretary

ACKNOWLEDGMENTS

I thank the following publishers:

American Journal of Forensic Psychiatry for quotations from Dr. Berlin's "Pedophilia: Diagnostic Concepts, Treatment, and Ethical Considerations".

American Journal of Psychiatry for quotations from "Gender Identity in Childhood and Later Sexual Orientation Follow-Up of 78 Males" by Richard Green.

American Psychiatric Association for the use of the *Diagnostic and Statistical Manual*, third edition.

Associated Book Publishers, London, England for permission to quote from Elizabeth Moberly, *Psychogenesis: The Early Development of Gender Identity*.

Attic Press, Greenwood, S.C. for quotations from *Homosexuality: A New Christian Ethic* by Elizabeth Moberly.

Ayd Medical Communications for quotations from Dr. Fred Berlin's article on pedophilia in *The Medical Moral Newsletter*.

Commonweal for quotations from "Catholic Homosexuals" by Gregory Baum.

Colin Cook for use of "Homosexuals Anonymous Tape Album: The Fourteen Steps" and quotations from *Homosexuality: An Open Door?*

Crossway Books for quotations from *The Broken Image* by Leanne Payne.

The Devin Adair Company for quotations from *The Homosexual Network* by Enrique Rueda.

DIGNITY/New York, Inc. for quotations from its monthly newsletter, *Calendar*.

Dignity International, Inc., Washington, D.C. for quotations from monthly newsletters. (The president of Dignity/USA has informed us that quotations from local newsletters or convention proceedings may not reflect the position of Dignity/USA.)

Dr. Bernard Fryshman, from whose unpublished paper I quoted copiously, "Societal Rights and Homosexual Rights".

Harvard Medical School Mental Health Letter for quotation from "Homosexuality: Nature vs. Nurture", Oct. 1985, by Judd Marmor.

Harvest News, vol. 1, no. 2 (Spring 1986), ed. John Freeman for a quotation from "Where Does a Mother Go to Resign" by Barbara Johnson.

Homosexuals Anonymous (H.A.), Reading, Pa. for use of the Fourteen Steps.

Ignatius Press for use of quotations from Gene Antonio's *The AIDS Cover-Up?*

Interaction, an International Newsletter, promoting the Integration of Values and Counseling (vol. 13, 1986, p. 6) for quotes from "Freedom from Homosexuality: The Third Option" by Daniel K. Roberts.

The Jurist for quotations from "Marriage Annulments for Gay Men and Lesbian Women" by Paul K. Thomas.

John McNeill, S.J., and National Catholic Reporter for use of material from "The Homosexual and the Church", *NCR*, Oct. 5, 1973.

University of Notre Dame Press for quotations from *Catholic Moral Theology in Dialogue* by Charles Curran.

Our Sunday Visitor Press for quotations from John Cavanagh's *Counseling the Homosexual* and May-Lawlor-Boyle's *Catholic Sexual Ethics*.

Paulist Press for quotations from *Courage to be Chaste* by Father Benedict Groeschel, O.F.M., Cap.

Praeger, A Division of Greenwood Press, Inc., N.Y. for quotations from Gerald van den Aardweg's *On the Origins and Treatment of Homosexuality*.

Regeneration News, Sept. 1986, for quotation from "Dignity Regenerated" by Brother Joe.

Richard M. Restak, M.D. for quotations from "Worry about Survival First, Then AIDS Victims' Rights" in *The Washington Post*.

Servant Publications, Ann Arbor, Michigan for quotations from *Homosexuality and Hope* by Gerald van den Aardweg.

Sheed and Ward for quotations from *AIDS: A Catholic Call to Compassion* by Eileen Flynn.

The American Spectator for quotations from "The Coming of AIDS" (March 1986) by James Grutsch, Jr. and A. D. J. Robertson.

University Press of America, Inc. for quotations from *Homosexuality and the Christian Way of Life* by Edward Malloy, C.S.C.

INDEX OF PROPER NAMES

INDEX OF SUBJECTS